PURITANISM AND THE AMERICAN EXPERIENCE

Edited by Michael McGiffert
University of Denver

ADDISON-WESLEY PUBLISHING COMPANY
Reading, Massachusetts
Menlo Park, California · London · Don Mills, Ontario

THEMES AND FORCES IN AMERICAN HISTORY SERIES
Under the editorship of Robin W. Winks

Purpose: To explore major influences on the development of American society and character.

Preface

America is what it is partly because some resolute Englishmen, known to history as Puritans, planted permanent settlements on these shores early in the seventeenth century. They were running an "errand into the wilderness"; though their performance would fall far short of their purpose, in both the power and the disaster of their undertaking they would set a durable mark on American culture. Therefore, as Perry Miller, the late master of Puritan studies in the United States, once wrote, "without some understanding of Puritanism, . . . there is no understanding of America."[1] This collection of documents and interpretations gives some account of our present understanding of Puritanism and its relevance to the American experience. The volume's three sections are concerned, respectively, with the social intent of the Puritans' "errand," with the modifications of character and outlook which took place as the Puritans adjusted to life in the American "wilderness," and with the legacy of Puritanism in American culture and character.

The motive of the Puritans' trans-Atlantic enterprise was essentially religious, and their objectives were explicitly corporate. They crossed the ocean to practice what in England they had preached (or had been forbidden to preach) and to flee the wrath that God seemed about to let fall on England for her sins. More was contemplated than the salvation of individual souls; collectively, by the act of migration, they committed themselves to attempt to create a new and holier society, "a Citty upon a Hill," as John Winthrop called it, wherein

---

[1] PERRY MILLER and THOMAS H. JOHNSON, eds., *The Puritans* (New York: American Book Co., 1938), p. 1.

iii

79263

God's particular people might live together lovingly under His rule and grace. This city was intended to be a model of righteousness for all the world, or at least all Christendom, to emulate—less a new England than a new Zion, a suburb of Heaven itself. The Puritan mission was thus one of spiritual redemption, communally defined; it was to be worked out by men and women who, in Winthrop's words, were "knitt together" by the "bond of loue."

Of course they failed. Even these dedicated people, who cracked their heads on Calvin, their hands on New England granite, and their hearts on the rock of salvation, proved unable, as generations passed, to sustain the intensity of spirit and discipline that their mission demanded. New England began as a reformation; it became an administration,[2] and the administrators, originally an oligarchy of "saints," grew less saintly. They also lost their audience: even before the city had been firmly set on its hill, the world that was supposed to pay attention was looking elsewhere for edification and diversion. Consequently, the creative moment went quickly by, the vision of the righteous community soon faded, and Boston turned out to be just another small provincial capital, commercially busy but spiritually insignificant—no longer a fit stage for the sublime drama of grace. Meanwhile the stage itself expanded. Rather than sitting tight in the city and keeping a moral, as well as a physical, distance from the wilderness, the Puritans moved out over their inland domain, possessed it, tamed it, and called it home. They learned to use their American environment for purposes other than those propounded by Winthrop. In the upshot, they swapped their godly birthright for "a mess of *American Pottage*," and when they came to think of it, some deplored the transaction but many more deemed the bargain good.

Historians have traced the Americanization of the Puritans. They have also reflected on the Puritanization of America, recognizing that, as Max Savelle remarks, "Puritanism . . . was firmly rooted in the American experience and in the emerging American mind of the eighteenth century, and from New England as a center it has radiated its influence in American civilization, for good or ill, from that day to this;

---

[2] PERRY MILLER, *The New England Mind: From Colony to Province* (Cambridge: Harvard University Press, 1953), p. 11.

and the end is not yet." [3] Though a definitive study of the influence of Puritanism in American thought and life has yet to be written, scholars have examined important aspects of the subject. Their findings are discussed by Richard Schlatter, who also sketches the historiography of American Puritanism, in the essay that follows this preface. The scholarship on which Professor Schlatter's observations are based is sampled in the third section of this volume.

Throughout the book, typographical errors in the sources have, where caught, been silently corrected, and almost all footnotes have been omitted by permission. Grateful acknowledgment goes to the University of Denver for funds to support the secretarial costs of this work.

Denver, Colorado   M. McG.
January, 1969

---

[3] MAX SAVELLE, *Seeds of Liberty: The Genesis of the American Mind* (New York, 1948), p. 27.

Contents

Introductory Essay

The Puritan Strain
RICHARD SCHLATTER

The most famous ship in American history, the *Mayflower*, anchored off what is now Plymouth, Massachusetts, in November 1620. A vessel of about 180 tons, bearing an undistinguished name common to other ships of the period, the *Mayflower* had made the voyage from Southampton in about sixty-four days. (The *Queen Elizabeth*, 86,673 tons, crosses in four and a half days, but is a less famous ship.) One hundred and two English passengers came ashore and founded the first permanent settlement in New England. The Plymouth Colony, founded by the Pilgrim Fathers, maintained its separate existence until 1691 when it merged with its more powerful neighbor, the Massachusetts Bay Colony.

The *Arbella*, a ship of 350 tons, less famous but perhaps more important than the *Mayflower*, led a flotilla to Boston Bay in 1630 to found the Bay Colony. Two thousand English people had settled in the Bay Colony by the end of that year. During the Great Migration, 1630–40, the population of New England grew to about 20,000. A small colony was founded at Providence, Rhode Island, in 1636, and at New Haven, Connecticut, in 1638. New England had 50,000 inhabitants in 1675, and about 100,000 in 1700. Boston, the largest town in seventeenth-century America, had about 1,200 inhabitants in 1640; 2,400 in 1660; 3,200 in 1680; and 6,700 in 1700. Rarely have so few been so famous and so much studied by historians.

The founders of New England were Puritans. Just what percentage of even the earliest settlers were in whole-hearted sympathy with

Reprinted by permission from John Higham, ed., *The Reconstruction of American History* (New York: Harper & Brothers, 1962; published in Great Britain by Hutchinson Publishing Group Ltd.).

the religious views of the leaders is hotly debated by present-day historians. But all scholars agree that it was the Puritan leaders who shaped the culture of New England, whatever the rank and file may have wanted. Government, religion, Church-State relations, education and learning, literature and the arts, family life, customs, morality, and the philosophical assumptions of the whole culture, bore the Puritan hallmark.

Consequently, historians of New England must begin their studies by trying to define Puritanism. No one definition can permanently satisfy. Drawing on the immense labors of modern historical scholarship in Europe and England, American scholars have put together an image of the Puritans as Protestants, English Protestants, Congregationalists; the heirs of Augustine, Calvin, Ramus, Cartwright, and Perkins; the Christian revolutionists whose slogans were predestination, justification by faith, and the Bible an all-sufficient guide; one branch of the English religious party, which formed in the days of Elizabeth, cut off the head of Charles I, suffered under Charles II, and petered out soon after 1688.

The founders of New England were Puritans, but they were also seventeenth-century Englishmen. Their Puritanism gave a distinctive hue to their culture and for its sake they were ready to leave England, which they loved, and settle in a wilderness which had for them no romantic attractions. Nevertheless, perhaps 90 per cent of their ideas, manners, prejudices, and beliefs were those of all, seventeenth-century Englishmen. Historians, consequently, must try to see the Puritanism of New England in perspective, against the common background of seventeenth-century English and Western culture. The exact discrimination of these various strands is one of the major tasks of modern Puritan historiography.

The impulse to study the Puritans intensively is easily understood. Their history is an important chapter—one of the opening chapters—in the story of the United States. For nearly 100 years Puritans dominated New England; and New England was the most populous and richest area in America. Puritanism, as a living religious tradition, died out in the course of the eighteenth century, but elements of the tradition lived on. Descendants of the original Puritan families—Cabots, Saltonstalls, Conants, Bradfords, Coolidges, Winthrops, Hoars, Chaunceys—are still leading citizens. New Englanders settled the Ohio Valley and the Middle West. Until far into the nineteenth century American literature was mostly New England literature written by Puritans and their descendants; American colleges were mostly New England colleges founded by Puritans or their descendants, and New England still has more colleges than any other section of the country. Most of the modern historians of Puritanism are professors in New England colleges; and Harvard, the oldest and most Puritan of all, is the source of many of the best modern studies of Puritanism. Until quite recently New England dominated American culture and New England was wholly Puritan in origin. Reason enough, then, for studying the Puritans.

The study of the Puritans takes place, not in isolation, but within the characteristic framework of American historical studies. American scholars have seen their total culture as originating in waves of European influence washing up on the American continent. The waves were christened in Europe before they journeyed to America—Romantic, Industrial, Conservative, Protestant, Catholic, Feudal, Monarchic, Republican, Egalitarian, Imperial, Constitutional, Federal, Utilitarian, Mercantile, Rational, Transcendental, Natural, Real, Social, Capital, Liberal, each with 'ism' added to make it substantive, are the more familiar. And 'Puritanism' is the first. Having identified the European 'isms' 'flying from the depravations of Europe to the American strand,' as Cotton Mather put it, the next task of the American historian has been to discover how these 'isms' were modified by the American environment. This leads him to try to define the environment: the Great Plains, the Mississippi Valley, the Appalachians and the Rockies, Tidewater and Piedmont, and the like, are all familiar words in American historical studies. They are all included in the grand idea 'frontier' which Frederick Jackson Turner made a central concept in American historiography at the turn of the last century. Ever since, much of American history, including the history of Puritanism, has been the story of how the 'isms,' the European inheritance, were modified by the 'frontier,' the characteristic American environment. Much of the best writing, many of the most interesting controversies, have been attempts to define the terms exactly, and get the relationships straight.

In so far as the historians are able to do all this, they are helping to solve the great American riddle—what is an American, what is the American character, what is the American tradition? The compulsive desire to solve this riddle is a function of the shortness of the American past, the diversity of the national origins, and the derivative nature of American culture. Americans do not know who they are and are always trying to find out. An Englishman does not ask himself, 'What does it mean to be an Englishman?'; a Frenchman does not ask himself, 'How can I write a French novel?'; a German does not ask himself, 'Is there such a thing as the German language?'; nor are there Un-English, Un-French, or Un-German Activities Committees officially charged with keeping the national tradition pure. Only American historians would try to define the peculiar national characteristics of their own scholarship.

Here, then, are the principal assumptions and motives which direct American studies of New England Puritanism. One of the most eminent of the historians of New England has written:

> *Puritanism may be described empirically as that point of view, code of values, carried to New England by the first settlers. These were English Protestants, and in their fundamental convictions were at one with the Protestants, or at least the Calvinistic Protestants, of all Europe. But the peculiar isolation of the New England colonies—the homogeneous people, the sparse soil, the climate, the economic struggle—quickly made these Protestants a peculiar people. Because their societies were tightly organized, and above all because they were a highly articulate people, the New Englanders established Puritanism—for better or worse—as one of the continuous factors in American life and thought. It has played so dominant a role because descendants of the Puritans have carried traits of the Puritan mind into a variety of pursuits and all the way across the continent. Many of these qualities have persisted even though the original creed is lost. Without some understanding of Puritanism, and that at its source, there is no understanding of America.*

This is an accepted view today. Nevertheless, until the 1920's the best historians of the colonial period were less interested in Puritan culture than in other aspects of early New England history. The monumental volumes of Herbert L. Osgood and Charles McLean Andrews belong to that era of American historiography which focussed on imperial history—the relations of colonies and mother country. Osgood and Andrews studied imperial constitutional history in an attempt to understand the Revolution. They were not much interested in Puritan culture and ideas, although Andrews's rich work touches on every phase of colonial life.

Those historians before 1920 who were interested in Puritan culture were mostly pious New England antiquarians. The books of Henry M. Dexter, John G. Palfrey, and Williston Walker are still consulted by specialists collecting facts. But the important books on the Puritans have been written by . . . Samuel Eliot Morison, Kenneth B. Murdock, and Perry Miller, to name the three most eminent, in whose work Harvard piety and provincial pride are incidental.

After the First World War, in an atmosphere of isolationism and disillusionment with the politics and culture of Europe, American critics lost interest in the older history which had tried to see colonial America in its imperial setting as an offshoot of British culture. They now sought for the unique in American history, the peculiar American character, the separate American tradition. In doing this they took a new look at Puritanism.

One group came to the straightforward conclusion that Puritanism was un-American and no part of the true American heritage. The most effective satirist of the 1920's, H. L. Mencken, identified Puritanism with canting hypocrisy, inhibitions, joylessness, witch-hunting, and tyranny masquerading as moral earnestness. Prohibition, Blue Laws, Fundamentalism, the narrow-minded censoring of books and plays and pictures, public and legal interference with private behaviour, together with a sniggering licentiousness behind the scenes—this has been the popular meaning of Puritanism since the 1920's as it was once before in Restoration England.

More sophisticated and scholarly versions of the anti-Puritanism of the 1920's are *The Founding of New England* (1921) by James Truslow Adams and V. L. Parrington's *Colonial Mind* (1927). Adams's book is still the best one-volume synthesis of New England history in the seventeenth century (an up-to-date re-doing would be useful), but it is especially weak on Puritan culture and religion. An exponent of the economic interpretation of history which dominated American historiography in the 1920's, Adams read Puritan theology and philosophy as an ideology constructed to further the ambitions of an economic class: Puritanism is 'the reasoned expression of the middle-class state of mind.' As an admirer of eighteenth-century liberalism, he was repelled by 'repression and conformity, the two key-notes of Puritan New England, [which] were to continue to mould the life of her people throughout the long "glacial age" of her early history.' Bigotry, intolerance, and censorship 'nullified, to a great extent, the benefits which might have been derived from her "educational" system. . . . In the other colonies, men may have been more ignorant of books, but they were healthy-minded.' Finally, an admirer of the 'Greek picture of the perfect life as the fullest development of the entire man, body and soul,' Adams was impatient with a Calvinism which proposed 'the utter surrender of one's own will to the divine will as expressed in minuteness of detail . . . even to the style of hats for a minister's wife, in the old Semitic writings' and which stripped 'God of every shred of what we consider moral character.'

V. L. Parrington's *Colonial Mind* is the first volume of his great work, *Main Currents in American Thought*. A Westerner, a supporter of the Progressive Movement, Parrington had originally meant his work to be called *A History of American Liberal Thought*. And he described Puritanism as the enemy of that liberalism which was, or which he wanted to make, the heart of the American tradition. Of their 'reactionary theology,' he wrote:

> *To the formalist who demanded an exact system, and to the timid who feared free speculation, the logical consistency of Calvinism made irresistible appeal . . . academic thinkers and schoolmen, men whom the free spaces of thought frightened and who felt safe only behind secure fences, theologians like John Cotton and his fellows, made a virtue of necessity and fell to declaiming on the excellence of those chains wherewith they were bound. How narrow and cold was their prison they seem never to have realized.*

To Parrington, theology was essentially political ideology: 'That Calvinism in its primary assumptions was a composite of oriental despotism and sixteenth-century monarchism, modified by the medieval conception of the city-state, is clear enough today to anyone who will take the trouble to translate dogma into political terms.' Anti-democratic, opposed to religious toleration, orthodox Puritanism was foreign to the progressive American tradition: 'Later critics of Puritanism discover in the theocratic experiment of Massachusetts Bay a preposterous attempt to turn back the pages of history.' Parrington's true Americans were the rebels and heretics—Roger Williams, Anne Hutchinson, and their like: 'In banishing the Antinomians and Separatists and Quakers, the Massachusetts magistrates cast out the spirit of liberalism from the household of the Saints.' Finally, Parrington's judgment of Puritanism is summed up in his paragraph on the imprecatory sermons of Jonathan Edwards, the last and greatest of Puritans:

> *Unfortunate as those sermons were in darkening the fame of an acute thinker . . . we cannot regret that Edwards devoted his logic to an assiduous stoking of the fires of hell. The theology of Calvin lay like a heavy weight upon the soul of New England, and there could be no*

surer way to bring it in to disrepute, than to thrust into naked relief the brutal grotesqueries of those dogmas. . . . Once the horrors that lay in the background of Calvinism were disclosed to common view, the system was doomed. . . . In this necessary work of freeing the spirit of New England, no other thinker played so large or so unconscious a part as Jonathan Edwards.

The accounts of Adams and Parrington do not satisfy recent students of Puritanism. To judge the Puritans by the yardstick of nineteenth-century liberalism is old-fashioned and unhistorical. Worse, the historians' firm conviction that the Puritans were a repulsive crew made it difficult for them to read Puritan works with scholarly care and patience. Adams and Parrington found New England sermons—the principal literary crop of the region—as hard going as most of us find *Mein Kampf*. Samuel Eliot Morison's judgment is just: '*The Colonial Mind* . . . is a brilliant synthesis of history and literature, but the writer shows little evidence of having read carefully the works of the authors he writes about.'

The writers of the 1920's who saw Puritanism as un-American revived interest in the subject. But the men who initiated the new study lacked the sympathetic open-mindedness and the patience for painstaking scholarship which precedes full understanding and just judgment. They made the study of Puritan culture a battleground of ideas and touched off a most remarkable outburst of scholarship. Historians became interested, for the first time, in New England intellectual history and made the study of that history one of the great successes of modern American historiography.

Three years before Parrington published his *Colonial Mind*, the first important work in the new historiography of Puritanism had already appeared.

Kenneth B. Murdock's *Increase Mather* (1925) is a full-length study of Puritanism in the modern style of scholarship. Increase Mather, the second in the powerful ministerial dynasty that dominated the intellectual, religious, and political life of seventeenth-century Boston, a prominent figure in the witchcraft scandals, a Puritan of Puritans, was not a sympathetic figure in the America of the 1920's. Parrington referred to the book as 'a somewhat meticulous defense . . . an extraordinarily painstaking document, that has added to our knowledge of Increase Mather's life and work, but it was unhappily conceived in the dark of the moon, a season congenial to strange quirks of fancy.' Of Harvard studies of the Puritans, Parrington wrote:

'[They] are excellent in their way, but a consciousness of dealing with Harvard worthies would seem to have laid the writers under certain inhibitions. Exposition too easily slides into apologetics.'

Parrington's criticisms are just, but they miss the point. *Increase Mather* has all the faults of a Ph.D. thesis which tries to overturn custom-hardened stereotypes by proving too much, claiming too much, and giving the hero the benefit of all doubts. Nevertheless, *Increase Mather* is a work of disciplined scholarship—Murdock has read the sources. And his sympathy with Mather and Puritan culture, which is sometimes strained and does sometimes slip into apologetics, is nevertheless the very quality which made it possible for him to read the documents with imaginative understanding. This is the stance of modern historical writing about the Puritans. Historians disagree about the meaning of particular facts; they differ as to what the essence of Puritan culture was; they admire or dislike this or that Puritan leader and their differences of judgment are often personal differences of taste. But all agree that exact scholarship and a willing suspension of disbelief sufficient to give the historical imagination scope are both essential. Since 1925 Murdock has gone on adding to our knowledge and understanding of Puritan culture.

The reconstruction of the Puritan story began with a biography and the next important work was also biographical. In 1930 Samuel Eliot Morison published *The Builders of the Bay Colony*. The preface to that volume is the manifesto of that modern Puritan historiography which grew to maturity in the 1930's and which still flourishes:

> *Most of the people described in this book would have led obscure lives but for a dynamic force called puritanism which drove them to start life anew in a wilderness. The commonwealth which they helped to create was not a large one in their time. . . . The total population was something between fourteen and sixteen thousand persons in 1640. . . . Search the modern world, where will you find another community of like extent and age, containing so many outstanding, pungent individuals as those described herein? . . . It is not easy to describe these people truthfully, yet with meaning to moderns. For the men of learning and women of gentle nurture who led a few thousand plain folk to plant a new England on ungrateful soil were moved by purposes utterly foreign to the present America. Their object was not to establish prosperity or prohibition, liberty or democracy, or indeed anything of currently recognized value. Their ideals were comprehended vaguely in the term puritanism, which nowadays has acquired various secondary and degenerate meanings. These*

ideals, real and imaginary, of early Massachusetts, were attacked by historians of Massachusetts long before 'debunking' became an accepted biographical mode; for it is always easier to condemn an alien way of life than to understand it. My attitude toward seventeenth-century puritanism has passed through scorn and boredom to a warm interest and respect. The ways of the puritans are not my ways, and their faith is not my faith; nevertheless they appear to me a courageous, humane, brave, and significant people.

The Builders of the Bay Colony, Morison's *Puritan Pronaos* (1936), and his three fat volumes on the history of Harvard (the founding, 1035, the seventeenth century, 2 vols., 1936) are learned and attractively written accounts of real men and women. To replace the comic-book caricatures of the Puritans manufactured by Mencken-esque journalists of the 1920's with believable people has been one of the major achievements of American historical scholarship in the twentieth century, and the honor is Morison's. From him we have learned to think of John Winthrop as a 'Puritan Squire' and a wise man of practical affairs, of John Hull, the goldsmith, as an artist and shrewd man of business, and of John Winthrop, Jr., as an industrial pioneer; from him we have learned that the private libraries and bookshops of seventeenth-century Boston were better, relatively, than those of any American city in later centuries, and that New England produced a remarkable number of Fellows of the Royal Society. Morison's Puritans are not only believable humans who loved good beer and gay clothing; they are admirable men and women who preserved in the midst of the wilderness a passion for learning and education unique in modern history.

What that learning was, what place it held in Puritan culture, we now know. Perry Miller's two volumes on *The New England Mind* (1939, 1953) are works unsurpassed in the whole corpus of American historical scholarship. They are not easy, and the second is more graceful and mature than the first; but together they are models of what learned intellectual history should be.

The first volume is an 'anatomy of the Puritan mind' in which Miller is 'concerned with defining and classifying the principal concepts of the Puritan mind in New England, of accounting for the origins, inter-relations, and significances of the ideas,' on the assumption that 'Puritanism was one of the major expressions of the Western intellect, that it achieved an organized synthesis of concepts which are fundamental to our culture, and that therefore it calls for the most

serious examination.' Miller has elucidated Non-Separating Congregationalism, the Federal Theology, and the Half-way Covenant; he has
traced the origins of Puritan thought and showed how large a place
reason held in the theology; he has given us a detailed picture of
Puritan cosmology, anthropology, and sociology.

The second volume is the story of how that synthesis of concepts
changed in the concrete setting of New England from 1620 to 1720. 'It
is a case history of the accommodation to the American landscape of
an imported and highly articulate system of ideas.' Here we see in
detail the original Puritan philosophy slowly metamorphosing into the
philosophy of the enlightenment—'somehow, in a century of American experience, the greatness of man's dependency had unaccountably
become a euphemism for the greatness of man.' By accounting for that
change, Miller's work is much more than an intensive study of a small
group which happened, in the lottery of history, to become the founders of America; it is a splendid study of an important era in the
intellectual history of Western man.

However, even twentieth-century Harvard historians are sometimes provincial. Morison's apologetics sometimes make the Puritans
too human: 'One gets the impression of a healthy and hearty community, untroubled by the inhibitions and prohibitions that have made
latter-day Puritanism so unpopular. . . . They were a free and happy
people.' After all, some Puritans, some of the time, were ascetics with a
prurient interest in obscenity and a pathological fear of witchcraft, and
no Puritan would have subscribed to the statement that any earthly
city could be free and happy. And Morison sees J. T. Adams's stric-
tures on the Puritans, not merely as exaggerations, which they are, but
as treasonable attacks on the honor of the builders of the Bay Colony.

In addition, the outsider suspects that Plymouth, Rhode Island,
and Connecticut have received less attention than they deserve from
the scholars of the Massachusetts Bay Colony. In Cambridge and
Boston, but not in the rest of America, the *Arbella* is a more notable
ship than the *Mayflower*. Perry Miller too easily rejects the old theory
that the aristocratic intellectuals of Massachusetts Bay derived part of
their church government from the Plymouth Pilgrims—'a small and
earnest band of simple souls,' 'home-spun, hardworking farmers,' 'a
relatively insignificant community, completely overshadowed by Massachusetts Bay' (but a community which produced in Bradford's *History* the best work of early New England literature). The issue is

important since the Puritan theory of church government had an influence on later American theories of democracy. To argue that if the leaders of the Bay Colony took their theories from Plymouth, 'How can we have much respect for the intellectual development of these people?' is unconvincing.

In emphasizing the literature, learning, and ideas of the Puritans, the Harvard historians may also connect them too closely with Renaissance humanism. One gets the impression that the founders of New England were intellectuals, followers of Erasmus and Ramus, whose piety and religion were secondary concerns. But 'the essence of Puritanism,' Alan Simpson reminds us, 'is an experience of conversion which separates the Puritan from the mass of mankind and endows him with the privileges and the duties of the elect. The root of the matter is always a new birth, which brings with it a conviction of salvation and a dedication of warfare against sin.'

All criticisms aside, historians of New England Puritanism have succeeded dramatically and admirably in rewriting the first chapter of New England history. But what have we learned about its relation to the rest of the story? What residues of Puritan experience have survived into our own time? After a generation of work, the question still cannot be answered precisely.

Kenneth Murdock has stated the problem with characteristic moderation:

> *It is pretty generally admitted that somewhere in America's total cultural heritage and the complex of qualities which make up the "American character" there are traces of Puritanism. It is very difficult, however, to be sure just what these traces are, partly because the continuing influence in intellectual history of any past "state of mind" is always hard to assess, and partly because the special "state of mind" of the New England colonists has often been misunderstood. . . . The fertilizing tradition is a matter of spirit and idea; the fruitful heritage of the past comes from ways of thought and feeling, fundamental intellectual and emotional points of view, which have the power to stimulate new attempts to map the changing current of life. Such things are hard to categorize; their nature defies precise definition. . . . The evidence is rarely conclusive enough to support dogmatic assertions, but there are bases for reasonable conjectures. Even guesses have value, since they bear upon a strain in American intellectual history the existence of which few historians would doubt even though its exact nature may be impossible to define.*

The discussion of the Puritan tradition in America has centered around five or six major topics which are themselves summaries of what the modern historian sees as the essence of Puritanism.

1. Morality and religion. We have now a juster understanding of the original Puritan moral code and we no longer blame the Puritans of the seventeenth century for the canting, genteel piety and the stuffy respectability which Mencken attacked in the twentieth century. But we do recognize that the moral and religious tone of much British and American criticism—economic, political, artistic, etc.—is partly Puritan in origin.

Fundamentalism, revivalism, and sectarian splintering in American religious history are all connected in complex ways with what happened in early New England. But again, our perspective has changed. Puritan Fundamentalism was intellectually respectable; it dovetailed with the best learning and science of the day. Seventeenth-century Puritans were not ignorant, superstitious bigots who had to reject biology, physics, geology, and historical criticism, in order to maintain their dogma. In fact, the religion of the Puritans was a highly intellectual religion and it is used by contemporary critics as a stick to beat the sentimental, tender-minded, anti-intellectual and genteel religiosity of the twentieth century. The recent neo-Calvinist movement in theology has tried to revive some parts of the Puritan's religious philosophy.

2. Education and literature. The Puritan respect for learning has come to be the quality which modern historians find most admirable. Certainly no other colonists in the history of the world have set up a university six years after settling in the wilderness. The foundation of Harvard College in 1636 is a unique and awe-inspiring achievement. 'After God had carried us safe to *New England,* and we had builded our houses, provided necessaries for our livelihood, reared convenient places for God's worship, and settled the civil government: One of the things we looked for, and looked after was to advance *Learning* and perpetuate it to Posterity; dreading to leave an illiterate Ministry to the Churches, when our present Ministers shall lie in the dust.' These words from *New England's First Fruits* (1643), reprinted more than once by recent historians, have become a part of the American heritage. The history of Puritan colleges, elementary and grammar schools, and of Puritan libraries has been zealously studied, and no one doubts that the tradition of learning and education is continuous from the seventeenth century to the present.

In literature, perhaps, the line of descent from the Puritans is clearest. The 'plain style,' biography and autobiography which reveal the inner life of the subject, historical writing, and a continuous tradition of symbol and allegory running through Hawthorne, Melville, Emerson, Thoreau, and James have all been traced back to their seventeenth-century origins.

3. The Puritan ethic in business life. The major studies of the relation between the Puritan ethic and the spirit of capitalism were made by Weber and Tawney and other European scholars. But American historians have asked the same questions of the American record and there is general agreement that some connection can be traced between Puritanism and a later American business ethic—business as a 'calling,' the moral significance of profits and thrift, the moral dignity of work, a distrust of aristocratic leisure and dilettantism, the suspicion that the poor are ungodly and hence shiftless, the conviction that Andrew Carnegie and John D. Rockefeller are numbered with the Elect because God has prospered them—all these are somehow and complexly related to the attitudes of seventeenth-century New England.

4. Democracy and limited government. English historiography about the Civil Wars and Commonwealth, perhaps because the political thought and activities of English Puritans is so rich and varied and well documented, is precise and definite on the subject of Puritanism and politics. The American historian works with relatively meager materials. Certainly the Puritan strands in American political thought and practice are exceedingly difficult to unravel. Here, perhaps, the simple-minded liberal interpretations of Puritanism have been at their weakest: nothing is accomplished by a rapid scanning of the sources and a separating of the apparently 'democratic' statements of the seventeenth century from the apparently 'theocratic.' Out of context, John Winthrop's speech on liberty (3 July 1645) sounds pretty much like an example of what Isaiah Berlin has called the totalitarian concept of 'positive' liberty; in its setting, as Edmund S. Morgan's recent biography of Winthrop makes clear, it appears much less sinister.

The founders of New England were not democrats; but there was an irrepressible democratic dynamic in Puritan theology which could not be stifled. The congregational idea of voluntary churches bound together by covenant eventually, in the American environment, passed over into politics: the Mayflower Compact—the first formal social contract in modern history, the Fundamental Orders of Connecticut, the writings of John Wise, and much else, are part of the democratic tradition in America.

As seventeenth-century English opponents of Stuart absolutism, the Puritans naturally supported constitutionalism and limited government, although John Winthrop was tempted in the early days of the Bay Colony to claim unbounded authority for himself and his fellow magistrates. Here, too, the 'Puritan conscience' plays its ambiguous role. The Protestant doctrine that the conscience of the individual is the ultimate judge of right becomes, in politics, the subversive doctrine that a man must refuse to obey a law, however legitimately promulgated, which violates his own sense of right. When Ralph Waldo Emerson said of the Fugitive Slave Law, enacted by Congress, signed by the President, and declared constitutional by the Supreme Court, 'I will not obey it, by God' his Puritan conscience was at work. Whatever leanings the magistrates of the Bay Colony had toward absolutism were bound to be defeated by this built-in principle of nonconformity:

> *Boston never wanted a good principle of rebellion in it, from the planting until now; there is always a minority unconvinced . . . some protester against the cruelty of magistrates to the Quakers . . . some defender of the slave against the politician and the merchant; some champion of the first principles of humanity against the rich and luxurious . . . some noble protestant, who will not stoop to infamy when all are gone mad, but will stand for liberty and justice, if alone, until all come back to him.*

5. *Frustrated Utopianism.* The most-quoted phrases of Puritan literature are those of John Winthrop, written aboard the *Arbella* in 1630: 'Men shall say of succeeding plantations: the lord make it like that of New England: for we shall be as a City set upon a Hill, the eyes of all people are upon us.' The sense that they are a peculiar people, designed by Providence to live in a more perfect community than any known in the Old World, the sense that it is America's mission to set an example to other nations, is part of America's Puritan inheritance. It echoes through the *Battle Hymn of the Republic,* the Gettysburg Address, and the crusade to make the world safe for democracy. At its

worst it becomes the vulgar, naive, chauvinistic idealism of the innocent abroad and the *Quiet American.*

Finally, the Puritans who sought to build a holy community ended in frustration and disillusionment. Their failures were the more bitter since their hopes had been so high. One of the recurring themes in American culture is the bitterness of failure, the frustration of never achieving the ideal. Americans see themselves as the standard-bearers of freedom and democracy, and Little Rock is the town in the headlines of every newspaper in the world. America has rejected the militarism and imperialism of the Old World, but Hiroshima and 'Yanks Go Home' are familiar phrases.

But an exact description of the Puritan contribution to American culture is not easy. Professor Murdock has outlined some of the difficulties in the passage already quoted, and there are others. How can we distinguish that which has been a continuous element from the seventeenth century to the present from that which was forgotten and then revived by a later generation as an analogy, a paradigm, or a metaphor? When Perry Miller says his 'mission of expounding' American history came to him as a 'sudden epiphany' on the banks of the Congo, he is translating Gibbon's 'musing amid the ruins of the Capitol' into Puritanese: this is obviously a conscious metaphorical revival, not an unbroken tradition of language and idea. But in the large picture of American culture as a whole the distinctions are not so easy. We will not be able to identify with precision the elements of the Puritan tradition in modern America until we have patiently and carefully studied the whole record. Until we do know the story in detail, talk about the Puritan tradition in America will be mostly speculation.

To thumb hastily through the record looking for the good and bad which Puritanism has contributed to the modern American character is a Puritan way of writing history and it ends in propaganda. The result is either unhistorical apologetics or the vilification which disfigures, for example, the work of J. T. Adams and V. L. Parrington. The result was implicit when they began by asking what was truly American in the Puritan tradition instead of asking what Puritanism was, in its own terms.

Perry Miller asks the question rhetorically in his prefaces, but writes like a historian in his texts, and gives no bald, dogmatic answers. He still speaks of 'the uniqueness of the American experience' (how can it be more unique than any other historical experience?), but he actually tells the 'massive story of the movement of European culture into the vacant wilderness of America,' and gives us profound case-studies of the relation of ideas to communal experience. The second volume of *The New England Mind*—the best single book on American Puritanism and a classic of modern historiography—attempts no formal answers to questions about the uniqueness of the American tradition and experience; yet its rich narrative, immensely learned and powerfully imagined, tells us what the first century of New England experience was, and answers the questions by implication.

Compared with the historiography of English Puritanism, the historiography of American Puritanism appears to be almost exclusively the history of ideas. English historians, following R. H. Tawney, have produced rich studies of the social and economic aspects of Puritanism and since the 1930's, influenced by Marxist and English socialist ideas, have studied intensively the class structure and the political character of Puritanism. But in America the Harvard historians reacted strongly against the economic and social interpretations of the 1920's, especially Parrington and J. T. Adams, and concentrated on the history of ideas. In doing so they sometimes left out of account the circumstances, the concrete times and places and social networks in which the thinkers lived. But this is the American part of the story— the wilderness which produced the American modifications in the transplanted European intellectual system. The Puritan contribution to American culture can be described only by looking at all aspects of Puritanism and all aspects of American culture. Puritan historiography in America has been too exclusively intellectual.

But now the force of the reaction appears to be spent. Miller's second volume is a history of Puritan ideas in action in seventeenth-century New England. A new generation of historians of New England, for whom the debates of the 1920's are historiographical rather than personal, are widening the angle of vision to include all aspects of colonial life: among the most notable recent books are Edmund S. Morgan's *Puritan Dilemma: The Story of John Winthrop* (1958), Bernard Bailyn, *The New England Merchants in the Seventeenth Century* (1955), and Anthony N. B. Garvan, *Architecture and Town Planning in Colonial Connecticut* (1951).

The work of the historian is never, of course, done. Every new generation of historians of Puritanism will discover hiatuses, blind spots, limited perspectives, and errors in the work of its predecessors; but contemporary scholarship devoted to seventeenth-century New England has achieved the level of learning and objectivity, grace and sophistication, of the best historical writing of the twentieth century.

Part One

THE PURITAN VISION: "A CITTY UPON A HILL"

Introduction

No man had more right to lecture his fellow voyagers on the ends and means of their mission than John Winthrop, the principal lay leader of the Puritan undertaking to America. He was one of the organizers of the Massachusetts Bay Company and its first governor; he directed the fleet that sailed in 1630; in Massachusetts he served fifteen years as governor or deputy governor, "at all times," writes Perry Miller, the colony's "leading citizen and most influential personage."[1]* Winthrop's sermon, "A Modell of Christian Charity" (2),† probably delivered on board the flagship *Arbella* during the crossing, is the classic statement of Puritan social and political philosophy, applied to the immediate task of erecting the holy community.

Note that though Winthrop assumes, as did all Englishmen of his time, that social order depends on fixed inequalities of rank, each person keeping in the position allotted to him by God, the main stress of his argument lies on the obligations of brotherly love that are incumbent on high and low, rich and poor, alike. The city on a hill was to be, above all else, a place where love prevailed, the more so because these venturers would be environed in a "community of perils." Note, too, Winthrop's use of the idea of the covenant as a sanction for fraternity: the covenant not only defined the goals of the mission; it was also an instrument of cohesion and discipline. As such it was the more effective because the commitments it entailed were understood to be voluntary. No one was required to go to New

---

* Raised numbers are keyed to the references listed at the end of the introduction to each section.
† Numbers in parentheses identify the readings appearing in this book.

23

England; hence each wayfarer was presumed to have freely taken upon himself the strenuous duties of God's commission. By Winthrop's reasoning, each one thus became personally responsible for the welfare of the whole community, and the outcome of the enterprise would depend directly on his performance. From this it followed that public exigencies would "oversway all private respects" in Winthrop's "due forme of Government." Though the Puritans individualized responsibility, there would be small scope in Massachusetts for the free expression of variant, private individualities. Finally, it is worth calling attention to Winthrop's lofty sense of the significance of what he and his colleagues were proposing to do: they meant to drive the Reformation to a glorious conclusion, demonstrating before "the eies of all people" that a social system could be founded on the principle of Christian charity. To explicate and magnify this vision was Winthrop's purpose in the *Arbella* sermon; to its realization he devoted his entire energy in Massachusetts.

By 1646, when Peter Bulkeley, minister at Concord, published *The Gospel-Covenant* (3), the Puritan experiment could be accounted a success. Threats from England had been repelled, and the Indians had been crushed. The economic difficulties of the early 1640's had been overcome. Deviationists such as Roger Williams, Anne Hutchinson, Samuel Gorton, and merry Thomas Morton had been expelled or suppressed. The "due forme of Government," somewhat modified by experience, seemed to be working well: a code of public law had been enacted, and soon the churches would adopt a body of regulations proposed to them by the Cambridge Synod of 1646–1648. A small but vigorous college had been founded. A loose confederation for mutual defense had been formed by Massachusetts, Plymouth, Connecticut, and New Haven. Most important, the saints, though perhaps not as holy as they should have been, were manifestly holier than any people elsewhere in the world. These several achievements justified the ministers and magistrates in believing that New England—excepting that sink of errors, Rhode Island—had been set in the right way, that the "first Foundation, both of Religion and Righteousness, Doctrine and Discipline, Church and Commonwealth," had been securely laid.[2] Indeed, New England now had a lesson of uniformity, serenity, and purity to teach to old England where, in the stress of civil war, the Puritan program of reform was jeopardized by a mushroom growth of left-wing sects, provoking New Englanders to warn against the dangers of religious toleration, since "such cracks and flaws in the new building of the Reformation, portend a fall." [3]

So large were New England's blessings, especially in contrast to England's agonies, that clergymen like Bulkeley now found it needful to caution the saints against complacency. God had singularly favored the Puritan venture but, if the people failed to fulfill the articles of the covenant, He would turn His favor into a curse. Hence there must be no relaxation, no subsidence of zeal, no wavering of commitment. Bulkeley's admonition of 1646, memorialized by Cotton Mather as "the dying charge of a Moses to an Israel in the wilderness," [4] strikes the same themes as Winthrop's pronouncement of 1630: its controlling imagery is that of the holy city; it stresses the rule of love and invokes the covenant to enforce that rule; it insists on the voluntary character of the covenant. Yet for all the similarity, there is a subtle difference, marking the disparity between a great work to be undertaken and the same great work largely completed. Winthrop told the people what they would have to do to be saved; so does Bulkeley, but he also tells them—and in the telling celebrates—what has already been done. For him, New England has become the actual "modell of Christian charity"; the pattern of righteousness has been localized there, and the mission is no longer to create but to conserve. The issue lurking in Bulkeley's homily is the same one that was raised by John Cotton's assertion that "it is for us to doe all the good we can, and to leave nothing to those that shall come after us, but to walk in the righteous steps of their fore-Fathers." [5] Whether the holy community could so sustain itself, once the reformation had become an administration, would be the crucial question of the rising generation. Bulkeley's tract suggests that the question had already become pertinent.

The fact was that in New England, as in old, the new building of the Reformation showed cracks and flaws. There were recurrent disputes between congregations and their ministers: Bulkeley himself went through a quarrel that racked the Concord church, occasioned the calling of a council of arbitrators from other churches, and ended in the dismissal of Concord's ruling lay elder.[6] There were also signs that the superstructure of civil institutions rested on an unstable base. Now and again popular sentiment heaved against the magistracy, expressing what Cotton Mather was later to call "the touchy jealousie of the people about their liberties." [7] One such eruption occurred in the village of Hingham in 1645 over the election of a militia officer; the squabble rose to the General Court where it pitted the magistrates, among them John Winthrop, against the deputies from the several towns. Having offended some citizens of Hingham by exercising against them his power as justice of the peace, Winthrop was im-

peached by the deputies for exceeding his commission. Acquitted, he
delivered a speech on liberty and authority (4)—the finest exposition
of the political theory of the Puritan commonwealth. As in his *Arbella*
sermon, Winthrop here employs the disciplinary device of the covenant, now expanded to include a covenant between the people and
their officials. Moreover, while denying that the power of God's appointed magistrates is in any sense arbitrary, he draws a firm distinction between license and civil liberty, the latter being "a liberty to that
only which is good, just, and honest." Liberty and authority are
reconciled, through the covenant, by defining liberty as cheerful submission to holy rule; this, says Winthrop, "is of the same kind of liberty
wherewith Christ hath made us free." Evidently the Hingham protest-
ers were pacified, or perhaps abashed, by Winthrop's "address from
the throne"; at any rate, they made no formal retort. Yet the very fact
that Winthrop felt compelled to speak as he did points to a basic
incongruity between the magisterial concept of government and the
political realities of the Bay Colony.

In the interpretive readings that follow, these matters of theory
and practice are treated by Perry Miller, Ralph Barton Perry, and
Darrett B. Rutman (5, 6, 7). Miller published his essay in 1938 when,
on the morning after the tercentenary celebrations of the founding of
Massachusetts and Harvard College—acclaimed as fountainheads of
American liberty, civility, and republicanism—he thought it needful to
emphasize the authoritarian, even the totalitarian, elements of Puritan
politics. Nearly twenty years later, when America was believed by
many intellectuals to be menaced by gray-flannel conformity, Miller
noted that historians faced a different temptation, namely, "to dwell
upon the inherent individualism, the respect for private conscience,
the implications of revolution" that Puritan theology was supposed to
have nurtured. He added, however, that "from neither resistance to
the *Zeitgeist* will come more than a partial apprehension of the reality" of historical Puritanism.[8] That being so, Miller's interpretation is
accompanied in this collection by Perry's philosophical reflections on
the "ultimate individualism" of the Puritan ethos and by Rutman's
strong argument, directed explicitly against Miller, for a deeper appreciation of the diversities and internal strains of early New England
society and thought. It is worth noting that the present volume reflects, in its design, the model of Puritanism that Rutman sharply
attacks. It should also be remarked that, as historians restudy New
England "town by town and church by church," they are amassing

evidence to support Rutman's main contentions.[9] Much more work will have to be done, however, before the outlines of a new model come convincingly clear.

1. PERRY MILLER and THOMAS H. JOHNSON, eds., *The Puritans* (New York: American Book Co., 1938), p. 126.

2. THOMAS SHEPARD, quoted in PERRY MILLER, *The New England Mind: The Seventeenth Century* (New York: Macmillan, 1939), p. 471.

3. THOMAS SHEPARD, *New Englands Lamentation for Old Englands present errours* (London, 1645), p. 2.

4. COTTON MATHER, *Magnalia Christi Americana*, I (Hartford, 1855), p. 402.

5. PERRY MILLER, *The New England Mind: The Seventeenth Century*, p. 471.

6. See MATHER, *Magnalia*, I, p. 402.

7. *Ibid.*, p. 127.

8. PERRY MILLER, *Errand into the Wilderness* (Cambridge, Mass.: The Belknap Press of Harvard Univ. Press, 1956), p. 141.

9. For studies in the local and institutional history of early New England, see the bibliography at the back of this book.

2

A Modell of Christian Charity

JOHN WINTHROP

God Almightie in his most holy and wise providence hath soe disposed of the Condicion of mankinde, as in all times some must be rich some poore, some highe and eminent in power and dignitie; others meane and in subieccion.

1. REASON: *First*, to hold conformity with the rest of his workes, being delighted to shewe forthe the glory of his wisdome in the variety and

Reprinted from *Winthrop Papers*, II (Boston: Massachusetts Historical Society, 1931), courtesy Massachusetts Historical Society.

differance of the Creatures and the glory of his power, in ordering all these differences for the preservacion and good of the whole, and the glory of his greatnes that as it is the glory of princes to haue many officers, soe this great King will haue many Stewards counting himselfe more honoured in dispenceing his guifts to man by man, then if hee did it by his owne immediate hand.

2. Reason: *Secondly*, That he might haue the more occasion to manifest the worke of his Spirit: first, vpon the wicked in moderateing and restraineing them: soe that the riche and mighty should not eate vpp the poore, nor the poore, and dispised rise vpp against theire superiours, and shake off theire yoake; 2ly in the regenerate in exerciseing his graces in them, as in the greate ones, theire loue mercy, gentlenes, temperance etc., in the poore and inferiour sorte, theire faithe patience, obedience etc:

3. Reason: *Thirdly*, That every man might haue need of other, and from hence they might be all knitt more nearly together in the Bond of brotherly affeccion: from hence it appeares plainely that noe man is made more honourable then another or more wealthy etc., out of any perticuler and singuler respect to himselfe but for the glory of his Creator and the Common good of the Creature, Man; Therefore God still reserues the propperty of these guifts to himselfe as Ezek: 16. 17. he there calls wealthe his gold and his silver etc. Prov: 3. 9. he claimes theire seruice as his due honour the Lord with thy riches etc. All men being thus (by divine providence) rancked into two sortes, riche and poore; vnder the first, are comprehended all such as are able to liue comfortably by theire owne meanes duely improued; and all others are poore according to the former distribution. There are two rules whereby wee are to walke one towards another: JUSTICE and MERCY. . . . There is likewise a double Lawe by which wee are regulated in our conversacion one towardes another: in both the former respects, the lawe of nature and the lawe of grace, or the morrall lawe or the lawe of the gospell, to omitt the rule of Justice as not propperly belonging to this purpose otherwise then it may fall into consideracion in some perticuler Cases: By the first of these lawes man as he was enabled soe withall [is] commaunded to loue his neighbour as himselfe vpon this ground stands all the precepts of the morrall lawe, which concernes our dealings with men. To apply this to the works of mercy this lawe requires two things first that every man afford his help to another in every want or distresse Secondly, That hee performe this

out of the same affeccion, which makes him carefull of his owne good according to that of our Saviour Math: [7.12] Whatsoever ye would that men should doe to you. . . .

The Lawe of Grace or the Gospell hath some differance from the former as in these respectes first the lawe of nature was giuen to man in the estate of innocency; this of the gospell in the estate of regeneracy: 2ly, the former propounds one man to another, as the same fleshe and Image of god, this as a brother in Christ allsoe, and in the Communion of the same spirit and soe teacheth vs to put a difference betweene Christians and others. Doe good to all especially to the household of faith; vpon this ground the Israelites were to putt a difference betweene the brethren of such as were strangers though not of the Canaanites. 3ly. The Lawe of nature could giue noe rules for dealeing with enemics for all arc to be considered as freinds in the estate of innocency, but the Gospell commaunds loue to an enemy. proofe. If thine Enemie hunger feede him; Loue your Enemies doe good to them that hate you Math: 5. 44.

This Lawe of the Gospell propoundes likewise a difference of seasons and occasions there is a time when a christian must sell all and giue to the poore as they did in the Apostles times. There is a tyme allsoe when a christian (though they giue not all yet) must giue beyond theire abillity, as they of Macedonia. Cor: 2. 6. likewise community of perills calls for extraordinary liberallity and soe doth Community in some speciall seruice for the Churche. Lastly, when there is noe other meanes whereby our Christian brother may be releiued in this distresse, wee must help him beyond our ability, rather then tempt God, in putting him vpon help by miraculous or extraordinary meanes. . . .

The diffinition which the Scripture giues vs of loue is this Loue is the bond of perfection. First, it is a bond, or ligament. 2ly, it makes the worke perfect. There is noe body but consistes of partes and that which knitts these partes together giues the body its perfeccion, because it makes eache parte soe contiguous to other as thereby they doe mutually participate with eache other, both in strengthe and infirmity in pleasure and paine, to instance in the most perfect of all bodies, Christ and his church make one body: the severall partes of this body considered aparte before they were vnited were as disproportionate and as much disordering as soe many contrary quallities or elements but when christ comes and by his spirit and loue knitts all these partes to himselfe and each to other, it is become the most perfect and best proportioned body in the world Eph: 4. 16. "Christ by whome all the body being knitt together by every ioynt for the furniture thereof according to the effectuall power which is in the measure of every perfeccion of partes a glorious body without spott or wrinckle the ligaments hereof being Christ or his loue for Christ is loue 1 John: 4. 8. Soe this definition is right Loue is the bond of perfeccion.

From hence wee may frame these Conclusions.

1. First all true Christians are of one body in Christ 1. Cor. 12. 12. 13. 17. [27.] Ye are the body of Christ and members of [your?] parte.

2ly. The ligamentes of this body which knitt together are loue.

3ly. Noe body can be perfect which wants its propper ligamentes.

4ly. All the partes of this body being thus vnited are made soe contiguous in a speciall relacion as they must needes partake of each others strength and infirmity, ioy, and sorrowe, weale and woe. 1 Cor: 12. 26. If one member suffers all suffer with it, if one be in honour, all reioyce with it.

5ly. This sensiblenes and Sympathy of each others Condicions will necessarily infuse into each parte a natiue desire and endeavour, to strengthen defend preserue and comfort the other. . . .

From the former Consideracions ariseth these Conclusions.

1. First, This loue among Christians is a reall thing not Imaginarie.

2ly. This loue is as absolutely necessary to the being of the body of Christ, as the sinewes and other ligaments of a naturall body are to the being of that body.

3ly. This loue is a divine spirituall nature free, actiue strong Couragious permanent vnder valueing all things beneathe its propper obiect, and of all the graces this makes vs nearer to resemble the virtues of our heavenly father.

4ly, It restes in the loue and wellfare of its beloued, for the full and certaine knowledge of these truthes concerning the nature vse, [and] excellency of this grace, that which the holy ghost hath left recorded 1. Cor. 13. may giue full satisfaccion which is needfull for every true member of this louely body of the Lord Jesus, to worke vpon theire heartes, by prayer meditacion continuall exercise at least of the speciall [power] of this grace till Christ be formed in them and they in him all in eache other knitt together by this bond of loue.

It rests now to make some applicacion of this discourse by the present designe which gave the occasion of writeing of it. Herein are 4 things to be propounded: first the persons, 2ly, the worke, 3ly, the end, 4ly the meanes.

1. For the persons, wee are a Company professing our selves fellow members of Christ, In which respect onely though wee were absent from eache other many miles, and had our imploymentes as farre distant, yet wee ought to account our selves knitt together by this bond of loue, and liue in the exercise of it, if wee would have comforte of our being in Christ . . .

2ly. for the worke wee haue in hand, it is by a mutuall consent through a speciall overruleing providence, and a more then an ordinary approbation of the Churches of Christ to seeke out a place of Cohabitation and Consorteshipp vnder a due forme of Government both ciuill and ecclesiasticall. In such cases as this the care of the publique must oversway all private respects, by which not onely conscience, but meare Ciuill pollicy doth binde vs; for it is a true rule that perticuler estates cannott subsist in the ruine of the publique.

3ly. The end is to improue our liues to doe more seruice to the Lord the comforte and encrease of the body of christe whereof wee are members that our selues and posterity may be the better preserued from the Common corrupcions of this euill world to serue the Lord and worke out our Salvacion vnder the power and purity of his holy Ordinances.

4ly for the meanes whereby this must bee effected, they are 2fold, a Conformity with the worke and end wee aime at, these wee see are extraordinary, therefore wee must not content our selues with vsuall ordinary meanes whatsoever wee did or ought to haue done when wee liued in England, the same must wee doe and more allsoe where wee goe: That which the most in theire Churches maineteine as a truthe in profession onely, wee must bring into familiar and constant practise, as in this duty of loue we must loue brotherly without dissimulation, wee must loue one another with a pure hearte feruently wee must beare one anothers burthens, wee must not looke onely on our owne things, but allsoe on the things of our brethren, neither must wee think that the lord will beare with such faileings at our hands as hee dothe from those among whome wee haue liued . . .

Thus stands the cause betweene God and vs, wee are entered into Covenant with him for this worke, wee haue taken out a Commission, the Lord hath giuen vs leaue to drawe our owne Articles wee haue professed to enterprise these Accions vpon these and these ends, wee haue herevpon besought him of favour and blessing: Now if the Lord shall please to heare vs, and bring vs in peace to the place wee desire, then hath hee ratified this Covenant and sealed our Commission, [and] will expect a strickt performance of the Articles contained in it, but if wee shall neglect the observacion of these Articles which are the ends wee haue propounded, and dissembling with our God, shall fall to embrace this present world and prosecute our carnall intencions, seekeing greate things for our selues and our posterity, the Lord will surely breake out in wrathe against vs be revenged of such a periured people and make vs knowe the price of the breache of such a Covenant.

Now the onely way to avoyde this shipwracke and to provide for our posterity is to followe the Counsell of Micah, to doe Justly, to loue mercy, to walke humbly with our God, for this end, wee must be knitt together in this worke as one man, wee must entertaine each other in brotherly Affeccion, wee must be willing to abridge our selues of our superfluities, for the supply of others necessities, wee must vphold a familiar Commerce together in all meekenes, gentlenes, patience and liberallity, wee must delight in eache other, make others Condicions our owne reioyce together, mourne together, labour, and suffer together, allwayes haueing before our eyes our Commission and Community in the worke, our Community as members of the same body, soe shall wee keepe the vnitie of the spirit in the bond of peace, the Lord will be our God and delight to dwell among vs, as his owne people and will commaund a blessing vpon vs in all our wayes, soe that wee shall see much more of his wisdome power goodnes and truthe then formerly wee haue beene acquainted with, wee shall finde that the God of Israell is among vs, when tenn of vs shall be able to resist a thousand of our enemies, when hee shall make vs a prayse and glory, that men shall say of succeeding plantacions: the lord make it like that of New England: for wee must Consider that wee shall be as a Citty vpon a Hill, the eies of all people are vppon vs; soe that if wee shall deale falsely with our god in this worke wee haue vndertaken and soe cause him to withdrawe his present help from vs, wee shall be made a story and a by-word through the world, wee shall open the mouthes of enemies to speake euill of the wayes of god and all professours for Gods sake; wee shall shame the faces of many of gods worthy seruants, and cause theire prayers to be turned into

Cursses vpon vs till wee be consumed out of the good land whether wee are goeing: And to shutt vpp this discourse with that exhortacion of Moses that faithfull seruant of the Lord in his last farewell to Israell Deut. 30. Beloued there is now sett before vs life, and good, deathe and euill in that wee are Commaunded this day to loue the Lord our God, and to loue one another to walke in his wayes and to keepe his Commaundements and his Ordinance, and his lawes, and the Articles of our Covenant with him that wee may liue and be multiplyed, and that the Lord our God may blesse vs in the land whether wee goe to possesse it: But if our heartes shall turne away soe that wee will not obey, but shall be seduced and worshipp [serue *cancelled*] othor Codo our pleasures, and proffitts, and serue them; it is propounded vnto vs this day, wee shall surely perishe out of the good Land whether wee passe over this vast Sea to possesse it;

> *Therefore lett vs choose life,*
> *that wee, and our Seede,*
> *may liue; by obeyeing his*
> *voyce, and cleaueing to him,*
> *for hee is our life, and*
> *our prosperity.*

3

A Willing and Voluntary Subjection
PETER BULKELEY

. . . And thou *New-England*, which art exalted in privilodgcs of the Gospel above many other people, know thou the time of thy visitation, and consider the great things the Lord hath done for thee. The Gospel hath free passage in all places where thou dwellest; oh that it might be glorified also by thee. Thou enjoyeth many faithful witnesses, which have testified unto thee, the Gospel of the grace of God. Thou hast

Reprinted from Peter Bulkeley, *The Gospel-Covenant; or the Covenant of Grace opened*, 2nd ed. (London, 1651).

many bright starres shining in thy firmament, to give thee the *knowledge of salvation from on high, to guide thy feet in the way of peace:* Be not high-minded, because of thy priviledges, but feare, because of thy danger. The more thou hast committed unto thee, the more thou must account for. No peoples account will be heavier then thine, if thou doe not walke worthy of the meanes of thy salvation. The Lord looks for more from thee, then from other people; more zeale for God, more love to his truth, more justice and equity in thy wayes; Thou shouldst be a speciall people, an onely people, none like thee in all the earth: oh be so, in loving the Gospel and Ministers of it, having them *in singular love for their works sake.* Glorifie thou that word of the Lord, which hath glorified thee. Take heed lest for neglect of either, God remove thy Candlesticke out of the midst of thee; lest being now as *a Citie upon an hill,* which many seek unto, thou be left like *a Beacon upon the top of a mountaine,* desolate and forsaken. If we walke unworthy of the Gospel brought unto us, the greater our mercy hath been in the enjoying of it, the greater will our judgement be for the contempt. Be instructed, and take heed. . . .

Seeing this is one of the blessings of the covenant of grace, to have God above us and over us, to guide and rule us, this must teach us when we enter into covenant with God, not to count our condition then a state of liberty, as if we might then walk after our owne desires, and wayes, as if there were none to command us and rule over us. Indeed, there is a spirituall liberty from our enemies, but there is subjection required to the Lord. We must not look onely after gifts, mercies, kindnesses, pardon, and such tokens and pledges of grace, but looke also for this, to be under God, and to set up him on high to be a God and Lord over us; And let us not count this our misery, but our blessednesse, that we are brought under his gracious government. Herein the Lord sheweth his marvellous kindnesse, that he will take care of us. . . . Now we are but poore ants and wormes upon earth, but the Lord of Heaven offereth to take the government of us upon himself; This is infinite mercy; whether would our unruly hearts carry us? if he should leave us to our selves? Who is there that hath an experience of the sinfull evils that are in his heart, but will acknowledge this to be a benefit, that the Lord should rule over him with an out-stretched arme? . . . The more contrariety and opposition that there is in us to the will of God, the greater mercy it is that he will be King over us. Learne therefore to count it no small blessing, and when God beginneth with us to overrule the rebelliousnesse of our hearts, and to bring them into order, take heed that wee spurne not with the heele, nor lift up ourselves: But let us humble our selves, and submit our selves to him, that he may take the guidance of us into his own hands. . . .

How may we know that the Lord hath taken us into his government, and that we are ruled by him alone?

By these foure things we may know it.

First, Where the Lord sets himselfe over a people, he frames them unto a willing and voluntary subjection unto him, that they desire nothing more then to be under his government, they count this their felicity, that they have the Lord over them, to governe them. As the servants of *Solomon* were counted happie that they might stand before him, and minister unto him; so it is the happinesse of Gods people, that they are under him, and in subjection unto him: The Lords government is not a *Pharaoh*-like tyranny, to rule them with rigour, and make them sigh and groane, but it is a government of peace; he rules them by love, as he first wins them by love. He conquers them indeed by a mighty strong hand, but withall he drawes them by the cords of love. He overcometh our evill with the abundance of his goodnesse; therefore his spirit, though sometime it be called a *spirit of power,* yet it is also a *spirit of love, joy, and peace;* though the spirit put forth his power in vanquishing our *enemies* that held us in bondage, yet it overcometh *us* by love, making us to see what a blessed thing it is to have the Lord to be over us. Thus when the Lord is in Covenant with a people, they follow him not forcedly, but as farre as they are sanctified by grace, they submit willingly to his regiment. Therefore those that can be drawne to nothing that is good, but by compulsion and constraint, it is a signe that they are not under the gracious government of the Lord God.

Secondly, If God be God over us, governing us by the government of his grace, wee must yeeld him universall obedience in all things. He must not be over us in one thing, and under us in another, but he must be over us in every thing; Gods authoritie is cast away by refusing obedience to one Commandment, as well as by refusing obedience unto all. His authoritie is seene in one, as well as in another. And he that breaketh one, doth in effect breake all. . . . When God cometh to rule, he cometh with power, to cast down *every strong hold,* and *every* high thought that is exalted against the power of Christ. He cometh to lay waste the whole kingdome of sinne, all must downe, not a stone left of that *Babel.* The Lord will reigne in the whole soule, he will have no God, no King with him. And therefore herein looke unto it, if he be God over us, he alone must rule over us, and no other with him. Consider whether Gods dominion hath its full extent in us; whether there be not some corruption which thou hast desirest to be spared in: Canst thou give up thy selfe wholly to the power of grace, to be ruled by it? Canst thou part with thy *Absalom,* thy beloved lust, and be content that God should set up his kingdom in thy whole soule? Then is God over thee, and thou in covenant with him. But if thou canst not submit that the life of some darling lust should goe; if there be any sinne that is dearer to thee, then to obey God; if thou hast thy exceptions, and reservations, and wilt not yeeld universall obedience, then art thou an alien from God and his Covenant; God is no God unto thee, nor art thou one of his people.

Thirdly, Where the Lord governeth and setteth up his kingdome over the soule, he carries & lifts up the heart to an higher pitch, and above that which flesh and bloud could or would attaine unto. And that both in the things themselves, & the ends which they ayme at in them. He makes a man undertake such things as his own heart would refuse and turne from. . . . This also we see in *Abraham* when he was commanded to sacrifice his own son, though he loved him, yet he loved God more, and therefore obeyed, which nature alone could never have done. In all these they wrought against the streame, doing that which flesh & bloud could never have done. Againe, the power of Gods grace in his government lifts up the soule to higher ends and aymes, then flesh and bloud can attain unto. The kingdome of Gods grace, is called the *kingdome of heaven,* his aymes and ends are on high, not earthly but heavenly; his government is an heavenly regiment, the Lord governeth the hearts of his people to the same end which he hath propounded to himselfe. Gods ends & our ends meet in one, which is the glorifying of his Name. This putteth the difference between all formall hypocrites, and those that are ruled by the spirit of grace: hypocrites are ruled by their own spirit, & they never ayme at higher then their own ends, their own honour, credit, profit, &c. Though their *actions* may be *spirituall,* yet their *ends* are *carnall;* but when God taketh the heart into his guidance, then he maketh us to set up him as highest in the throne, and all is done for his honour. It makes a man to use and imploy himselfe, wisdome, strength, riches, credit, and esteeme in the Church, & all for God, not for himselfe; God is his last end in every thing, as most worthy to be glorified by all. Indeed a man in Covenant with God may do many things for himselfe,

ayming at the furtherance of his own good both spirituall and tempo-
rall, and also ayme at the good of other men, but this is not in
opposition, but in subordination to God and his glory; that last and
maine end must sway all other ends. Nothing must be done to crosse
and hinder his glory; this is the government of Gods Grace. . . .

Fourthly, The government of Gods grace causeth the peace of
God to lodge in that soule in which it ruleth. . . . Grace and peace goe
hand in hand; There is a reigne and rule of grace. And so there is of
peace. As under the reigne of *Solomon,* there was abundance of peace,
so there is under the government of Christ, he is the King of *Salem.*
And the more the soule is subjected unto his government, the more
peace it finds. And that may be seene in these two things.

First, In the dispensations and administrations of Gods providence, though things go crosse against us, we meet with many troubles, Gods providences seeme to crosse his promises, yet there is peace
to the soule in it. . . . Certain it is, that if ever our hearts be out of
quiet, it is because there is some sedition and trayterous conspiracy,
which hath been rising up against the kingdome of Christ, and this
workes trouble; but where the soule is subjected to the regiment of
grace, it maketh it to rest in peace; In all wrongs, injuries, and crosses,
it knows the Lord will right them; In all wants, it knows that he will
provide; In all kinds of tryalls, that he will with the temptation give an
issue in due time. But the heart that is unsubdued to Gods kingdome,
is ready to fret against God, and sit downe discontented when any
thing crosseth him.

Secondly, As it resteth in peace under the dispensations of Gods
providences, so it rests in peace in regard of the spirituall enemies of
our salvation, which fights against our souls. Whatsoever threatens our
ruine, the soule shrowds it selfe under the wing of the Almighty. . . .
Let us examine our selves by these things, and we may see whether we
be under the government of God, and so whether we be in Covenant
with him.

4

Authority and Liberty
JOHN WINTHROP

. . . The great questions that have troubled the country, are about the authority of the magistrates and the liberty of the people. It is yourselves who have called us to this office, and being called by you, we have our authority from God, in way of an ordinance, such as hath the image of God eminently stamped upon it, the contempt and violation whereof hath been vindicated with examples of divine vengeance. I entreat you to consider, that when you choose magistrates, you take them from among yourselves, men subject to like passions as you are. Therefore when you see infirmities in us, you should reflect upon your own, and that would make you bear the more with us, and not be severe censurers of the failings of your magistrates, when you have continual experience of the like infirmities in yourselves and others. We account him a good servant, who breaks not his covenant. The covenant between you and us is the oath you have taken of us, which is to this purpose, that we shall govern you and judge your causes by the rules of God's laws and our own, according to our best skill. When you agree with a workman to build you a ship or house, etc., he undertakes as well for his skill as for his faithfulness, for it is his profession, and you pay him for both. But when you call one to be a magistrate, he doth not profess nor undertake to have sufficient skill for that office, nor can you furnish him with gifts, etc., therefore you must run the hazard of his skill and ability. But if he fail in faithfulness, which by his oath he is bound unto, that he must answer for. If it fall out that the case be clear to common apprehension, and the rule clear also, if he transgress here, the error is not in the skill, but in the evil of the will: it must be required of him. But if the case be doubtful, or the rule doubtful, to men of such understanding and parts

Reprinted from James Savage, ed., *The History of New England from 1630 to 1649. By John Winthrop, Esq.* [Winthrop's Journal] (Boston, 1826), II, 228–30.

as your magistrates are, if your magistrates should err here, yourselves must bear it.

For the other point concerning liberty, I observe a great mistake in the country about that. There is a twofold liberty, natural (I mean as our nature is now corrupt) and civil or federal. The first is common to man with beasts and other creatures. By this, man, as he stands in relation to man simply, hath liberty to do what he lists; it is a liberty to evil as well as to good. This liberty is incompatible and inconsistent with authority, and cannot endure the least restraint of the most just authority. The exercise and maintaining of this liberty makes men grow more evil, and in time to be worse than brute beasts: omnes sumus licentia deteriores. This is that great enemy of truth and peace, that wild beast, which all the ordinances of God are bent against, to restrain and subdue it. The other kind of liberty I call civil or federal, it may also be termed moral, in reference to the covenant between God and man, in the moral law, and the politic covenants and constitutions, amongst men themselves. This liberty is the proper end and object of authority, and cannot subsist without it; and it is a liberty to that only which is good, just, and honest. This liberty you are to stand for, with the hazard (not only of your goods, but) of your lives, if need. be. Whatsoever crosseth this, is not authority, but a distemper thereof. This liberty is maintained and exercised in a way of subjection to authority; it is of the same kind of liberty wherewith Christ hath made us free. The woman's own choice makes such a man her husband; yet being so chosen, he is her lord, and she is to be subject to him, yet in a way of liberty, not of bondage; and a true wife accounts her subjection her honor and freedom, and would not think her condition safe and free, but in her subjection to her husband's authority. Such is the liberty of the church under the authority of Christ, her king and husband; his yoke is so easy and sweet to her as a bride's ornaments; and if through frowardness or wantonness, etc., she shake it off, at any time, she is at no rest in her spirit, until she take it up again; and whether her lord smiles upon her, and embraceth her in his arms, or whether he frowns, or rebukes, or smites her, she apprehends the sweetness of his love in all, and is refreshed, supported, and instructed by every such dispensation of his authority over her. On the other side, ye know who they are that complain of this yoke and say, let us break their bands, etc., we will not have this man to rule over us. Even so, brethren, it will be between you and your magistrates. If you stand for your natural corrupt liberties, and will do what is good in your own eyes, you will not endure the least weight of authority, but will murmur, and oppose, and be always striving to shake off that yoke; but if you will be satisfied to enjoy such civil and lawful liberties, such as Christ allows you, then will you quietly and cheerfully submit unto that authority which is set over you, in all the administrations of it, for your good. Wherein, if we fail at any time, we hope we shall be willing (by God's assistance) to hearken to good advice from any of you, or in any other way of God; so shall your liberties be preserved, in upholding the honor and power of authority amongst you.

5

The Puritan State and Puritan Society
PERRY MILLER

It has often been said that the end of the seventeenth and the beginning of the eighteenth century mark the first real break with the Middle Ages in the history of European thought. Even though the Renaissance and Reformation transformed many aspects of the Western intellect, still it was not until the time of Newton that the modern scientific era began; only then could men commence to regard life in this world as something more than preparation for life beyond the grave. Certainly if the eighteenth century inaugurated the modern epoch in natural sciences, so also did it in the political and social sciences. For the first time since the fall of the Roman Empire religion could be separated from politics, doctrinal orthodoxy divorced from loyalty to the state, and the citizens of a nation be permitted to worship in diverse churches and to believe different creeds without endangering the public peace. Various factors contributed to effecting this revolution; the triumph of scientific method and of rationalism

Reprinted by permission of the publishers from Perry Miller, *Errand into the Wilderness* (Cambridge, Mass.: The Belknap Press of Harvard University Press). Copyright, 1956, by the President and Fellows of Harvard College.

made impossible the older belief that government was of divine origin; the rise of capitalism, of the middle class, and eventually of democracy, necessitated new conceptions of the role of the state. Social leadership in England and America was assumed by a group of gentlemen who were, by and large, deists or skeptics, and to them all religious issues had become supremely boring. At the same time the churches themselves, particularly the newer evangelical denominations, were swinging round to a theology that made religious belief the subjective experience of individual men, entirely unrelated to any particular political philosophy or social theory.

In order to understand Puritanism we must go behind these eighteenth-century developments to an age when the unity of religion and politics was so axiomatic that very few men would even have grasped the idea that church and state could be distinct. For the Puritan mind it was not possible to segregate a man's spiritual life from his communal life. Massachusetts was settled for religious reasons, but as John Winthrop announced, religious reasons included "a due forme of Government both ciuill and ecclesiasticall," and the civil was quite as important in his eyes as the ecclesiastical. Only in recent years has it become possible for us to view the political aspects of Puritanism with something like comprehension and justice. For two centuries our social thinking has been dominated by ideas that were generated in the course of a sweeping revolt against everything for which the Puritans stood; the political beliefs of the Puritans were forgotten, or, if remembered at all, either deplored or condemned as unfortunate remnants of medievalism. Puritanism has been viewed mainly as a religious and ethical movement. But of late years the standards of the eighteenth century have for the first time come under serious criticism and in many quarters are showing the strain. In these circumstances the social philosophy of Puritanism takes on a new interest, and quite possibly becomes for us the most instructive and valuable portion of the Puritan heritage.

The Puritan theory of the state began with the hypothesis of original sin. Had Adam transmitted undiminished to his descendants the image of God in which he had been created, no government would ever have been necessary among men; they would all then have done justice to each other without the supervision of a judge, they would have respected each other's rights without the intervention of a policeman. But the Bible said—and experience proved—that since the Fall, without the policeman, the judge, the jail, the law, and the magistrate, men will rob, murder, and fight among themselves; without a coercive state to restrain evil impulses and administer punishments, no life will be safe, no property secure, no honor observed. Therefore, upon Adam's apostasy, God Himself instituted governments among men. He left the particular form to be determined by circumstance—this was one important human art on which the Puritans said the Bible was *not* an absolute and imperious lawgiver—but He enacted that all men should be under some sort of corporate rule, that they should all submit to the sway of their superiors, that no man should live apart from his fellows, that the government should have full power to enforce obedience and to inflict every punishment that the crimes of men deserved.

There was, it is true, a strong element of individualism in the Puritan creed; every man had to work out his own salvation, each soul had to face his maker alone. But at the same time, the Puritan philosophy demanded that in society all men, at least all regenerate men, be marshaled into one united array. The lone horseman, the single trapper, the solitary hunter was not a figure of the Puritan frontier; Puritans moved in groups and towns, settled in whole communities, and maintained firm government over all units. Neither were the individualistic business man, the shopkeeper who seized every opportunity to enlarge his profits, the speculator who contrived to gain wealth at the expense of his fellows, neither were these typical figures of the original Puritan society. Puritan opinion was at the opposite pole from Jefferson's feeling that the best government governs as little as possible. The theorists of New England thought of society as a unit, bound together by inviolable ties; they thought of it not as an aggregation of individuals but as an organism, functioning for a definite purpose, with all parts subordinate to the whole, all members contributing a definite share, every person occupying a particular status. "Society in all sorts of humane affairs is better then Solitariness," said John Cotton. The society of early New England was decidedly "regimented." Puritans did not think that the state was merely an umpire, standing on the side lines of a contest, limited to checking egregious fouls but otherwise allowing men free play according to their abilities and the breaks of the game. They would have expected *laissez faire* to result in a reign of rapine and horror. The state to them was an active instrument of leadership, discipline, and, wherever necessary, of coercion; it legislated over any or all aspects of human behavior, it not merely regulated misconduct but undertook to inspire and direct all conduct. The commanders were not to trim their policies by the desires of the people, but to drive ahead upon the predetermined course; the people were all to turn out as they were ordered, and together they were to crowd sail to the full capacity of the vessel. The officers were above the common men, as the quarter-deck is above the forecastle. There was no idea of the equality of all men. There was no questioning that men who would not serve the purposes of the society should be whipped into line. The objectives were clear and unmistakable; any one's disinclination to dedicate himself to them was obviously so much recalcitrancy and depravity. The government of Massachusetts, and of Connecticut as well, was a dictatorship, and never pretended to be anything else; it was a dictatorship, not of a single tyrant, or of an economic class, or of a political faction, but of the holy and regenerate. Those who did not hold with the ideals entertained by the righteous, or who believed God had preached other principles, or who desired that in religious belief, morality, and ecclesiastical preferences all men should be left at liberty to do as they wished—such persons had every liberty, as Nathaniel Ward said, to stay away from New England. If they did come, they were expected to keep their opinions to themselves; if they discussed them in public or attempted to act upon them, they were exiled; if they persisted in returning, they were cast out again; if they still came back, as did four Quakers, they were hanged on Boston Common. And from the Puritan point of view, it was good riddance.

These views of the nature and function of the state were not peculiar to the Puritans of New England; they were the heritage of the past, the ideals, if not always the actuality, of the previous centuries. That government was established by God in order to save depraved men from their own depravity had been orthodox Christian teaching for centuries; that men should be arranged in serried ranks, inferiors obeying superiors, was the essence of feudalism; that men should live a social life, that profit-making should be restrained within the limits of the "just price," that the welfare of the whole took precedence over any individual advantage, was the doctrine of the medieval church, and of the Church of England in the early seventeenth century. Furthermore, in addition to these general principles, there were two or three more doctrines in the New England philosophy which also were common to the age and the background: all the world at that moment believed with them that the church was to be maintained and protected by the civil authority, and a certain part of the world was contending that government must be limited by fundamental law and that it takes its origin from the consent of the people.

Every respectable state in the Western world assumed that it could allow only one church to exist within its borders, that every citizen should be compelled to attend it and conform to its requirements, and that all inhabitants should pay taxes for its support. When the Puritans came to New England the idea had not yet dawned that a government could safely permit several creeds to exist side by side within the confines of a single nation. They had not been fighting in England for any milk-and-water toleration, and had they been offered such religious freedom as dissenters now enjoy in Great Britain they would have scorned to accept the terms. Only a hypocrite, a person who did not really believe what he professed, would be content to practice his religion under those conditions. The Puritans were assured that they alone knew the exact truth, as it was contained in the written word of God, and they were fighting to enthrone it in England and to extirpate utterly and mercilessly all other pretended versions of Christianity. When they could not succeed at home, they came to America, where they could establish a society in which the one and only truth should reign forever. There is nothing so idle as to praise the Puritans for being in any sense conscious or deliberate pioneers of religious liberty—unless, indeed, it is still more idle to berate them because in America they persecuted dissenters for their beliefs after themselves had undergone persecution for differing with the bishops. To allow no dissent from the truth was exactly the reason they had come to America. They maintained here precisely what they had maintained in England, and if they exiled, fined, jailed, whipped, or hanged those who disagreed with them in New England, they would have done the same thing in England could they have secured the power. It is almost pathetic to trace the puzzlement of New England leaders at the end of the seventeenth century, when the idea of toleration was becoming more and more respectable in European thought. They could hardly understand what was happening in the world, and they could not for a long time be persuaded that they had any reason to be ashamed of their record of so many Quakers whipped, blasphemers punished by the amputation of ears, Antinomians exiled, Anabaptists fined, or witches executed. By all the lights which had prevailed in Europe at the time the Puritans had left, these were achievements to which any government could point with pride. In 1681 a congregation of Anabaptists, who led a stormy and precarious existence for several years in Charlestown, published an attack upon the government of Massachusetts Bay; they justified themselves by appealing to the example of the first settlers, claiming that like themselves the founders had been nonconformists and had fled to New England to establish a refuge for persecuted consciences. When Samuel Willard, minister of the Third Church in Boston, read this, he could hardly believe his eyes; he hastened to assure the authors that they did not know what they were talking about:

> *I perceive they are mistaken in the design of our first Planters, whose business was not Toleration; but were professed Enemies of it, and could leave the World professing they died no Libertines. Their business was to settle, and (as much as in them lay) secure Religion to Posterity, according to that way which they believed was of God.*

For the pamphlet in which Willard penned these lines Increase Mather wrote an approving preface. Forty years later, he and his son Cotton participated in the ordination of a Baptist minister in Boston, and he then preached on the need for harmony between differing sects. But by that time much water had gone under the bridge, the old charter had been revoked, there was danger that the Church of England might be made the established church of the colonies, theology had come to be of less importance in men's minds than morality, the tone of the eighteenth century was beginning to influence opinion —even in Boston. Increase was old and weary. Puritanism, in the true sense of the word, was dead.

Of course, the whole Puritan philosophy of church and state rested upon the assumption that the Word of God was clear and explicit, that the divines had interpreted it correctly, and that no one who was not either a knave or a fool could deny their demonstrations. *Ergo*, it seemed plain, those who did deny them should be punished for being obstinate. John Cotton said that offenders should not be disciplined for their wrong opinions, but for persisting in them; he said that Roger Williams was turned out of Massachusetts not for his conscience but for sinning against his own conscience. Roger Williams and John Cotton debated the question of "persecution" through several hundred pages; after they had finished, I think it is very doubtful whether Cotton had even begun to see his adversary's point. And still today it is hard to make clear the exact grounds upon which Roger Williams became the great apostle of religious liberty. Williams was not, like Thomas Jefferson, a man to whom theology and divine grace had become stuff and nonsense; on the contrary he was pious with a fervor and passion that went beyond most of his contemporaries. So exalted was his conception of the spiritual life that he could not bear to have it polluted with earthly considerations. He did not believe that any man could determine the precise intention of Scripture with such dreadful certainty as the New England clergy claimed to possess. Furthermore, it seemed to him that even if their version were true, submission to truth itself was worth nothing at all when forced upon men by the sword. Williams evolved from an orthodox Puritan into the champion of religious liberty because he came to see spiritual truth as so rare, so elevated, so supernal a loveliness that it could not be chained to a worldly establishment and a vested interest. He was a libertarian because he contemned the world, and he wanted to separate church and state so that the church would not be contaminated by the state; Thomas Jefferson loved the world and was dubious about the spirit, and he sought to separate church and state so that the state would not be contaminated by the church. But John Cotton believed that the state and church were partners in furthering the cause of truth; he knew that the truth was clear, definite, reasonable, and undeniable; he expected all good men to live by it voluntarily, and he was sure that all men who did not do so were obviously bad men. Bad men were criminals, whether their offense was theft or a belief in the "inner light," and they should be punished. Moses and Aaron, the priest and the statesman, were equally the vice-regents of God, and the notion that one could contaminate the other was utter insanity.

The two other ideas derived from the background of the age, rule by fundamental law and the social compact, were also special tenets of English Puritanism. For three decades before the settlement of Massachusetts the Puritan party in England had been working hand in glove with the Parliament against the King. The absolutist Stuarts were allied with the bishops, and the Puritan agitator and the Parliamentary leader made common cause against them both. As a result of this combination, the Puritan theorists had taken over the essentials of the Parliamentary conception of society, the contention that the power of the ruler should be exercised in accordance with established fundamental law, and that the government should owe its existence to a compact of the governed. Because these ideas were strategically invaluable in England, they became ingrained in the Puritan consciousness; they were carried to the New England wilderness and were preached from every pulpit in the land.

The Puritans did not see any conflict between them and their religious intentions. In New England the fundamental law was the Bible. The magistrates were to have full power to rule men for the specific purposes to which the society was dedicated; but they as well as their subordinates were tied to the specific purposes, and could not go beyond the prescribed limits. The Bible was clear and definite on the form of the church, on the code of punishments for crimes, on the general purposes of social existence; its specifications were binding on all, magistrates, ministers, and citizens. Consequently, the Puritans did not find it difficult to conclude that in those matters upon which the Bible left men free to follow their own discretion, the society itself should establish basic rules. The New England leaders and the people frequently disagreed about what these rules were, or how detailed they should be made, but neither side ever doubted that the community must abide by whatever laws had been enacted, either by God or by the state. The government of New England was, as I have said, a dictatorship, but the dictators were not absolute and irresponsible. John Cotton was the clerical spokesman for the Massachusetts rulers, but he stoutly demanded "that all power that is on earth be limited."

The belief that government originated in the consent of the governed was equally congenial to the Puritan creed. The theology is often enough described as deterministic, because it held that men were predestined to Heaven or Hell; but we are always in danger of forgetting that the life of the Puritan was completely voluntaristic. The natural man was indeed bound in slavery to sin and unable to make exertions toward his own salvation; but the man into whose soul grace had been infused was liberated from that bondage and made free to undertake the responsibilities and obligations of virtue and decency. The holy society was erected upon the belief that the right sort of men could of their own free will and choice carry through the creation and administration of the right sort of community. The churches of New England were made up of "saints," who came into the church because they wanted membership, not because they were born in it, or were forced into it, or joined because of policy and convention. Though every resident was obliged to attend and to pay taxes for the support of the churches, no one became an actual member who did not signify his strong desire to be one. The saints were expected to act positively because they had in them a spirit of God that made them capable of every exertion. No doubt the Puritans maintained that government originated in the consent of the people because that theory was an implement for chastening the absolutism of the Stuarts; but they maintained it also because they did not believe that any society, civil or ecclesiastical, into which men did not enter of themselves was worthy of the name.

Consequently, the social theory of Puritanism, based upon the law of God, was posited also upon the voluntary submission of the citizens. As men exist in nature, said Thomas Hooker, no one person has any power over another; "there must of necessity be a mutuall ingagement, each of the other, by their free consent, before by any rule of God they have any right or power, or can exercise either, each towards the other." This truth appears, he argues, from all relations among men, that of husband and wife, master and servant; there must be a compact drawn up and sealed between them.

> *From* mutuall acts *of consenting and ingaging each of other, there is an impression of* ingagement *results, as a* relative bond, *betwixt the contractours and confederatours, wherein the* formalis ratio, *or* specificall nature *of the covenant lieth, in all the former instances especially* that of *corporations. So that however it is true, the rule bindes such to the duties of their places and relations, yet it is certain, it requires that they should* first freely ingage *themselves in such covenants, and* then be carefull to fullfill *such duties. A man is allowed freely to make choice of his wife, and she of her husband, before they need or should perform the duties of husband and wife one towards another.*

The rules and regulations of society, the objectives and the duties, are erected by God; but in a healthy state the citizens must first agree to abide by those regulations, must first create the society by willing consent and active participation.

These ideas, of a uniform church supported by the civil authority, of rule by explicit law, of the derivation of the state from the consent of the people, were transported to the wilderness because they were the stock ideas of the time and place. What the New England Puritans added of their own was the unique fashion in which they combined them into one coherent and rounded theory. The classic expression of this theory is the speech on liberty delivered by John Winthrop to the General Court in 1645. In that year Winthrop was serving as lieutenant governor, and as such was a justice of the peace; a squabble broke out in the town of Hingham over the election of a militia officer; Winthrop intervened, committing one faction for contempt of court when they would not give bond to appear peaceably before the legislature and let the affair be adjudicated. Some of the citizens were enraged, and the lower house of the General Court impeached Winthrop for exceeding his commission and going beyond the basic law of the land. He was tried and acquitted; thereupon he pronounced his magnificent oration, setting before the people the unified theory of the Puritan commonwealth.

As he expounds it, the political doctrine becomes part and parcel of the theological, and the cord that binds all ideas together is the covenant. Winthrop argues that individuals, in a natural state, before grace has been given them, are at absolute liberty to do anything they can, to lie, steal, murder; obviously he is certain that natural men, being what they are, will do exactly these things unless prevented. But when men become regenerate they are then at "liberty" to do only what God commands. And God commands certain things for the group as a whole as well as for each individual. Regenerate men, therefore, by the very fact of being regenerate, come together, form churches and a state upon explicit agreements, in which they all promise to live with one another according to the laws and for the purposes of God. Thus the government is brought into being by the act of the people; but the people do not create just any sort of government, but the one kind of government which God has outlined. The governors are elected by the people, but elected into an office which has been established by God. God engenders the society by acting through the people, as in nature He secures His effects by guiding secondary causes; the collective will of regenerate men, bound together by the social compact, projects and continues the will of God into the state. As John Davenport expressed it, "In regular actings of the creature, God is the first Agent; there are not two several and distinct actings, one of God, another of the People: but in one and the same action, God, by the Peoples suffrages, makes such an one Governour, or Magistrate, and not another." So, when men have made a covenant with God they have thereby promised Him, in the very terms of that agreement, to compact among themselves in order to form a holy state in which His discipline will be practiced. As one of the ministers phrased it:

> *Where the Lord sets himselfe over a people, he frames them unto a willing and voluntary subjection unto him, that they desire nothing more then to be under his government. . . . When the Lord is in Covenant with a people, they follow him not forcedly, but as farre as they are sanctified by grace, they submit willingly to his regiment.*

When men have entered these covenants, first with God, then with each other in the church and again in the state, they have thrice committed themselves to the rule of law and the control of authority. Winthrop can thus insist that though the government of Massachusetts is bound by fundamental law, and though it takes its rise from the people, and though the people elect the officials, still the people's liberty in Massachusetts consists in a "liberty to that only which is good, just and honest." By entering the covenant with God, and the covenant with each other, the citizens renounce all natural liberty, surrender the right to seek for anything that they themselves might lust after, and retain only the freedom that "is maintained and exercised in a way of subjection to authority."

The theory furnishes an excellent illustration of the intellectual ideal toward which all Puritan thought aspired; in the realm of government as of nature, the Puritan thinker strove to harmonize the determination of God with the exertion of men, the edicts of revelation with the counsels of reason and experience. On one side, this account exhibits the creation of society as flowing from the promptings and coaction of God; on the other side it attributes the origination to the teachings of nature and necessity. The social compact may be engineered by God, but it is also an eminently reasonable method of bringing a state into being. Delimitation of the ruler's power by basic law may be a divine ordinance to restrain the innate sinfulness of men, but it is also a very natural device to avoid oppression and despotism; the constitution may be promulgated to men from on high, but it is in fact very much the sort which, had they been left to their own devices, they might have contrived in the interests of efficiency and practicality. Men might conceivably have come upon the erection of governments through explicit compacts, in which they incorporated certain inviolable regulations and a guarantee of rights, quite as much by their own intelligence as by divine instruction. As always in Puritan thought, there was no intention to discredit either source, but rather to integrate the divine and the natural, revelation and reason, into a single inspiration. "Power of Civil Rule, by men orderly chosen, is Gods Ordinance," said John Davenport, even if "It is from the Light and Law of Nature," because "the Law of Nature is God's Law." The Puritan state was thus from one point of view purely and simply a "theocracy"; God was the sovereign; His fiats were law and His wishes took precedence over all other considerations; the magistrates and ministers were His viceroys. But from another point of view, the

Puritan state was built upon reason and the law of nature; it was set up by the covenant of the people, the scope of its power was determined by the compact, and the magistrates and ministers were the commissioned servants of the people.

As this theory stands on paper it is, like so many edifices of the Puritan mind, almost perfect. When it was realized in practice, however, there were at least two difficulties that soon became apparent. For one, not all the people, even in New England, were regenerate; in fact, the provable elect were a minority, probably no more than one-fifth of the total population. But this did not dismay the original theorists, for they had never thought that mere numerical majorities proved anything. Consequently, though the social compact furnished the theoretical basis of society in New England, nevertheless it was confined to the special few; the election of officers and the passing of laws was given to those only who could demonstrate their justification and sanctification. The congregational system, with its membership limited to those who had proved before the church that they possessed the signs of grace, offered a ready machinery for winnowing the wheat from the chaff. Therefore, under the first charter the suffrage in Massachusetts was limited to the church members. In Connecticut the franchise was not officially restrained in this fashion, but other means served as well to keep the electorate pure and orthodox. The "citizens," as they were called, elected delegates to the General Court, chose judges, and passed laws. The others, the "inhabitants," had equality before the law, property rights, police protection; they were taxed no more than the citizens or submitted to no indignities, but they were allowed no voice in the government or in the choice of ministers, and only by the mere force of numbers gained any influence in town meetings.

The restriction of the franchise to church membership seemed to solve the first difficulty confronted by the Puritan theorists. But in time it only brought them face to face with the second and more serious problem: the whole structure of theory which Winthrop outlined in his speech, and which the sermons of the 1660's and 1670's reiterated, fell apart the moment the "citizens" were no longer really and ardently holy. Just as soon as the early zeal began to die down, and the distinction between the citizens and the inhabitants became difficult to discern, then the purely naturalistic, rational, practical aspect of the political theory became detached from the theological, began to stand alone and by itself. As the religious inspiration waned, there remained no reason why all the people should not be held partners to the social compact; the idea that God worked His ends through the covenant of the people grew vague and obscure, while the notion that all the people made the covenant for their own reasons and created the state for their own purposes took on more and more definite outlines. As toleration was forced upon the colonies by royal command, or became more estimable as religious passions abated, the necessity for the social bond being considered a commitment of the nation to the will of God disappeared. Instead, men perceived the charms and usefulness of claiming that the compact had been an agreement of the people, not to God's terms, but to their own terms. The divine ordinance and the spirit of God, which were supposed to have presided over the political process, vanished, leaving a government founded on the self-evident truths of the law of nature, brought into being by social compact, instituted not for the glory of God, but to secure men's "inalienable rights" of life, liberty, and the pursuit of happiness. Except that, until Jefferson rewrote the phrase, the sacred trinity of interests which government could not tamper with were more candidly summarized as life, liberty—and property. . . .

6

The Ultimate Individual
RALPH BARTON PERRY

. . . Individualism is the antithesis of two universalisms, abstract and organic. The individual is the concrete particular rather than the abstract nature therein embodied—for example, Socrates rather than man; and the individual is the constituent member rather than the organic whole—for example, Socrates rather than the Athenian society. Puritanism is individualistic in both senses. Neither can be construed absolutely. Men have a common abstract nature, and this will always remain a part of the truth; but there can be no man without men. It is impossible to ignore man's social organization, but it is also impossible to ignore the fact that a social organization is composed of individuals. Similarly, the religious life involves some degree of union between man and God; but without some degree of separateness this union would lose its meaning. If man and God were identical, there might still be a universe, but there could be no religious life, which consists of the dealings of God with men and of men with God. The core of Christian faith and worship lies in a man's finding of God after an estrangement, and his enjoying a God in some degree distinct from himself.

It is a question, then, of relative emphasis as between the terms and the relationship. Which is fundamental and which is derivative— in being, in genesis, in causal explanation, in authority, or in perfection? In this relative sense puritanism is indubitably individualistic. Its stubborn individualism determines its economic and political affinities, and is of the utmost importance in determining its place in the development of modern American institutions. This individualism also distinguishes puritanism from pantheistic and mystical forms of religion, whether Occidental or Oriental.

In puritanism the concrete human individual is known as the 'soul,' and the emphasis which it receives represents puritan individualism in the first sense, the sense, namely, opposed to abstract universalism. But the nature of the soul conditions the relations into which it is qualified to enter, whether with other human souls or with a higher being of the same type, such as a personal God. In discussing the soul, therefore, we shall be laying the ground for a subsequent examination of the puritan's second individualism—his rejection, namely, of organic universalism, whether social or theological. . . .

We have, then, first to note that souls were concrete. In proportion as philosophers are, as they tend to be, governed by an intellectual bias, they assign the highest place in the order of being and value to abstract universals. Concrete particulars tend to be disparaged as signifying the minimum of intelligibility, and as the objects of 'mere' sense, affection, or action. Insofar as Christian belief has been interpreted and formulated by such philosophers, as it often has been, abstract deity has been exalted above the persons of the Trinity, an abstract humanity above particular suffering and sinful mortals, a timeless logical order above the creative acts of a temporal will, and the contemplation of abstract truth above the love of particular individuals.

To the naïve Christian believer, however, concrete particulars are not mere negations of intellect, but presentations of experience and primary certainties. The Christian narratives are not allegories or myths in which the higher truths of the intellect are hidden; or symbols substituted for ideas. The ultimate meaning and the popular representation are one and the same. Creation means that God *did* bring man and the natural world into existence—in a distant past looked back upon from the actual present. It is a part of history antecedent to and continuous with the history of Abraham and Moses, of Jesus and the foundation of the Church, and of the Last Judgment. The future life means the *future* life, a more or less remote tomorrow reckoned forward from today. God created the world by the causal efficacy of his will and from the motive of love; will and love being construed in accordance with their plain human meaning. Adam sinned, and transmitted to his descendants a sinfulness which only God's redeeming love can cure. Through that love certain fortunate individuals are saved and restored to the innocence and joy which Adam forfeited.

All of these and like dogmas have, no doubt, their aspect of mysteriousness and their aspect of rationality, the one of which can be allocated to blind faith and the other to reason. But thus to judge them from the standpoint of the intellect, as lying either within or beyond its domain, is to ignore that positive meaning which they have in terms of experience itself: a meaning which is neither blind nor rational, and which commends them to the plain man. He needs no philosopher to tell him the meaning of creative action, of will, of persons, of sin, of repentance, and of love.

Love, as we have seen, is the supreme principle of Christian piety, and also, as we have yet to see, the highest attribute of God. The world as seen with the eye of love is a world of individuals, love being, as Royce pointed out, an "exclusive" passion, which, once it has fastened on its object, is satisfied by no other, even of the same kind. It is directed to the individual on his own account—felt toward the individual for himself. It is a fondness and solicitude evoked by the concrete man, however much or little of the ideal he may embody. Jesus taught that with God not one sparrow is forgotten, and that since men are of more value than many sparrows, they may count, each and every one, on the same untiring and sleepless providence.

Christian love is directed to the existent particular, in that time and place, and in that kind and blend of qualities, by which it is unique. This is most adequately represented by the attitudes of familial love. In terms of Christian love men are children or brothers, and God is the father, in whom parental love is perfected. The loving parent knows his own children, one by one, with a particular love for each. His children are not mere exemplifications of human attributes, which, once they have served their symbolic purpose, become redundant. The multiplication of children is not a repetitive process, or a series of experiments which, once the essence is grasped, may then be terminated without loss. Each unit adds value, as well as number; and if any individual were lacking, so much value would be lost to the universe. Each individual has a proper, as well as a generic, name; and is precious to the loving parent for being *this one* and no other.

Christianity considered as a body of ideas is an intermingling of Christian experience and tradition with such secular instruments of thought as were available to the Mediterranean world in the early centuries of the Christian era; and these instruments were largely forged by the pagan philosophers. It is impossible to divest any specific Christian doctrine altogether of this pagan ingredient. It is possible, however, to distinguish it, and to note the proportion in which it is mixed with the specifically Christian ingredient. We may then say that puritanism represents here, as elsewhere, an effort to purify Christianity; which, in this case, means to credit the plain statements of Scripture, naïvely and literally construed, and to accept the beliefs most immediately involved in the attitudes and emotions of the average Christian worshiper.

The pagan ingredient in Christian doctrine reflected the intellectualism and the abstract universalism of Plato and Aristotle. Its adoption as an integral part of Christian thought is represented by the great system of Thomas Aquinas, now recognized as the official Catholic philosophy. Puritan thought, on the other hand, adhered more closely to religious common sense. As it sought to regain the pristine simplicity of worship, so it sought likewise to recover the pristine simplicity of mind; and to accept as authentic that view of God and man which was prior to the influence of Greek philosophy, and which is accessible to the humble believer as well as to the learned doctors. The puritan's religious consciousness was not interpreted and reconstructed by philosophy; it *was* his philosophy. The puritan's world was a dramatic and historical world, in which events were unique in time and place, and in which the principal agents were particular persons, called by proper names and enumerable in a cosmic census. His representations were perceptual and his imagination was pictorial. If he disparaged the senses, this was because of their limited range or their association with the baser appetites, and not because of the concreteness and particularity of their objects. . . .

This conception of the individual soul as the concrete human being, moral in its internal structure and at the same time corporeal in its external relations—an inner ascendancy of the love of God over lower passions, having at the same time a local habitation and a name —is confirmed by the puritan conception of the relations between man and God. God has created concrete persons; and it is such that God loves, and seeks to save and perfect. He loves them neither abstractly nor collectively, but each by each with a particular love. "God took me aside," said Thomas Goodwin, "and as it were privately said unto me, do you now turn to me, and I will pardon all your Sins." The elect are individually nominated to Christ:

> *The* Father *said unto the Son,* such an elect Soul there is, that I will bring into thy Fold, and thou shalt undertake for that Soul, as a Sufficient and an Eternal Saviour. *Wherefore, I am now, in thy Hands, O my Lord; Thy Father hath putt mee there; and I have putt myself there; O save mee! O heal mee! O work for mee, work in mee, the good Pleasure of thy Goodness.*

The particular human individual, whatever his destiny, whether salvation or damnation, is thus through God's interest elevated to a place of exalted dignity in the actual world.

God, in his own nature, is also a soul, a moral entity actuated by unerring and omnipotent love of the good and of the creatures he has fashioned in his image. In his second person, as Christ, God's nature is expressly humanized. In order that God may be man he must live on earth, in a specific time and place, and through an earthly body engage in reciprocal intercourse with a local environment. The humanity of God is represented by Jesus at Gethsemane. Pascal's rendering of this experience in his *"Le mystère de Jésus"*—the blend of loneliness, of patience, of tender compassion, of a faith which holds firm on the verge of despair, and of a suffering borne willingly for the sake of others lonely and suffering like himself—might well be taken as a summary of the essence of the Christian life.

This humanization of God is not a degradation. Never is God so divine, so evocative of love, so clearly entitled to worship and obedience, as in this aspect of triumphant suffering. And his humanity is the same thing as the divinity of man, both consisting in the victory of the moral will over temptation, amidst an environment which is at one and the same time an impediment and a sphere of opportunity. God, in order to be a God of religion, that is, an adorable and saving God, must become a particularized, a struggling, an acting, and a suffering individual. The relation of God to man and of man to God cannot be expressed save as an intercourse between two such souls—save in terms of *moi* and *toi*.

The pneumatic aspect of the Christian soul receives further light from the conception of the Holy Spirit. Waiving the metaphysical difficulties which beset the doctrine of the Trinity, the underlying motive is clear. God is not merely a supreme and providential power, and a moral individual, but also a mobile and palpable force capable of operating locally. When God is considered as working in the individual man and reinforcing his moral will; or as dwelling in the collective life of believers in such wise as to unite them into the body of the church; then he is referred to as the Holy Spirit. The experience of the Holy Spirit is the sense of an access of love, of light, of assurance, and of energy that seems to come from 'without' or 'above.' . . .

In puritanism, the individual human soul is both the subject and the scene of salvation. Doctrines such as predestination and election suggest that a man's salvation consists in his having his name registered, and that this is effected by a sort of absent treatment of which the fortunate beneficiary is himself unaware. Nothing could be further from the truth as the puritan saw it. A man's being saved meant that something happened to him of which he was fully aware, and in which he participated. He was saved by the grace of God, and he was saved irresistibly—but not unwillingly or unwittingly. Salvation was not a bequest written in God's testament from the beginning of time, opened only at the Last Judgment, and distributed only after the resurrection. The saved entered upon their patrimony here and now. Salvation happened within the life-cycle of the soul and at the very core of its humanity. This general truth I shall now examine under its three aspects: faith, retribution, and regeneration.

Faith is the beginning, albeit the mere threshold or dawning, of a new life. It marks a crucial point, defining a new direction which diverges to ever enlarging distances—the first step on a long journey. It is a human act which initiates the progressive achievement of God's saving grace. This doctrine, together with insistence on the right of private judgment as applied to Scripture, and on the priesthood of believers, forms part of that radically individualistic creed which distinguishes puritan protestantism within the larger stream of Christianity.

The fact that faith is an "evidence of things unseen" must not be allowed to obscure the fact that it is an intellectual act, involving both understanding and inference as well as acceptance. The reading of the Bible and the application of its teachings to life involve a grasp of its meaning and its implications. These acts of the intellect, however restricted, are acts of the same human individual who is their beneficiary: the believer interprets the gospel himself, and accepts it for himself. The minister, instead of being the source or vehicle of magical powers, is the teacher and preacher, who expounds ideas and presents their evidence to other minds. When Cotton Mather in his youth was disturbed by his impediment of speech, he said: "Another thing that much exercised mee was, that I might not bee left without necessary Supplies of *Speech* for my Ministry." That his anxiety was needless, or his prayer, at any rate, answered, is proved by his lifelong volubility. The priesthood of all believers is not a mere rejection of the priestly caste, but an extension to all believers of the priestly vocation of teaching and preaching.

Preaching, with its odor of intrusiveness, differs only in its tone and manner from that more blessed thing called teaching. Teaching and preaching imply both an art of communicating ideas and a capacity to receive them. The idea that these functions should be exercised in some degree by all believers directed attention to free and universal education. The encouragement of intellectual attainment on the part of the ministry requires a similar qualification on the part of their congregations. It is not an accident that Geneva, Scotland, and puritan New England should have played an important role in the history of public education.

The puritan's homiletic volubility and addiction to theological combativeness were conducive to that practice of discussion, that interchange and cross-examination of opinion, which is the life-blood of free institutions. He sowed the seeds of that very tolerance which in his theocracy he sought to suppress. For if you seek to persuade a man, you assume that evidence and not external force is the fit instrument by which to deal with dissenting minds. You assume that each mind has a power and a right to reach its own conclusions, and that the most that another mind can do is to provide the options of intellectual choice. If you wish to persuade, and not merely induce a gesture of outward conformity, then you must wish for others that same receptivity to evidence through which your own conclusions acquire their force of truth. You cannot seek to persuade your neighbor without wishing him to be *open* to persuasion, and if you open his mind, other ideas may find lodgment there. And pending the moment of his persuasion you must accept a contrariety of opinion, and protect it by an appropriate form of liberty.

The right of private judgment implies that the truth is accessible to the isolated individual. The individual who sees or represents the object as it is, possesses all that is necessary to truth—not the whole truth, but the quality of truth. The agreement of other minds is an effect, and not a condition, of truth; minds which direct or yield themselves to the same object will tend to a sameness of judgment or belief. This is the precise reverse of the view that minds governed by the same internal principles, or united as parts of the same over-individual mind, will construct the same object. Puritanism, in common with the whole Christian tradition, was 'realistic' rather than 'idealistic' in its theory of knowledge. Puritan belief was not aware of this issue, being innocent of those subjectivisms, relativisms, and corporate authoritarianisms which, implanted in the European mind in the nineteenth century, have had such tragic consequences in the twentieth. But beneath its specific cosmology and moral code there lay the deeper and more general presupposition of a common objective world and scale of values which reveal themselves to man through his cognitive faculties; or, if not through his natural intellect, then through the added light of revelation.

Faith is belief, and belief has, over and above its intellectual character, an aspect of firmness, persistence, and subjective certainty. Burke attributed the "fierce spirit of liberty" in America partly to the religion of the northern provinces, which he said "is a refinement on the principle of resistance; it is the dissidence of dissent; and the protestantism of the protestant religion."

Puritanism was distinguished not only by its spirit of dissent, but by its stubborn adherence to a creed. This attitude was not only different from, but also contrary to, those acts of understanding, inference, and persuasion with which it was associated. The puritan's guilt is, however, mitigated by the unavoidable difficulty which puritanism here shares with all mankind.

The puritan was not a pharmacologist, but a doctor and a patient; he both prescribed and took his medicine. Now to believe, in the practical sense, implies a degree of commitment which the theorist is privileged to avoid; to *live* by an idea requires some degree of fidelity and partisanship. The inevitable effect is to harden acceptance and repel unsettling evidence. In such a situation, which is the universal lot of men who must both think and live and live by what they think, there is a subtle and often insidious contamination of the intellect by passion and will. The will to believe is confused with the light of reason, and the certainty begotten by constancy or by the heat of polemics is mistaken for insight and theoretical demonstration. But if the puritan may be cited as a warning, it is only fair to add that he fell into error through eagerness to make his ideas not only conformable to evidence, but effective in practice.

The puritan is charged with pride of opinion and contentiousness. Individual minds, poorly endowed, scantily furnished, and little disciplined, were turned loose upon the Scriptures, with the assurance that they might there find the ultimate verities for themselves. That text should be divorced from context, and used to support crude individual vagaries; that private opinions should multiply; that their adherents should become their partisans; that dissent should issue in dissension —all this was inevitable. It rightly gave offense to the sweet reasonableness of Richard Hooker:

> *Nature worketh in us all a love to our own counsels. The contradiction of others is a fan to inflame that love. Our love set on fire to maintain that which once we have done, sharpeneth the wit to dispute, to argue, and by all means to reason for it. . . .*

> *O merciful God, what man's wit is there able to sound the depth of those dangerous and fearful evils, whereinto our weak and impotent nature is inclinable to sink itself, rather than to shew an acknowledgment of error in that which once we have unadvisedly taken upon us to defend, against the stream as it were of a contrary public resolution! . . .*

> *Think ye are men, deem it not impossible for you to err; sift unpartially your own hearts, whether it be force of reason or vehemency of affection, which hath bred and still doth feed these opinions in you.*

Puritan contentiousness was not merely an offense to contemporary taste; it was a seed of inner weakness. It drove puritans themselves to a definition and enforcement of orthodoxy that belied their own principles. It proved their lack of certain indispensable qualities:

moderation and flexibility of opinion, regard for the body of collective wisdom and for the authority of competent and learned minds, a modest admission of fallibility.

It is not inconsistent with the right of private judgment that a man should learn from others, or reckon on the possibility that his opponent may be right. This is a matter of temper rather than of principle; and the puritan's temper was often arrogant and combative. Let us admit this, and add to it the charge, no less relevant and just, that to impute the capacity for truth to every man not only elevates the man, but debases the truth. There still remains a large credit to the puritan's account from his doctrine of faith and private judgment: the internality of thought and belief to the individual human soul; the individual as the unique subject of rational assent, and as the object of persuasion; the interrelation within an integral individual of thought and will, so that he may act from his own inner convictions. If these are commonplaces, so much the better; but they need perpetual reaffirmation in a world in which most men are still ready to let others do their thinking for them. . . .

When a man's salvation is consummated, he achieves a certain condition of which he is himself aware. Salvation is something that has happened *to* him, and not something that has merely happened *about* him. Call it 'regeneration,' 'sanctification,' or what you will, the fruit of the gospel, in fact, the most perfect and precious fruit of creation itself, is to be found within the circumference of the individual soul. It is experienced there; and if it is not experienced there, then it has not occurred. This is the most fundamental and most radical part of puritan individualism.

Like other elements of puritanism, this idea was not invented, but was selected from the general body of Christian teaching for special emphasis both in theory and in practice. It is consistent with other puritan ideas: the sweeping away or drastic simplification of the whole liturgical, sacramental, and ecclesiastical system in order to bring the individual man face to face with God; the equal dignity of all believers; the sharp demarcation between the elect and the damned; the conception of the visible church as a congregation of saints; the rigors of discipline and the practice of self-examination. . . .

The experience of regeneration consists in a sense of power and of certainty, felt by the individual as a relief from frustration and as a resolution of doubt. These experiences can be verified without resort to speculation or dogma. He who is saved knows the goodness of God in the act of loving him; he knows his exceeding goodness, in loving him above all other loves. He derives a new power from the integration of his life—the resolution of inner conflict, the unification and convergence of his total motivation. That of which the 'fall' had deprived him was a capacity to recognize and choose the good. He has now recovered his 'freedom,' in the positive sense of a freedom to love God and to obey him from love, in place of a compulsion to obey him from fear, or to disobey him blindly. Of this surpassing goodness, and of its effect upon himself, he is the direct witness. He is aware of the new orientation of his affections, he tastes its sweetness, and he feels a reinvigoration flowing from his new harmony and single-mindedness.

To the puritan this was by no means the whole of the story. In his sense of assurance he did unquestionably claim, and seem to witness, an intervention from abroad. He seemed to see the hand, as well as the goodness, of God. The presence of this second, and external, factor is evident in prayer. It was characteristic of puritanism that the personal and spontaneous aspect of prayer should have been emphasized. Prayer was the believer's direct resort to God, without intermediaries. It was an exercise in submission and in the direction of the emotions to their supreme object. But it was at the same time a petition that called for an answer.

Unquestionably the average puritan believed that God exerted a transforming influence upon the soul. He found abundant scriptural support for this view in St. Paul; who, while he stressed the moral content of the Spirit, continually spoke of it as from God, as "working on" the soul, and as "delivering" it from the dominion of the flesh. "The fruit of the Spirit is love, joy, peace, longsuffering, gentleness, goodness, faith." Of the fruit, since it ripens within his own breast, the human individual is the most reliable witness. But the puritan was, for better or for worse, committed to a theistic metaphysics. It was presupposed in his sense of security. For the saved soul felt not only purified, exalted, and invigorated, but destined to enjoy that state in perpetuity. His salvation meant that he was not only saved, but safe; and the guarantee of this finality of salvation, expressed in the doctrines of perseverance and irresistibility, could be afforded only by an identity between the forces to which he owed his regeneration and the forces that controlled the future course of the universe.

Any critical appraisal of the puritan's idea of personal salvation must therefore distinguish these two components: an immediate experience of inner moral change, and a belief in its divine spiritistic cause. Each has its characteristic difficulties and dangers.

The first is exposed to the danger of excessive emotionality. In St. Paul's exhortation, "be not drunk with wine, wherein is excess; but be filled with the Spirit," it is to be noted that he did not encourage men to be "drunk," even with the Spirit. Emotion imbibed to excess is as fatal as wine to those qualities which the apostle himself enumerated in the same context: "For the fruit of the Spirit is in all goodness and righteousness and truth. . . . See then that ye walk circumspectly, not as fools, but as wise."

It is easy to confuse moral regeneration with emotional intoxication. A sense of elation, in which tensions are relieved and the individual is flooded with fresh streams of energy, may be no more than a phase of manic-depressive psychosis. Emotion may act as an anesthetic, and remove the symptoms of disorder without effecting its cure: taken as a sedative or stimulant, it may make a man a drug addict rather than a saint. The forces of suggestion and contagion may be deliberately created in order to induce a toxic effect. Emotionality, like disease, assumes an acute form when it becomes epidemic, its intensity increasing in proportion to its volume. Divorced from any specific ideational or practical content, liberated from every control, and having acquired a momentum of its own, it may violate every standard of taste, decency, or public order. A specious regeneration, like a fever, will be followed by a chill. Requiring the repetition of exciting stimuli, it will not bear the test of everyday living.

These evils, which mark the history of evangelical revivalism, were known to the puritan and were frequently the occasion of doubts and warnings. They were characteristic of the protestantism of the extreme left, and provided a motive for those puritan persecutions which are usually remembered only as evidences of intolerance. Jonathan Edwards, puritan leader of the Great Awakening, was aware that its emotional manifestations must be strictly judged by standards of piety and right conduct. In his *Treatise Concerning Religious Affections* he took pains to distinguish their mere "fluency and fervour" from the trustworthy signs of their "graciousness." The religious affections, he said, are truly "holy" only when they incline the heart to God, possess a "beautiful symmetry and proportion," and bear fruit in

Christian practice. If Edwards's *Faithful Narrative of the Surprising Work of God* is a penetrating analysis of the phenomena of conversion, his longer *Thoughts on the Revival of Religion in New England* is a most thorough appraisal of these phenomena—an appraisal in which the writer, while accepting the whole as a manifestation of the spirit of God, is at great pains to point out its dangerous excesses.

The Reverend Charles Chauncy, who was a contemporary of Jonathan Edwards, but stood apart from the Great Awakening, felt himself to be in the best puritan tradition when he warned his contemporaries that a feeling of regeneration may be purely delusionary unless it is confirmed by conscience, by works, by systematic thought, and by the test of durability. In the spirit of the Enlightenment he distrusted what Bishop Butler called "superstition, and the gloom of enthusiasm."

Puritanism itself, then, realized the need of objective checks, in order to avoid too great a reliance on subjective experience. Although it stressed the individual religious experience, it resisted anarchy, both intellectual and moral. It sought through intellectual sobriety to restrain vagaries of opinion, holding to the idea that thinking minds are brought to agreement by the common truth. It sought through moral sobriety to combat antinomianism, perpetually reaffirming the moral validity which is founded on conscience. And the critic, whether puritan or nonpuritan, must at least concede this much to the defendant: that he was a witness of the immediate goodness and transforming power of love; and that here he was face to face with original data of the moral and religious life. . . .

In his individualism the puritan testified to moral and spiritual realities of which he was in immediate possession. It was his role to impress on his age and his posterity the prerogatives of the human soul. He knew it as the sphere of those linkages which constitute the life of thought and will, and as both the scene and the witness of salvation. He symbolizes those ideas of individual integrity and responsibility and of personal dignity and destiny to which the American mind has so persistently clung through all its phases of historical change. He is qualified to be their symbol because in him they were carried to excess and allowed to eclipse other truths which have become more evident to a later age.

7

The Mirror of Puritan Authority

DARRETT B. RUTMAN

"Puritanism" is a time-honored word in American history. On the highest level of scholarship it signifies a concept dear to historians who have made a life's work defining the New England "mind" and its role in the evolution of a peculiar American "mind." On the lowest level it is one of many catchwords and slogans which serve to half-educate our youth, a capsule description to distinguish the New England colonies from those to the south and explain the course of New England's institutional and political development. On either level, the historians' "Puritanism" would seem to be their own creation, a stereotype which, as any intimate view of a "Puritan" community will show, has little to do with reality in New England.

The stereotype has arisen as the result of a tendency among historians of early New England, and particularly the intellectual historians who have dominated the field in the last generation, to limit themselves to the study of the writings of the articulate few, on the assumption that the public professions of the ministers and magistrates constitute a true mirror of the New England mind. The historian seeking to understand a New England concept of authority, for example, has familiarized himself with the literature of England and Europe relative to the nature of man in society. He has scanned the works of such lay leaders of early New England as John Winthrop, noting his "little speech" on liberty of July 1645 and his earlier "A Modell of Christian Charity": "God Almightie in his most holy and wise providence hath soe disposed of the Condicion of mankinde, as in all times some must be rich some poore, some highe and eminent in power and dignitie; others meane and in subjeccion." He has thumbed through the ministerial writings to find Thomas Hooker: "However it is true, [that] the rule bindes such to the duties of their places and relations, yet it is certain, it requires that they should *first freely ingage* themselves in such covenants, and *then* be carefull to fullfill

Reprinted by permission from *Law and Authority in Colonial America*, George A. Billias, editor. Barre Publishers, Barre, Massachusetts, 1965.

such duties." Or perhaps he has dipped into the pages of John Cotton: "It is evident by the light of nature, that all civill Relations are founded in Covenant. For, to passe by naturall Relations between Parents and Children, and Violent Relations, between Conquerors and Captives; there is no other way given whereby a people . . . can be united or combined into one visible body, to stand by mutuall Relations, fellow-members of the same body, but onely by mutuall Covenant; as appeareth between husband and wife in the family, Magistrates and subjects in the Commonwealth, fellow Citizens in the same Citie."

On occasion, the historian has turned also to the law, noting that it is replete with examples of the intrusion of authority into every aspect of New England life: "Taking into consideration the great neglect of many parents and masters in training up their children in learning, and labor, and other implyments which may be proffitable to the common wealth," it is ordered that the selectmen of every town "shall henceforth stand charged with the care of the redresse of this evill"; "forasmuch as in these countryes, where the churches of Christ are seated, the prosperity of the civil state is much advanced and blessed of God" and the ministers' preaching of the word "is of generall and common behoofe to all sorts of people, as being the ordinary meanes to subdue the harts of hearers not onely to the faith, and obedience to the Lord Jesus, but also to civill obedience, and allegiance unto magistracy" it is ordered that "every person shall duely resort and attend" to church services; it is ordered that "hereafter, noe dwelling howse shalbe builte above halfe a myle from the meeteing howse."

From such sources modern historians have drawn a picture of a highly cohesive and ordered social structure in which authority was omnipresent—the authority of the father in the family, of the minister in the church, of the magistrate in town and commonwealth. Both the cohesiveness of society and the authority were God-ordained, for man from the moment of Adam's fall was a degenerate being who required the oversight of his fellows in order to avoid the worst of sins. ("*In multitude of counsellers is safetie*," Cotton was fond of saying.) Within the family, the father's authority was a natural concomitant to parenthood. But for the rest, man chose for himself. He submitted himself to the oversight of a congregation and through it a presbytery of ministers and elders, and to the civil authority of a king or prince or magistrate. Having submitted, however, he was bound by a godly duty to "faithe patience, obedience." Thus the ministers wrote that the congregations were obliged to "yeeld obedience to their Overseers, in whatsoever they see and hear by them commanded to them from the Lord"; the magistrates that "we have our authority from God, in way of an ordinance, such as hath the image of God eminently stamped upon it, the contempt and violation whereof hath been vindicated with examples of divine vengeance." To further the interests of the community as a whole, the individual's personal aspirations were to be sublimated. "Goe forth, everyman that goeth, with a publicke spirit, looking not on your owne things onely, but also on the things of others," Cotton commanded the settlers who sailed with Winthrop in 1630. And Winthrop echoed him: "Wee must be knitt together in this worke as one man." Magistrates and ministers, too, were committed to the welfare of the entire community. The ministry was to guide the community in the way of God's truth. The civil authorities were to preserve the community in its liberty to do "that only which is good, just, and honest." The "ultimate and supreme" goal of both was that "the common Good of the Society, State or Kingdom" be preserved and *"God in all things . . . glorified."*

The current view of New England Puritanism, of which this view of New England authority is but a part, rests upon two major implicit assumptions. The first is that there is such a thing as "Puritanism"—a term impossible perhaps to define, but capable nevertheless of being described—and that the acme of Puritan ideals is to be found in New England during the years 1630–1650. After that date, it is asserted, degeneration set in and there was a gradual falling away from the Puritan ideal. George L. Haskins, the outstanding writer on law and authority in early Massachusetts, reflects this assumption when he writes that "the initial decades of the Bay Colony's existence were the formative years" when, "under the pervasive influence of Puritan doctrine," government, law, ecclesiastical polity, and social structure were fully shaped; "the early social and political structure was to endure for several decades, but it gradually crumbled as primitive zeals began to wane and the religious aspects of life were subordinated to commercial interests."

Haskins owes an unacknowledged debt to Cotton Mather and other New England Jeremiahs, for the notion of Puritan quintessence and decline goes back to Mather's day. Sitting down to pen his *Magnalia Christi Americana* at the end of the seventeenth century, Mather was convinced that the years in which he was living were degenerate ones, that the years preceding his—the founding years— had constituted a golden age of which he was one of the few pure survivors. By telling the story of the past and its leaders he hoped to call his own time to the dutiful obedience to God's will (in both religious and social matters) which had previously prevailed. Mather's motive was succinctly set forth in the introduction to his sketches of the lives of the early ministers: "Reader, behold these *examples;* admire and follow what thou dost behold *exemplary* in them. They are offered unto the publick, with the intention . . . that *patterns* may have upon us the force which *precepts* have not."

This first assumption, though old, has proved of great pragmatic value to the modern historian. Having established that the first decades of New England were the acme of Puritanism, the historian can then turn around and describe Puritanism in terms of what he has found in New England during those early years. Hence, he can avoid the problem of defining Puritanism, a task which Samuel Eliot Morison once found distasteful but necessary. The historian can also evade the issue of separating those facets of New England thought and character which were uniquely Puritan from those which merely reflected the way of life in England. Moreover, by accepting Mather's progression from golden age to degeneration, the historian can conceptualize Puritanism by drawing upon a vast quantity of material without worrying whether his sources are being used out of context as regards time, place, or persons. If Puritanism can "best be described as that point of view, that philosophy of life, that code of values, which was carried to New England by the first settlers in the early seventeenth century" and became "one of the continuous factors in American life and thought," as a leading anthology by Perry Miller and Thomas H. Johnson asserts, then certainly (the historian reasons) one can postulate a unique and unchanging Puritan ideal of society in terms of the letters and tracts emanating from New England during the first two decades of settlement, and, with increasing caution in view of the degeneration, from the whole of the seventeenth century. The same anthology contains selections from Winthrop's 1630 "Modell of Christian Charity" through John Wise's 1717 *Vindication of the Government of New-England Churches* to exemplify a Puritan theory of state and society, and concludes that

> *the most obvious lesson of the selections printed herein is that . . . the theorists of New England thought of society as a unit, bound*

together by inviolable ties; they thought of it not as an aggregation of individuals but as an organism, functioning for a definite purpose, with all parts subordinate to the whole, all members contributing a definite share, every person occupying a particular status. . . . The society of early New England was decidedly 'regimented.' Puritans did not think the state was merely an umpire, standing on the side lines of a contest, limited to checking egregious fouls, but otherwise allowing men free play according to their abilities and the breaks of the game. . . . The state to them was an active instrument of leadership, discipline, and, wherever necessary, of coercion. . . . The commanders were not to trim their policies by the desires of the people, but to drive ahead upon the predetermined course. . . . There was no questioning that men who would not serve the purposes of the society should be whipped into line. The objectives were clear and unmistakable; any one's disinclination to dedicate himself to them was obviously so much recalcitrancy and depravity.

The second major assumption is that one is free to ignore the "if" in Winthrop's "little speech" on liberty: "If you stand for your natural corrupt liberties, and will do what is good in your own eyes, you will not endure the least weight of authority, but will murmur, and oppose, and be always striving to shake off that yoke." Winthrop had, of course, no call to speak of those who "stand" for natural liberties unless there were individuals who took such a point of view. Similarly, one assumes oneself free to ignore the nature of the law—that law reflects not merely the assumptions of society, but the antithesis of those assumptions. The law calling upon town selectmen to insure the proper upbringing of children when their parents were neglecting to educate them to serve the community indicates not only that children were expected to receive such an education, but implies strongly that some children were *not* being prepared in the prescribed manner. The law requiring settlers to build their houses within a half-mile of the agencies of social control—church and magistrates—not only echoes the ideal of a cohesive society, but the fact that some persons were perfectly willing to break with the ideal and scatter across the rich New England countryside. One indication that the law (and the ideal it reflected) was being disregarded is a 1639 letter written by the Plymouth congregation to Boston's First Church "concerning the holding of Farmes of which there is noe lesse frequent use with your selves then with us . . . by means of [which] a mans famylie is Divided so in busie tymes they cannot (except upon the Lord's day) all of them joyne with him in famylie duties." The repeal of the Massachusetts law in 1640 on the grounds that it was unenforceable is still further substantiation.

The assumption is not without its rationalization. If the historian accepts as a matter of faith that, as Richard Schlatter writes, "it was the Puritan leaders who shaped the culture of New England, whatever the rank and file may have wanted"—an extension of the notion of a Puritan oligarchy from the political to the social milieu—then it is easy to explain away those who disregarded the law or who stood for "natural corrupt liberties." Once again, Mather has provided the modern historian with a ready-made answer. To him incidents of social and religious dissent were merely the "continual *temptation* of the devil" which were, at least in the early years, overcome by the pure in heart.

That an ideal arrangement of society was visualized by some of the first comers to New England and that they contemplated realizing the ideal in the New World is patently obvious. One need only glance at Winthrop's "Modell of Christian Charity" to see it. But was the ideal uniquely Puritan? The thought that men, like the diverse parts of nature, ideally stood in ordered symmetry is to be found in Shakespeare's *Troilus and Cressida:*

> *The heavens themselves, the planets and this centre,*
> *Observe degree, priority and place.*
> *. . . . O, when degree is shaked,*
> *Which is the ladder of all high designs,*
> *The enterprise is sick! How could communities . . .*
> *Prerogative of age, crowns, sceptres, laurels,*
> *But by degree, stand in authentic place?*

The notion of men entering society by compact or covenant and thereby binding themselves to authority was a pervading theme in Western thought, although particularly relevant for the religious polemicists of the sixteenth and seventeenth centuries. One finds it, for example, in the *Vindiciae Contra Tyrannos* of the French Protestants and in Richard Hooker's *Ecclesiastical Polity.* In Hooker's work, too, is found the idea of the divine nature of authority once established by man: "God creating mankind did endue it naturally with full power to guide itselv, in what kind of societies soever it should choose to live," yet those on whom power "is bestowed even at men's discretion, they likewise do hold it by divine right" for "albeit God do neither appoint the thing nor assign the person; nevertheless when men have established both, who doth doubt that sundry duties and offices depending thereupon are prescribed in the word of God"; therefore, "we by the law of God stand bound meekly to acknowledge them for God's lieutenants."

More importantly, was the ideal—so often expressed by the articulate few and commented upon by the intellectual historians—ever a reality in New England? Certainly conditions in America were not conducive to it. The very ideal contained a flaw, for while in England the social and religious covenant was an abstract principle to be toyed with by logicians, in New England it was, in town and church, transformed into practice. How does one convince the generality that the forms and personnel of authority are within its province, but that once established they are in God's domain and are to be honored as such? What spokesman for New England orthodoxy could surpass Ireland's Cuchulinn in battling the waves of the sea? Moreover, the transition from old to New England constituted a break in the social fabric familiar to the individual. In an English borough or village the individual located himself according to well-established social and political relationships, but these were no more. Family ties in New England during the early years were relatively few. Ties to the traditional elements of authority—vestrymen, churchwardens, manor stewards, borough councillors, justices-of-the-peace—had disappeared, to be created anew in the New England town, it is true, but such new relationships lacked the sanctity of long familiarity. And even when new ties existed, there was little stability in the New Englander's place in the social and political order. What mattered the regular assertion that God had ordained some to ride and some to walk when those who walked one day could, by virtue of the absence of traditional leaders, the presence of New World opportunities, and the application of their own diligence, ride another?

Such musings give a hint of the answer as to whether the ideal was ever a reality in New England. For more than a hint, however, one must turn to the New Englander's own habitat, his town. For many historians such research necessitates a shift to an entirely different set of sources. It means leaving behind published sermons, tracts, and laws and turning instead to town and church records. It calls for an end to the relatively comfortable perusal of the writings of a few and undertaking the drudgery of culling local records to identify the persons in a given town—their backgrounds, landholdings, economic activities, social and economic affiliations, and politics. Research of such nature is time-consuming, but the rewards are rich.

One such study is that of Sudbury, Massachusetts, undertaken by Sumner Chilton Powell. Sudbury was a small interior town devoted to the raising of cattle. It was not directly affected by the turn to trade and commerce in the 1640s as were some other communities. Moreover, its population was relatively homogeneous during the period with which Powell dealt. One might expect, therefore, that all the generalizations respecting Puritan attitudes would be reflected in the activities of Sudbury's people. But Powell's story is far from that. The founders were acquisitive English yeomen, little touched by any formal Puritan movement in England. During the town's first years, its people were devoted to building and cultivating the land, using the "open-field" or common agricultural method which most of them had known in England. In the early 1650s, however, they felt the pinch of too little land and solicited the General Court for an additional tract. The subsequent enlargement opened Pandora's box. One segment of the town demanded a shift to closed agriculture—large tracts individually operated—and a division by which "every man shall enjoy a like quantity of land"; another resisted. This issue became entangled with a second, the desire of some to build a new meeting house. Matters were complicated still further by a third issue, the desire of the older settlers to limit the number of cattle allowed on the town meadow. The heated debates that followed involved every person in the town, including minister Edmund Brown. Town meetings became "exciting and well-attended"; tempers flared. In the end, the town split, one faction moving away to found Marlborough, Massachusetts.

The debates divided the town into warring factions, Peter Noyes and Edmund Goodnow representing the first settlers and heads of families, John Ruddock and John How leading the younger men of the town, and minister Brown acting largely in his own interest. At one point Goodnow declared that, "be it right or wrong, we will have [our way] . . . if we can have it no other way, we will have it by club law." At another point, How threatened secession by the young men: "If you oppresse the poore, they will cry out; and if you persecute us in one city, wee must fly to another." Pastor Brown called a meeting "to see to the constraining of youth from the profanation of the Lord's day in time of public service" and turned the session into a political harangue; subsequently the minister appeared at a town meeting to cry out he would "put it to a Vote, before I would be nosed by them." Townsmen refused to attend Sabbath lectures and services for fear of being "ensnared" by their political opponents. One party visited the minister "to desire him not to meddle" and Ruddock bluntly told his pastor that, "setting aside your office, I regard you no more than another man." The Reverend Mr. Brown ultimately attempted to have the dispute submitted to a council of elders drawn from neighboring churches, but the various factions refused on the grounds that "it was a civil difference." Where in this debate is there any indication that the New Englanders "thought of society as a unit, bound together by inviolable ties . . . all parts subordinate to the whole . . . every person occupying a particular status"?

In Boston, too, much the same story is to be found: actions quite contrary to attitudes so often generalized upon. In 1634, the generality —again, a relatively homogeneous populace—challenged the town's leadership by demanding an immediate division of all available land on an equal basis. The response of the leadership was to some extent based on attitudes made classic by historians. Winthrop, thinking in terms of the community, argued against the allocation of more land than an individual could use, partly out of his desire "to prevent the neglect of trades, and other more necessary employments" and "partly that there might be place to receive such as should come after." To him, it would be "very prejudicial" if newcomers "should be forced to go far off for land, while others had much, and could make no use of it, more than to please their eye with it." But the townsmen would have none of it. Land was too much a way to personal gain.

The issue reached a climax in December when a committee of seven was elected to divide the town lands. Winthrop "and other of the chief men" failed of election. The townsmen feared "that the richer men would give the poorer sort no great proportions of land" and chose "one of the elders and a deacon, and the rest of the inferior sort." All the advocates of an ordered society were brought to bear to overturn the election. Winthrop spoke of his grief "that Boston should be the first who should shake off their magistrates," and the Reverend Mr. Cotton of "the Lord's order among the Israelites" by which "all such businesses" were "committed to the elders." "It had been nearer the rule," Cotton argued, "to have chosen some of each sort." The generality gave way for the moment and agreed to a new election. Subsequently a more proper committee was chosen "to devide and dispose" of the land "leaving such portions in Common for the use of newe Commers, and the further benefitt of the towne, as in theire best discretions they shall thinke fitt."

The battle, however, was by no means over. The pursuit of individual gain continued to prompt political activity. The prevailing economic view (and one not uniquely Puritan) was that all phases of the economy were subject to government regulation. Town governments in Massachusetts had the authority to regulate land distribution, land usage, and the laying out of streets; in Boston, the town government established embryonic building codes and licensed inns and wharves. Given this actual exercise of power over the various avenues of opportunity, it was to one's advantage to participate in public affairs.

Land, for a time, continued to be the principal issue. The town had a limited area into which it could expand. By the second decade it had become difficult to find plots for newcomers or additional acreage for older settlers. In 1641, popular pressure forced the selectmen to review the larger grants made in the 1630s, but this action served little purpose. Even where surveys indicated that a Winthrop, Oliver or Cotton held more land than had been allocated, the selectmen took no remedial action. During the following year, the selectmen—in order to obtain more room on Boston's tiny peninsula for house lots—resurrected an earlier order denying the inhabitants permanent possession of their lots in the Boston fields. The result was an angry town meeting in which the order was repealed "for peace sake, and for avoyding of confusion in the Towne."

Boston's turn to trade in the 1640s brought about a change. Opportunities for personal aggrandizement in land were gradually replaced by the better chances for advancement in commerce and allied crafts such as coopering, leatherworking, and shipbuilding. For the artisan, participation in local government was equally as important as it had been for those persons interested in land. The leatherworker or butcher, subject to the selectmen under local regulations regarding the cleanliness of his establishment, or even his very right to carry on his trade within the town, of necessity participated in the town meetings to elect the men who could, in a moment, curtail or end his business activities. The retailer, subject to the inspection of clerks of the market operating under commonwealth law, was quick to make known his choice for such officials. Almost everyone engaged in any kind of economic activity—the laws limiting the electorate notwithstanding —sought to vote for the deputies to the General Court and the

Assistants inasmuch as these men wrote the commonwealth ordinances governing economic activity.

On the inter-town level in Massachusetts, too, the desire for personal aggrandizement played havoc with the ideal of an orderly and cohesive society. Town rivalries arose; boundary disputes raged interminably between communities, the prize being a rich meadow or copse. Craftsmen in one town were jealous of those in another. Shoemakers outside Boston, for example, objected to shoemakers within that town organizing a company and seeking exclusive privileges regarding shoes sold in the Boston market. Do not allow "our Brethren of Boston" to "have power put into their hands to hinder a free trade," they wrote to the General Court. "Keeping out Country shoomakers from Coming into the Market," they continued, "wil weaken the hands of the Country shoomakers from using their trade, or occasion them to Remove to boston which wilbe hurtful to Other townes." Merchants and tradesmen in the northern towns—Ipswich, Salem, Newbury—bitterly resented the fact that "Boston, being the chiefest place of resort of Shipping, carries away all the Trade." They reacted in a series of political moves aimed at reducing Boston's central position in the commonwealth. An effort was made to move the seat of government from Boston; an attempt got underway to change the basis of representation in the House of Deputies to Boston's disadvantage; and an alliance was formed between northern towns and country towns to create a bloc within the House to oppose those towns immediately around Boston harbor.

The political activity in and among the towns suggests that the people of Massachusetts Bay, and one can extrapolate to include the other New England colonies, were not acting within the concept of authority and cohesive, ordered society which modern historians have so carefully delineated and pronounced to be characteristic of Puritanism and Puritan New England. Society was not something to which the people of the Bay commonwealth invariably subordinated their own interests. Indeed, the abstract concept of "society" seems to have held little meaning for a generality intent upon individual pursuits. Nor was authority a pervasive thing, obliging the individual through family, church, and state to sublimate his personal aspirations to the interests of the community as a whole. The "state" in Sudbury—in the form of either town or commonwealth government—could provide no other solution to the town's disputes than to permit the community to divide. The church—the Reverend Mr. Brown personally and the elders of the neighboring churches invited in by Brown—was unable to interpose its authority to settle matters. Family fidelity failed to check the personal aspirations of the "landless young sons" who followed Ruddock and How.

The people of Massachusetts, it would appear, were coming to view the elements of authority as being divided rather than united. In particular, they viewed the church and state as distinct entities with well-defined (and to a large extent mutually exclusive) areas of operation. In Sudbury, for example, Pastor Brown's intervention in a civil affair led to his being asked not to "meddle." In Boston, the calling of the Synod of 1646–48 by the commonwealth government roused strong opposition from those who lashed out against the interjection of "civil authority" in church business. The conflict so begun would eventuate in a full scale assault upon the imposition of ministerial authority within the church and of synodical authority among churches—further evidence that the historians' concept of authority and cohesiveness bears little resemblance to New England reality. The historians might cite as evidence of the concept the Cambridge *Platform* which emanated from the Synod and pronounced ministerial and synodical authority to be part of the New England Way, but the deathbed utterances of the Reverend John Wilson are more to the point. Wilson cited as "those sins amongst us, which provoked the displeasure of God" the rising up of the people *"against their Ministers . . . when indeed they do but Rule for Christ,"* and *"the making light of, and not subjecting to the Authority of* Synods, *without which the Churches cannot long subsist."*

The same dichotomy between church and state which one finds in the towns may be seen on the commonwealth level. The historians have noted all too often those laws passed by civil authorities to further the views of the church and those cases where the ministry advised the magistrates on civil matters. But they have paid far too little attention to the arduous efforts made to define the respective spheres of church and state. As John Cotton wrote in 1640, "the government of the Church is as the Kingdome of Christ is, not of this world, but spirituall and heavenly. . . . The power of the keyes is far distant from the power of the sword." To him church and state in Massachusetts were involved in the same task, "the Establishment of pure Religion, in doctrine, worship, and [church] government, according to the word of God: As also the reformation of all corruptions in any of these." Hence the ministers, in whose care the word of God was placed, could logically press for "sweet and wholsom" laws and "civil punishments upon the willfull opposers and disturbers" of the church. But for the things of this world—"the disposing of mens goods or lands, lives or liberties, tributes, customes, worldly honors, and inheritances"—"in these the Church submitteth, and refereth it self to the civill state."

For the most part, too, historians in the past few years have tended to overlook those cases where there was a clash between magistrates and ministers. In 1639, the General Court decided that too frequent and overly long church meetings were detrimental to the community and asked the elders "to consider about tho length and frequency of church assemblies." The ministers promptly denounced the magistrates. The request "cast a blemish upon the elders," they said, one "which would remain to posterity, that they should need to be regulated by the civil magistrates." The over-anxious intervention of an elder in a matter before the Assistants in 1643, on the other hand, drove one magistrate to exasperation. "Do you think to come with your eldership here to carry matters?" he shouted. On another occasion, when the elders of Essex County went beyond the bounds that Winthrop considered proper in espousing the cause of the northern towns against Boston—for when town argued with town the elders tended to identify with their communities—the governor lashed out. They "had done no good offices in this matter, through their misapprehensions both of the intentions of the magistrates, and also of the matters themselves, being affairs of state, which did not belong to their calling."

In the division of authority that was taking place, it would seem that the church was freely conceded the power of opening and closing the doors of heaven. To whatever extent the individual sought heaven, he honored the authority of the church in moral and theological matters. But the keys to personal aggrandizement in this world were lodged with the state, and the generality was coming to look upon the state in a peculiarly modern way. In one sense the state was the servant of the individual, obligated to foster his welfare and prosperity. At the same time, it was to protect him from the aspirations of others—acting, so to speak, as an umpire for society, exercising authority in such a way as to avoid collisions between members of the community who were following their individual yet concentric orbits. One can perceive such a view of society, however obliquely, in the political theory of the later New Englanders. For indeed, their writings on this matter are not all of a piece. There is a subtle difference between a Winthrop or Cotton for whom the goal of society was the pleasing of God; a Samuel Willard to whom a happy, contented people was most pleasing to God; and a John Wise to whom "the Happiness of the People, is the End of its [the state's] Being; or main Business to be attended and done."

The view of society discernible in the New England community is quite different from that expounded by intellectual historians who have turned to the writings of the articulate few—and little else—as their mirror of New England's mind. Are we to discard their mirror and the "Puritan" concepts which they have seen in it? The purpose of intellectual history is to delineate the ideological framework within which a people acted. If the actions of the people under consideration do not fall within the framework created, it follows that the framework is invalid. It is not that simple, of course. In the case of New England, the intellectual framework erected over the past years has been firmly based upon the writings of the leading laymen and clergy in the society. We must accept such works as a valid expression of their ideals, even though their ideals might not apply to the people as a whole.

But what are we to describe as "Puritan," the ideals of the articulate few which, relative to society and authority, were neither unique nor pervasive, or the actuality of the man in the street—more accurately, the man in the village lane—which does not fit the ideals? The very fact that such a question can be asked would seem to imply that the description of New England in terms of Puritanism, or of Puritanism in terms of New England, is erroneous. Certainly, the concept of a Puritan golden age, followed by decline, disappears. Mather's degeneration is, in large part, nothing more than the insistence by the generality upon a relationship between the individual and society rather different from that held to by the leaders. And the golden age, as Mather himself admitted, was marked by continual controversies which "made neighbours that should have been like *sheep,* to 'bite and devour one another'" and inspired "unaccountable *party-making*," a symptom of that different relationship.

The historian must, of course, address himself to the problem of New England's intellectuals. Isolated from reality as they were, they clung for almost half a century to ideals which grew more outdated with the passing of each day, and then gradually and subtly accommodated their ideals to the realities of the situation facing them. But their accommodation and the forces in society that caused them to make changes represent a much more important aspect of history than the mere description of "Puritanism." And the historian must dispense with the easy generalization that such leaders "shaped" New England's culture regardless of what "the rank and file may have wanted." He must seek instead to understand the rank and file, their motivations, aspirations, and achievements. For in the last analysis which is more vital, an ideological "Puritanism" divorced from reality which has received so much attention over the years, or the reality which has received so little attention but which was in essence laying down the basis for two-and-a-half centuries of American history ahead?

Part Two

THE PURITAN BECOMES AMERICAN

Introduction

In 1664 Roger Williams wrote to John Winthrop's son: "Sir, when we that have been the eldest . . . are rotting, (to-morrow or next day) a generation will act, I fear, far unlike the first Winthrops and their Models of Love: I fear that the common Trinity of the world, (Profit, Preferment, Pleasure) will here be the *Tria omnia*, as in all the world beside: . . . that God Land will be (as now it is) as great a God with us English as God Gold was with the Spaniards . . . ."[1] Even as Williams wrote, the social character of New England was changing; the offspring of the founders were playing out the drama of adaptation that would be performed in turn by each succeeding wave of immigrants, with the noteworthy difference that the Puritans occupied open land (if one discounts a few Indians), whereas subsequent newcomers would encounter an established cultural system, shaped partly by the Puritans themselves.

To surviving graybeards like Williams, adaptation meant degeneration: to say that the Puritans were becoming American was to confess that the great mission of redemption was failing. Winthrop had hoped to preserve posterity from "the Common corrupcions of this euill world," but posterity went whoring after false gods—God Profit, God Land, God Pleasure; they took to wearing decadent English fashions, including long hair, and to disporting themselves in taverns and "mixt Dancings." These apostasies were so diligently damned by the ministers that, by the close of the seventeenth century, an enormous mass of clerical agony had accumulated, signifying a crisis in the Puritan soul and a remarkable refraction of the Puritan vision. In the readings that follow, the homilies of Nicholas Noyes (8) and Increase Mather (9) exemplify the hortatory sermon, or jeremiad, that reflected, even while it bewailed, the "sad decay and diminution of the Glory" in New England.

A striking feature of the jeremiads was their preoccupation with New England itself. They were works of a parochial spirit, far removed from the cosmopolitanism of Winthrop, and they illustrate what Louis Hartz has described as a general law of cultural fragmentation: "When a cultural fragment leaves a larger context, it . . . forgets the context itself and elevates its own fragmentary ethos into a psychic absolute." [2] In the early 1650's Edward Johnson wrote of the first voyagers that "for England's sake they are going from England to pray without ceasing for England." [3] Fifty years later Cotton Mather emphasized less the desire to redeem England than the motive of escape from England's iniquities: "I write the WONDERS of the CHRISTIAN RELIGION, flying from the depravations of Europe, to the American strand." [4] Safe in the trans-Atlantic asylum, removed by birth and history from Europe's corruption, Mather's generation acted primarily for New England's sake and prayed chiefly for themselves. As Perry Miller observes in his essay, "Errand into the Wilderness" (10), they could no longer look back to the Old World for a definition of purpose or identity. Rather, they had to make meaning out of their own experience, contrive New World explanations of themselves, work out a peculiar *American* destiny.

This they would do partly by creating a myth of an original heroic age of piety and virtue, when saints were truly saintly. "When," Increase Mather asked, "will *Boston* see a COTTON, & a NORTON, again? When will *New-England* see a HOOKER, a SHEPARD, a MITCHEL, not to mention others?" The myth of ancestral glory could be used to lash a backsliding people to contrition; apart from its utility, however, it reveals New England's impulse to define itself in terms of its own past. It was, moreover, a mark of the Puritans' adjustment to America that the jeremiads, for all their gnashings and weepings, were shot through with expressions of love for New England and pride in the great works that had been accomplished there. "Ah dear New England! dearest land to me," cried Michael Wigglesworth in the midst of castigating New England's sins.[5] And Increase Mather insisted that the glory, though diminished, had not entirely departed: New England was still God's favored place (otherwise why should He chastise it so severely?), and its people were still His chosen people. This mixture of self-flagellation and self-congratulation is interpreted by Daniel J. Boorstin in his discussion of "The Puritans: From Providence to Pride" (11) as evidence of the Puritans' need "to seek their standards in their own experience" and "to find their purposes somehow implicit in their achievements."

God Profit, according to Roger Williams, was one of New England's principal idols—and not without reason, for by mid-century the economic viability of the Puritan colonies, based on fishing and the West Indian trade, was assured, and anxious ministers were warning that "Outward prosperity is a worm at the root of godliness, so that religion dies when the world thrives."[6] Ironically, however, those same ministers preached an ethic of behavior that galvanized the economic energies of their people. As Perry Miller remarks, they "deplored the effects of trade upon religion, but did not ask men to desist from trading; arraigned men of great estates, but not estates." What counted, morally, was motive and use: the root of evil was not money itself, if honestly earned and charitably spent, but the love of money for its own sake or for the sake of what it could buy in power, position, and pleasure. Far from urging withdrawal from the world where God Profit kept shop, Puritanism promoted activity in that world. All men, having received certain talents or abilities from God, and being called by Him to certain occupations, must serve Him in their daily toil. For the saint, moreover, there were special incentives to be up and doing: by godly works of enterprise and benevolence he should display his gratitude for the gift of grace and confirm his assurance of salvation. As befitted a religion of a rising middle class, Puritanism thus inculcated the code of economic virtues—industry, probity, frugality, sobriety, charity, and the like—that historians call the Protestant Ethic.

Not surprisingly, New England's adherence to the Protestant Ethic raised serious difficulties. As expounded by such first-generation clergymen as John Cotton, the ideal was corporate rather than individualistic: its object was the good and godliness of the commonwealth. Furthermore, each Christian was commanded, while pursuing his calling with all his might, to keep his heart disentangled from worldly lusts. He should strive in the marts of Mammon, but fix his gaze on Heaven. But—and this was the question that would rack the Puritan conscience—could even the saintliest saint live true to such injunctions? Could he grow rich in purse yet remain poor in spirit? Would he be able to sustain the corporate, otherworldly sense of his vocation when, by sedulous practice of the economic virtues, he found himself advancing on the way to wealth? Going this way, would he not end in Vanity Fair or, like Benjamin Franklin, in Philadelphia?

The case of Robert Keayne, the leading merchant of early Boston, strikes to the core of this dilemma, for both Keayne and his adversary Cotton drew their arguments from the scriptural sources of the Protestant Ethic, the one to justify his business conduct, the other to censure it (12, 13). The same strain appears in Cotton Mather's warning that while every man must have an "allowable" and "agreeable" occupation, "it cannot be a *Calling* where we shall be our selves *Befriended*" (14). Ultimately, the problem would devolve on Franklin, the archetype of the Yankeefied or ungodly Puritan, who, by divorcing morality from piety, would fix the Protestant Ethic on a secular base. But though he stripped away the theological sanctions of the economic code, Franklin maintained its traditional corporate emphasis: like Keayne a man of civic spirit, he used his wealth to improve the life and culture of his adopted town, thereby assisting Philadelphia to succeed Boston as, in a secular sense, America's city on a hill. In the selections below, Perry Miller (15) and Herbert W. Schneider (16) examine these changes and continuities in Puritan economic and social thought from Keayne and Cotton through Mather to Franklin.

If God Profit had his thousands of devotees, God Land had his tens of thousands. At first, the existence of open space benefited the Puritan community, for dissidents like Roger Williams and Anne Hutchinson could simply be dumped on the frontier where, if they were not altogether out of mind, they were at least out of sight. But as settlers moved into the hinterland—a process that began as early as 1636 when Thomas Hooker's congregation pulled up stakes at Newtown and trekked to the Connecticut River—the frontier became a problem. No matter how carefully the authorities regulated the planting of new villages, they found it increasingly difficult to maintain central discipline over a spreading population. The holy experiment required strict laboratory controls—a kind of air-tight or sin-tight seal. When those controls broke down, there was cause to ask, as Cotton Mather asked in 1694, "Do our *Old* People, any of them *Go Out* from the Institutions of God, Swarming into New Settlements, where they and their Untaught Families are like to *Perish for Lack of Vision?* . . . Think, here *Should this be done any more?*" Implicitly acknowledging that territorial expansion did not accord with the medieval image of the city on a hill, walled against the wilderness, Mather cautioned that "when men, for the Sake of Earthly Gain, . . . drive *Through the Wall*, . . . the *Angel of the Lord* becomes their Enemy." [7] Mather's charge would be echoed down American centuries by Eastern critics of the wildness of the West: on the raw moving fringe of settlement, morality, piety, civility, and orthodoxy all dissolved.

For an understanding of the Americanization of the Puritan, what matters, however, is something subtler and more basic than Mather's complaints, namely, the Puritans' changing attitude toward the land which they converted from wilderness to garden and in which, as generations passed, they felt increasingly at home. ". . . those who came were resolved to be Englishmen," wrote Stephen Vincent Benét,

> *Gone to world's end, but English every one,*
> *And they ate the white-corn kernels, parched in the sun,*
> *And they knew it not, but they'd not be English again.*[8]

So with the Puritans: at the outset they took possession of hostile country by the "forest labours" which Edward Johnson describes in his account of the settling of Concord (17). The land, to borrow a memorable line from Robert Frost, was then theirs, but they were not yet the land's.[9] But with Johnson's "watery swampes," "scorching plaine," and "lonesome condition," compare Samuel Sewall's apostrophe of 1697 (18) to the loved and lovely places of *his* generation's acquaintance, places he had delighted in from boyhood. Note also that though, as a merchant, Sewall moved in the great world of imperial commerce, his mentality was thoroughly provincial: visiting England, he found himself "a Stranger in this Land." [10] Observe, finally, how in the mid-eighteenth century, when Yankee pioneers were pressing beyond the Hudson, parochial sentiment yielded, among some descendants of the Puritans, to a larger vision that was both continental and transcendental. Thus Jonathan Edwards prophesied that all America would probably be the seat of glory in God's last dispensation. New England in particular, yet not New England alone but the whole continent, would be the ultimate suburb of Heaven, for "when God is about to turn the earth into a paradise," He begins "in a wilderness" (19). Reflecting on these and similar documents, Alan Heimert (20) concludes this discussion of the Americanization of the Puritans by showing how the Puritans' errand into the wilderness was redefined, both metaphorically and actually, by their experience in American space, as the wild land was tamed and the bones of the fathers were laid in American graves.

1. *The Complete Writings of Roger Williams* (New York: Russell and Russell, Inc., 1963), VI, 319.

2. LOUIS HARTZ, "American Historiography and Comparative Analysis: Further Reflections," *Comparative Studies in Society and History,* V (July, 1963), p. 365. For elaboration see HARTZ, *The Founding of New Societies* (New York: Harcourt, Brace and World, 1964).

3. EDWARD JOHNSON, *The Wonder-Working Providence of Sions Saviour in New England,* ed. J. Franklin Jameson (New York: Charles Scribner's Sons, 1910), p. 53.

4. COTTON MATHER, *Magnalia Christi Americana* (Hartford, 1855), I, 25.

5. MICHAEL WIGGLESWORTH, "God's Controversy with New-England," in PERRY MILLER and THOMAS H. JOHNSON, eds., *The Puritans* (New York: American Book Co., 1938), p. 616.

6. ELEAZER MATHER, *A Serious Exhortation,* quoted in THOMAS J. WERTENBAKER, *The Puritan Oligarchy* (New York: Charles Scribner's Sons, 1947), p. 203.

7. Quoted in FREDERICK JACKSON TURNER, *The Frontier in American History* (New York: Henry Holt and Co., 1920), p. 64.

8. STEPHEN VINCENT BENÉT, *Western Star* (New York: Farrar and Rinehart, Inc., 1943), p. 116.

9. ROBERT FROST, "The Gift Outright," *Complete Poems of Robert Frost* (New York: Rinehart and Winston, 1949), p. 467.

10. Quoted in BERNARD BAILYN, *The New England Merchants in the Seventeenth Century* (Cambridge: Harvard Univ. Press, 1955), p. 194.

THE VISION REFRACTED: "A MESS OF AMERICAN POTTAGE"

8

New Englands Duty

NICHOLAS NOYES

Some make as if *New-England* were already as sinful, as sinful can be; as bad, as bad can be. To which I reply, I have no design to speak diminutively of the Sins of the Countrey; I do acknowledge with grief, and shame, that they have been, and are very horrible; yet I think such Sayings are not justifyable in any. Some well-meaning holy men, being of dark melancholly Spirits, and little acquainted with the advances that Atheism, Idolatry, Superstition, Prophaneness, Iniquity and Sensuality have made in other professing parts of the World; are apt to *think so,* and in their indignation against sin & sinners to *say so.* But the truth is, Though we have cause to abhor our selves for being so bad as we are; and to meditate all ways possible to grow better; yet it cannot with truth be asserted, that as yet we are as bad as bad can be; for there is real danger of growing worse. There are other design-ing persons, that are of a vulture Spirit, that fly hastily over all the fair meadows and fields without eying of them; that they may pitch and prey upon some Carrion. These find nothing but faults in the *Govern-ment, Churches, Ministers,* and *Good people* of all ranks: & Sport themselves with the falls of here and there an Eminent Professor; or the infirmities, & real, or supposed mistakes of men much better than themselves; *These fools make a mock of sin;* and it serves their occasion, to blaspheme all the Work of God in the Wilderness; and traduce for Hypocrites, all those, that their evil example can't make loose or prophane. All I shall say to this latter sort is, That I have no design to justify our selves; Shame, and blushing, and confusion of

Reprinted from Nicholas Noyes, *New Englands Duty and Interest, To be an Habitation of Justice* (Boston, 1698).

face belongeth to us: for we are sinners. Yet if a comparative goodness would serve our turn (as it will not) we might possibly pass in this degenerate Age. We acknowledge we are very bad; but yet not so bad; but we are afraid of being worse.

Others make & speak as if we were as miserable already, as miserable we could be. To which I reply, I have no design to speak diminutively of the *Judgments of God*. I acknowledge they have been very terrible. *At this also my heart trembleth:* yet I think we ought not so to pore upon the *Judgments* of God, as to forget the *Mercies* of God; for in *Judgment God hath remembred Mercy.* I am sure such Speeches *forget Thanksgiving.* Unhumbled, Unthankful and peevish men, think to receive *only good from the hand of God: and not evil:* and under a merciful, moderate Affliction, say, it can't be worse. But such ought to know that the *holy and jealous God* hath *more,* and *more terrible* miseries & mischiefs to heap; and arrows to spend upon an *Unreformable Covenant people,* than ever yet, have come upon *New England.* . . .

Now as for *New England,* if the *First Planters* of it had dream'd that the very Situation or Climate of this Land had been crime enough to make men *aliens from the Covenants of promise;* they would not have Sold their *European Birthright* for a mess of *American Pottage.* For ought I can see to the contrary, our *Declensions* are the *worst Omen* and *Objection* against us; and *Reformation* would be the best *Answer* to them: and Hope and Prayer are powerful helps and inducements to it. . . . What I am about to speak, I speak that *New-England sin not;* yet if it should so come to pass, that *New-England* should yet be *more sinful & more miserable* than now it is (which God prevent *for his Mercys sake, which endureth for ever*) yet there is Scripture ground to hope, that after God had vindicated his Holiness by sore punishments on us, God would again *restore, reform* and *bless New-England;* and have a name, and a praise to himself, in the *Wilderness,* of the *Posterity of his People.* . . .

9

The Glory Departing from New England
INCREASE MATHER

God has not seemed to take pleasure in the American world, *so as to fix and settle His Glory therein.* The Scripture sayes, The Kingdom of God is like Leaven hid in *Three measures* of Meal until *the whole* was Leavened. *Luk.* 23. 22. Which some take to be a Prediction, that the Gospel should spread through *Asia, Europe* and *Africa,* then the only known parts of the world. What God will do for the future with *America,* is not for us to determine. Act. 1. 7. *It is not for you to know the Times, and the Seasons which the Father has put in His own power.* But it is our Duty humbly to observe his Providence. Now the Lord has not hitherto seen meet to shine upon this so as on the other *Hemisphere.* The greatest part of its Inhabitants are Pagans. Most of those that have any thing of the *Christian* Name are really *Anti-Christian.* And the generality of them that pretend unto the Protestant Religion, are a lose sort of men, and a Scandal to any Religion. There was an attempt (about an Hundred and Fifty Years since) to settle the Protestant Religion in the *Southern America,* and some Eminent Christians and Ministers, from *Geneva* were ingaged in it; but it soon come to nothing. And the late miscarriage of the *Caledonia* design is an awful Providence, and looks uncomfortably on *America.* There is more of the Divine Glory in *New-England* then in all *America* besides. We have the greater Cause not to be high-minded, but to fear. Especially if we

Consider . . . *That the Glory is in some measure, & in an awful degree removed from us already.* The Glory of the Lord seems to be on the wing. Oh! Tremble for it is going, it is gradually departing. Although there is that of the Divine Glory still remaining among us, which we ought to be very Thankful for; Nevertheless, much of it is gone, which thought should humble and abase us in the dust before

Reprinted from Increase Mather, *Ichabod. Or, A Discourse, Shewing what Cause there is to Fear that the Glory of the Lord is Departing from New-England* (Boston, 1702).

the Lord. . . . You that are Aged persons, and can remember what *New-England* was Fifty Years ago, that saw these Churches in *their first Glory;* Is there not a sad decay and diminution of the Glory? We may weep to think of it. . . . Ancient men, though they bless God for what they *Do* see of His Glory remaining in these Churches, they cannot but mourn when they remember what they *Have* seen, far surpassing what is at present. . . . Time was, when these Churches were *Beautiful as* Tirzah, *Comely as* Jerusalem, *Terrible as an Army with Banners.* What a glorious Presence of Christ was there in all His Ordinances? Many were Converted, and willingly Declared what God had done for their Souls: and there were added to the Churches daily such as should be Saved. But are not Sound Conversions become rare at this day, and this in many Congregations? *Discipline* in the Churches was upheld in the power of it; and a special Presence of the Lord Jesus Christ went along with it. . . . We may fall into Tears, considering how the power of Discipline is fallen in our Churches. Some Scandalous practices which not only the *Waldenses,* but the Reformed Churches in *France,* and in *Holland,* have in their Discipline declared to be Censurable Evils, are now indulged in some Churches in *New-England.* Look into Pulpits, and see if there is such a Glory there, as once there was? *New-England* has had Teachers very Eminent for Learning, & no less Eminent for Holiness, & all Ministerial accomplishments. When will *Boston* see a COTTON, & a NORTON, again? When will *New-England* see a HOOKER, a SHEPARD, a MITCHEL, not to mention others? No little part of the Glory was laid in the Dust, when those Eminent Servants of Christ were laid in their Graves. Look into our Civil State: Does Christ reign there as once He did? Is there that Glory in Courts as once there was? Is not our House in diverse parts of this Land, in some danger of falling for want of Pillars to support it? Look into *Towns:* How few do we find that are a Glory to the places where they live? When *Vacancies* are made, it is a difficult thing to find persons fit to make up those Breaches. And almost every where 'tis so, whether in our Ecclesiastical, Military, or Civil State. So that what our Great *Hooker* long since predicted, that the *People of* New-England *would be punished with the want of Eminent Men to manage Publick affairs, both in Church and State,* is in part sadly verified already. How many Churches, how many Towns are there in *New-England,* that we may Sigh over them, and say, *The Glory is gone!* Look into *Families:* Are there not those which once were *Glorious* ones because of the *Religion* which flourished in them, which now are not so. How many Children or Grand-Children are there in *New-England,* of whom it may be said, as in Judg. 2. 17. *They turned quickly out of the way, which their Fathers walked in, Obeying the Commandments of the Lord, but they did not so.* . . .

But, *Is there no way to prevent the Removal of the Glory from us?* Yes there is. I have not spoken these things that we should Despair, but that we might be *Awakened* to do what we may to prevent further and greater Removals of our Glory. *As yet,* our Day is not expired: *As yet* we have a Gracious *Time of Visitation: As yet,* we are under a *Probationary* dispensation. How long or how short that shall be, is with God. Only it does not use to last very long in a Land of such Light and means of Grace as *New-England* has been. *The brightest dayes are commonly short ones.*

But, *What then is to be done?* . . .

1. *Let the Life and Power of Godliness be revived.* That has been the singular Glory of *New-England:* The generality of the *First Planters* were men Eminent for Godliness. We are the Posterity of the *Good, Old Puritan Nonconformists* in *England,* who were a Strict and Holy people. Such were our Fathers who followed the Lord into this wilderness, when it was a Land not sown. Oh! That the present and succeeding Generations in *New-England* might be like the *First Generation* of Christians, who transplanted and settled themselves in this part of the world. Then might we with Confidence pray and believe that God would accomplish for us, that which *Solomon* pray'd for in the behalf of his People, I King. 8. 57. *The Lord our God be with us as He was with our Fathers, Let Him not leave us nor forsake us.* Yea, Let us be as our Fathers were, as to Holiness in all manner of Conversation, and the Lord our God *will be with us* as He was with them. We shall have the same Glory remaining with us which they had.

2. *Let us abide in those Truths respecting the Order of the Gospel, which our Fathers have left with us as a Legacy.* Herein is the difference between *New-England* and all other Plantations. As for other Plantations, they were settled with respect to *Trade,* or some other worldly interest: But it was not so with *New-England.* Our Fathers in coming into this part of the world, did not propose to themselves worldly advantages, but the contrary. It was purely on a Religious account that they ventured themselves and Little ones over the vast Ocean into this which was then a wast and *howling Wilderness.* Although of later Times we have too much changed that which

was our Glory, not *Seeking the Kingdom of God in the First place,* not making Religion, but Trade and Land, and Earthly accommodations our *Interest:* And God has remarkably smitten us in that which has been our *Idol.* In this we are degenerated from the Piety of our Ancestors. But what in Religion was it that induced them to come into this Land? Not the main *Articles of Faith,* for in those they differed not from other *Protestant Churches.* But it was regard to the *Order of the Gospel* that brought them hither. That so they might Erect a Spiritual Kingdom for the Lord Jesus Christ to Reign over. That they might Build Churches which should be *Ordered* in all Respects according to the mind of Christ declared in the *Gospel.* On which account a *Defection* from those Truths will in *New-England* be a greater Sin and Provocation to God, then in any other part of the world. Considering the Glorious Light which has been shining here, there are practices which in other parts of the world would be a great *Reformation,* but in *New-England* a *Degeneracy.* No one needs to Enquire *What is the Order of the Gospel!* You have it declared in *the Platform of Church Discipline,* agreed unto by the *Elders and Messengers of these Churches,* above Fifty Years ago. A *Platform* which is drawn out of the Scriptures of Truth, by men Eminent for Learning and Holiness, and such as were *Confessors* and great Sufferers for the Testimony which they had born to the Kingdom of Christ; and in those respects as likely to have the Truth revealed to them as any men in the world. And that Book was the result of many prayers and Extraordinary seekings to God for the sending forth of his Light and Truth in the matters which were to be debated, and are therein determined. Blessed Mr. *Norton* went to Heaven Exhorting these Churches to continue in the Profession and Practice of that *Discipline;* withal declaring that their safety and the presence of Christ with them depended thereon. Some of his words were these; *"Let our Polity be a Gospel Polity.* This is the very work of our Generation, and the very work we ingaged for into this wilderness; this is the scope and end of it: that which is written on the Forehead of NEW-ENGLAND, viz. *The compleat walking in the Faith of the Gospel according to the Order of the Gospel,*—You have the *Platform of Church Discipline* given to you in way of Counsel as the Confession of our Faith in this way of Church-Government—If any be departed from it, let them look to it—*Our Fidelity in this Cause is our Crown: See that it be not taken from us."* Thus did that Great man express himself, in the *last Sermon* that ever he Preached, which was but Three days before his translation to Glory. And if I, (who am not worthy to be compared with him) knew that this would be *the last Sermon* that ever I should Preach, (as I know not but it may be so) my *Dying Farewel* to these Churches should be the very same. For I know and am perswaded by the Lord Jesus, that if ever these Churches shall *Depart* from that *Holy Platform*, the *Glory* of the Lord will *Depart* from them. . . .

10

Errand into the Wilderness
PERRY MILLER

It was a happy inspiration that led the staff of the John Carter Brown Library to choose as the title of its New England exhibition of 1952 a phrase from Samuel Danforth's election sermon, delivered on May 11, 1670: *A Brief Recognition of New England's Errand into the Wilderness.* It was of course an inspiration, if not of genius at least of talent, for Danforth to invent his title in the first place. But all the election sermons of this period—that is to say, the major expressions of the second generation, which, delivered on these forensic occasions, were in the fullest sense community expression—have interesting titles; a mere listing tells the story of what was happening to the minds and emotions of the New England people: John Higginson's *The Cause of God and His People In New-England* in 1663, William Stoughton's *New England's True Interest, Not to Lie* in 1668, Thomas Shepard's *Eye-Salve* in 1672, Urian Oakes's *New England Pleaded With* in 1673, and, climactically and most explicitly, Increase Mather's *A Discourse Concerning the Danger of Apostasy* in 1677.

All of these show by their title pages alone—and, as those who have looked into them know, infinitely more by their contents—a deep

Reprinted by permission of the publishers from Perry Miller, *Errand into the Wilderness* (Cambridge, Mass.: The Belknap Press of Harvard University Press). Copyright, 1956, by the President and Fellows of Harvard College.

disquietude. They are troubled utterances, worried, fearful. Something has gone wrong. As in 1662 Wigglesworth already was saying in verse, God has a controversy with New England; He has cause to be angry and to punish it because of its innumerable defections. They say, unanimously, that New England was sent on an errand, and that it has failed.

To our ears these lamentations of the second generation sound strange indeed. We think of the founders as heroic men—of the towering stature of Bradford, Winthrop, and Thomas Hooker—who braved the ocean and the wilderness, who conquered both, and left to their children a goodly heritage. Why then this whimpering?

Some historians suggest that the second and third generations suffered a failure of nerve; they weren't the men their fathers had been, and they knew it. Where the founders could range over the vast body of theology and ecclesiastical polity and produce profound works like the treatises of John Cotton or the subtle psychological analyses of Hooker, or even such a gusty though wrongheaded book as Nathaniel Ward's *Simple Cobler,* let alone such lofty and rightheaded pleas as Roger Williams' *Bloudy Tenent,* all these children could do was tell each other that they were on probation and that their chances of making good did not seem very promising.

Since Puritan intellectuals were thoroughly grounded in grammar and rhetoric, we may be certain that Danforth was fully aware of the ambiguity concealed in his word "errand." It already had taken on the double meaning which it still carries with us. Originally, as the word first took form in English, it meant exclusively a short journey on which an inferior is sent to convey a message or to perform a service for his superior. In that sense we today speak of an "errand boy"; or the husband says that while in town on his lunch hour, he must run an errand for his wife. But by the end of the Middle Ages, errand developed another connotation: it came to mean the actual business on which the actor goes, the purpose itself, the conscious intention in his mind. In this signification, the runner of the errand is working for himself, is his own boss; the wife, while the husband is away at the office, runs her own errands. Now in the 1660's the problem was this: which had New England originally been—an errand boy or a doer of errands? In which sense had it failed? Had it been despatched for a further purpose, or was it an end in itself? Or had it fallen short not only in one or the other, but in both of the meanings? If so, it was indeed a tragedy, in the primitive sense of a fall from a mighty designation. . . .

. . . Since so much of the literature after 1660—in fact, just about all of it—dwells on this theme of declension and apostasy, would not the story of New England seem to be simply that of the failure of a mission? Winthrop's dread was realized: posterity had not found their salvation amid pure ordinances but had, despite the ordinances, yielded to the seductions of the good land. Hence distresses were being piled upon them, the slaughter of King Philip's War and now the attack of a profligate king upon the sacred charter. By about 1680, it did in truth seem that shortly no stone would be left upon another, that history would record of New England that the founders had been great men, but that their children and grandchildren progressively deteriorated.

This would certainly seem to be the impression conveyed by the assembled clergy and lay elders who, in 1679, met at Boston in a formal synod, under the leadership of Increase Mather, and there prepared a report on why the land suffered. The result of their deliberation, published under the title *The Necessity of Reformation*, was the first in what has proved to be a distressingly long succession of investigations into the civic health of Americans, and it is probably the most pessimistic. The land was afflicted, it said, because corruption had proceeded apace; assuredly, if the people did not quickly reform, the last blow would fall and nothing but desolation be left. Into what a moral quagmire this dedicated community had sunk, the synod did not leave to imagination; it published a long and detailed inventory of sins, crimes, misdemeanors, and nasty habits, which makes, to say the least, interesting reading. . . .

First, there was a great and visible decay of godliness. Second, there were several manifestations of pride—contention in the churches, insubordination of inferiors toward superiors, particularly of those inferiors who had, unaccountably, acquired more wealth than their betters, and, astonishingly, a shocking extravagance in attire, especially on the part of these of the meaner sort, who persisted in dressing beyond their means. Third, there were heretics, especially Quakers and Anabaptists. Fourth, a notable increase in swearing and a spreading disposition to sleep at sermons (these two phenomena seemed basically connected). Fifth, the Sabbath was wantonly violated. Sixth, family government had decayed, and fathers no longer kept their sons and daughters from prowling at night. Seventh, instead of people being knit together as one man in mutual love, they were full of contention, so that lawsuits were on the increase and lawyers were thriving. Under the eighth head, the synod described the sins of sex and alcohol, thus producing some of the juiciest prose of the period: militia days had become orgies, taverns were crowded; women threw temptation in the way of befuddled men by wearing false locks and displaying naked necks and arms "or, which is more abominable, naked Breasts"; there were "mixed Dancings," along with light behavior and "Company-keeping" with vain persons, wherefore the bastardy rate was rising. In 1672, there was actually an attempt to supply Boston with a brothel (it was suppressed, but the synod was bearish about the future). Ninth, New Englanders were betraying a marked disposition to tell lies, especially when selling anything. In the tenth place, the business morality of even the most righteous left everything to be desired: the wealthy speculated in land and raised prices excessively; "Day-Labourers and Mechanicks are unreasonable in their demands." In the eleventh place, the people showed no disposition to reform, and in the twelfth, they seemed utterly destitute of civic spirit.

"The things here insisted on," said the synod, "have been oftentimes mentioned and inculcated by those whom the Lord hath set as Watchmen to the house of Israel." Indeed they had been, and thereafter they continued to be even more inculcated. At the end of the century, the synod's report was serving as a kind of handbook for preachers: they would take some verse of Isaiah or Jeremiah, set up the doctrine that God avenges the iniquities of a chosen people, and then run down the twelve heads, merely bringing the list up to date by inserting the new and still more depraved practices an ingenious people kept on devising. I suppose that in the whole literature of the world, including the satirists of imperial Rome, there is hardly such another uninhibited and unrelenting documentation of a people's descent into corruption.

I have elsewhere endeavored to argue that, while the social or economic historian may read this literature for its contents—and so construct from the expanding catalogue of denunciations a record of social progress—the cultural anthropologist will look slightly askance at these jeremiads; he will exercise a methodological caution about taking them at face value. If you read them all through, the total effect, curiously enough, is not at all depressing: you come to the paradoxical realization that they do not bespeak a despairing frame of mind. There is something of a ritualistic incantation about them; whatever they may signify in the realm of theology, in that of psychology they are purgations of soul; they do not discourage but actually encourage the community to persist in its heinous conduct. The exhortation to a reformation which never materializes serves as a token payment upon the obligation, and so liberates the debtors. Changes there had to be: adaptations to environment, expansion of the frontier, mansions constructed, commercial adventures undertaken. These activities were not specifically nominated in the bond Winthrop had framed. They were thrust upon the society by American experience; because they were not only works of necessity but of excitement, they proved irresistible—whether making money, haunting taverns, or committing fornication. Land speculation meant not only wealth but dispersion of the people, and what was to stop the march of settlement? The covenant doctrine preached on the *Arbella* had been formulated in England, where land was not to be had for the taking; its adherents had been utterly oblivious of what the fact of a frontier would do for an imported order, let alone for a European mentality. Hence I suggest that under the guise of this mounting wail of sinfulness, this incessant and never successful cry for repentance, the Puritans launched themselves upon the process of Americanization.

However, there are still more pertinent or more analytical things to be said of this body of expression. If you compare it with the great productions of the founders, you will be struck by the fact that the second and third generations had become oriented toward the social, and only the social, problem; herein they were deeply and profoundly different from their fathers. The finest creations of the founders—the disquisitions of Hooker, Shepard, and Cotton—were written in Europe, or else, if actually penned in the colonies, proceeded from a thoroughly European mentality, upon which the American scene made no impression whatsoever. . . .

The titles alone of productions in the next generation show how concentrated have become emotion and attention upon the interest of New England, and none is more revealing than Samuel Danforth's conception of an errand into the wilderness. Instead of being able to compose abstract treatises like those of Hooker upon the soul's preparation, humiliation, or exultation, or such a collection of wisdom and theology as John Cotton's *The Way of Life* or Shepard's *The Sound Believer,* these later saints must, over and over again, dwell upon the specific sins of New England, and the more they denounce, the more they must narrow their focus to the provincial problem. If they write upon anything else, it must be about the halfway covenant and its manifold consequences—a development enacted wholly in this country—or else upon their wars with the Indians. Their range is sadly constricted, but every effort, no matter how brief, is addressed to the persistent question: what is the meaning of this society in the wilderness? If it does not mean what Winthrop said it must mean, what under Heaven is it? Who, they are forever asking themselves, who are we?—and sometimes they are on the verge of saying, who the Devil are we, anyway? . . .

. . . No less than John Milton was New England to justify God's ways to man, though not, like him, in the agony and confusion of defeat but in the confidence of approaching triumph. This errand was being run for the sake of Reformed Christianity; and while the first aim was indeed to realize in America the due form of government, both civil and ecclesiastical, the aim behind that aim was to vindicate the most rigorous ideal of the Reformation, so that ultimately all Europe would imitate New England. If we succeed, Winthrop told his audience, men will say of later plantations, "the lord make it like that of New England." There was an elementary prudence to be observed: Winthrop said that the prayer would arise from subsequent plantations, yet what was England itself but one of God's plantations? In America, he promised, we shall see, or may see, more of God's wisdom, power, and truth "then formerly wee have beene acquainted with." The situation was such that, for the moment, the model had no chance to be exhibited in England; Puritans could talk about it, theorize upon it, but they could not display it, could not prove that it would actually work. But if they had it set up in America—in a bare land, devoid of already established (and corrupt) institutions, empty of bishops and courtiers, where they could start *de novo*, and the eyes of the world were upon it—and if then it performed just as the saints had predicted of it, the Calvinist internationale would know exactly how to go about completing the already begun but temporarily stalled revolution in Europe.

When we look upon the enterprise from this point of view, the psychology of the second and third generations becomes more comprehensible. We realize that the migration was not sent upon its errand in order to found the United States of America, nor even the New England conscience. Actually, it would not perform its errand even when the colonists did erect a due form of government in church and state: what was further required in order for this mission to be a success was that the eyes of the world be kept fixed upon it in rapt attention. If the rest of the world, or at least of Protestantism, looked elsewhere, or turned to another model, or simply got distracted and forgot about New England, if the new land was left with a polity nobody in the great world of Europe wanted—then every success in fulfilling the terms of the covenant would become a diabolical measure of failure. If the due form of government were not everywhere to be saluted, what would New England have upon its hands? How give it a name, this victory nobody could utilize? How provide an identity for something conceived under misapprehensions? How could a universal which turned out to be nothing but a provincial particular be called anything but a blunder or an abortion?

If an actor, playing the leading role in the greatest dramatic spectacle of the century, were to attire himself and put on his makeup, rehearse his lines, take a deep breath, and stride onto the stage, only to find the theater dark and empty, no spotlight working, and himself entirely alone, he would feel as did New England around 1650 or 1660. For in the 1640's, during the Civil Wars, the colonies, so to speak, lost their audience. First of all, there proved to be, deep in the Puritan movement, an irreconcilable split between the Presbyterian and Independent wings, wherefore no one system could be imposed upon England, and so the New England model was unserviceable. Secondly—most horrible to relate—the Independents, who in polity were carrying New England's banner and were supposed, in the schedule of history, to lead England into imitation of the colonial order, betrayed the sacred cause by yielding to the heresy of toleration. They actually welcomed Roger Williams, whom the leaders of the model had kicked out of Massachusetts so that his nonsense about liberty of conscience would not spoil the administrations of charity.

In other words, New England did not lie, did not falter; it made good everything Winthrop demanded—wonderfully good—and then found that its lesson was rejected by those choice spirits for whom the exertion had been made. By casting out Williams, Anne Hutchinson, and the Antinomians, along with an assortment of Gortonists and Anabaptists, into that cesspool then becoming known as Rhode Island, Winthrop, Dudley, and the clerical leaders showed Oliver Cromwell how he should go about governing England. Instead, he developed the utterly absurd theory that so long as a man made a good soldier in the New Model Army, it did not matter whether he was a Calvinist, an Antinomian, an Arminian, an Anabaptist or even—horror of horrors—a Socinian! Year after year, as the circus tours this country, crowds howl with laughter, no matter how many times they have seen the stunt, at the bustle that walks by itself: the clown comes out dressed in a large skirt with a bustle behind; he turns sharply to the left, and the bustle continues blindly and obstinately straight ahead, on the original course. It is funny in a circus, but not in history. There is nothing but tragedy in the realization that one was in the main path of events, and now is sidetracked and disregarded. One is always able, of course, to stand firm on his first resolution, and to condemn the clown of history for taking the wrong turning: yet this is a desolating sort of stoicism, because it always carries with it the recognition that history will never come back to the predicted path, and that with one's own demise, righteousness must die out of the world. . . .

Many a man has done a brave deed, been hailed as a public hero, had honors and ticker tape heaped upon him—and then had to live, day after day, in the ordinary routine, eating breakfast and brushing his teeth, in what seems protracted anticlimax. A couple may win their way to each other across insuperable obstacles, elope in a blaze of passion and glory—and then have to learn that life is a matter of buying the groceries and getting the laundry done. This sense of the meaning having gone out of life, that all adventures are over, that no great days and no heroism lie ahead, is particularly galling when it falls upon a son whose father once was the public hero or the great lover. He has to put up with the daily routine without ever having known at first hand the thrill of danger or the ecstasy of passion. True, he has his own hardships—clearing rocky pastures, hauling in the cod during a storm, fighting Indians in a swamp—but what are these compared with the magnificence of leading an exodus of saints to found a city on a hill, for the eyes of all the world to behold? He might wage a stout fight against the Indians, and one out of ten of his fellows might perish in the struggle, but the world was no longer interested. He would be reduced to writing accounts of himself and scheming to get a publisher in London, in a desperate effort to tell a heedless world, "Look, I exist!"

His greatest difficulty would be not the stones, storms, and Indians, but the problem of his identity. In something of this sort, I should like to suggest, consists the anxiety and torment that inform productions of the late seventeenth and early eighteenth centuries—and should I say, some thereafter? It appears most clearly in *Magnalia Christi Americana,* the work of that soul most tortured by the problem, Cotton Mather: "I write the Wonders of the Christian Religion, flying from the Depravations of Europe, to the American Strand." Thus he proudly begins, and at once trips over the acknowledgment that the founders had not simply fled from depraved Europe but had intended to redeem it. And so the book is full of lamentations over the declension of the children, who appear, page after page, in contrast to their mighty progenitors, about as profligate a lot as ever squandered a great inheritance.

And yet, the *Magnalia* is not an abject book; neither are the election sermons abject, nor is the inventory of sins offered by the synod of 1679. There is bewilderment, confusion, chagrin, but there is no surrender. A task has been assigned upon which the populace are in fact intensely engaged. But they are not sure any more for just whom they are working; they know they are moving, but they do not know where they are going. They seem still to be on an errand, but if they are no longer inferiors sent by the superior forces of the Reformation, to whom they should report, then their errand must be wholly of the second sort, something with a purpose and an intention sufficient unto itself. If so, what is it? If it be not the due form of government, civil and ecclesiastical, that they brought into being, how otherwise can it be described?

The literature of self-condemnation must be read for meanings far below the surface, for meanings of which, we may be so rash as to surmise, the authors were not fully conscious, but by which they were troubled and goaded. They looked in vain to history for an explanation of themselves; more and more it appeared that the meaning was not to be found in theology, even with the help of the covenantal dialectic. Thereupon, these citizens found that they had no other place to search but within themselves—even though, at first sight, that repository appeared to be nothing but a sink of iniquity. Their errand having failed in the first sense of the term, they were left with the second, and required to fill it with meaning by themselves and out of themselves. Having failed to rivet the eyes of the world upon their city on the hill, they were left alone with America.

11

The Puritans: From Providence to Pride
DANIEL J. BOORSTIN

If ever there was a dogma fit to arm a weak settlement on a savage frontier, it was Puritanism. And yet the very success of the Puritan community on that frontier was to be the undoing of their philosophy. Their success induced them gradually to seek their standards in their own experience, to make what they had accomplished the yardstick of what they might have, or ought to have, accomplished. We shall see how the pragmatic spirit, the belief in "givenness," * seeped into the interstices of the Puritan dogma and was gradually to dissolve it into a more general faith in the magical definition of American purpose out of the American success.

It is doubtful if there has ever anywhere been a more subtle, a more comprehensive, or more beautifully put-together theory of society than that which the Pilgrims and Puritans brought with them in the early seventeenth century. One of its marvels was that it was equally capable of communication in heavy treatises like William Ames's *Marrow of Sacred Divinity* and in five-minute talks like John Winthrop's speech to the General Court. It was a miracle of logic, with its own way of asking and of answering any question you might put. Of all people in modern history, these early Puritans could be least accused of confusion about their ends or of that inarticulateness which I have described as a characteristic of American political thought. These people were eager to tell why they were here, what their

Reprinted from *The Genius of American Politics* by Daniel J. Boorstin by permission of The University of Chicago Press. Copyright 1953 by The University of Chicago.
* Elsewhere in the book from which this essay is taken, Professor Boorstin defines the idea of "givenness" as the "belief that values in America are in some way or other automatically defined: *given* by certain facts of geography or history peculiar to us," or, more succinctly, that "values are implicit in the American experience" (*The Genius of American Politics,* pp. 9, 23–24) [Ed.].

community was about, and where they were going. The Pilgrims came to the New World, William Bradford explains in his *History*, "not out of any newfanglednes, or other such like giddie humor, by which men are oftentimes transported to their great hurt and danger, but for sundrie weightie and solid reasons."

Not only did the early settlers come to New England with an explicit philosophy, but their philosophy, as I shall try to show, had characteristics which fitted it admirably to be a prop for people struggling in the wilderness. In the very beginning, at least, the American experience, far from corroding Puritan dogma, actually seemed its strongest possible proof. For a while, New England would give a dazzling vividness to their dogma. But only in the beginning. For, as the Puritans threw themselves into the struggle against nature, developed their equipment for that struggle, and finally succeeded in building Zion in the wilderness, they were increasingly subject to those influences which were to persist in American history. We can see the growing sense of "givenness," the growing tendency to make the "is" the guide to the "ought," to make America as it was (or as they had now made it) a criterion of what America ought to be. This was the breakdown of classic Puritanism which I have called the movement from providence to pride. . . .

There were several unique features of the American story which are significant for our purpose. Among them is the fact that in the long run Puritanism in New England was to decline, not because it was defeated, but, in a sense, because it had succeeded. It was its spectacular success in building churches and communities, a success all the more spectacular because it was accomplished against the backdrop of what the Puritans themselves called a "howling wilderness," that led the Puritans to trust increasingly to their own energies and accomplishments, to find their purposes somehow implicit in their achievements.

For better or worse, there is a kind of continuity between the Harvard of Roger Conant of Salem (a member of the first committee appointed by the town in 1636 to view a site for an English university in New England) and the Harvard of James Bryant Conant. For in New England there was no proper counterpart to the English Restoration of 1660; no decisive defeat of the Puritans. If the dogma of Puritanism eventually declined, the influence of Puritans remained unbroken; at virtually every period in the later history of New England, dominant groups have claimed spiritual, as well as genealogical, descent from the Puritans of the classic age. . . . Puritanism in New England was not so much defeated by the dogmas of anti-Puritanism as it was simply assimilated to the conditions of life in America. Never was it blown away by a hurricane. It was gradually eroded by the American climate.

A distinctive and paradoxical feature of the American story was that the decline actually came in part from the removal of many of those perils which had earlier confirmed the Puritan dogmas. The more secure the Puritans became on this continent, the more meager and unimpressive became the daily proofs of their dogma. At the same time, success nourished their pride and gave them a community to which they could point as the embodiment of their philosophy. In all this we shall see how the New England story re-enacted one of the familiar ironies of history: in the very act of establishing their community, they undermined the philosophy on which it was to have been founded.

Just as the conditions of America in the first generation were admirably suited to confirm the Puritan beliefs, so the gradual removal of those conditions within the next generations was destined to undermine them. The firm establishment of a community in New England was marked by a growing sense of security, a decline of many of the fears and uncertainties which had nourished a desperate dependence on God. The second generation owed its presence in New England, not to God's happy guidance across the perils of an ocean, but to the simple accident of birth. Puritan immigrants who came after the mid-century were met, not by the Indian arrows which had greeted the first Pilgrims, but by the embrace of their countrymen. Glowing fireplaces and full storehouses were ready for them. Their welcome now seemed less from God—or from Satan—than from their fellow-Puritans. . . .

As the fund of American experience increased, everyday events lost the magic of novelty and the mystery of the unexpected. More and more, life took on the air of the familiar, or even of the banal. The Puritans had now come to look for the bitter winter and the inspiriting spring of New England. The seasonal pattern of habits of the wild animals, the birds, and the fish was gradually discovered. Having learned the best ways of growing Indian corn, the Puritans saw more and more connection between their own efforts and the product of the soil. As they charted the Indian trails, named the hills, and followed the curves of the rivers, they built their own bridges and ferries and established the ways from one village to another. Now if one failed to reach his destination, he had to blame himself.

With remarkable rapidity the Puritans in New England built up their knowledge of the nature around them. The encyclopedic farmer's almanac displaced the catalogue of remarkable providences. As their interest in and mastery of natural history increased, New England Puritans—for example, Cotton Mather, John Leverett, Paul Dudley, John Winthrop, Jr., and Zabdiel Boylston—were enlisted in the Royal Society among the leaders of English science. In New England it was the clergy who propagated the new astronomy. The use of Charles Morton's *Compendium Physicae* and the growing laboratories of Harvard College attest the serious interest in what they called "experimental natural philosophy." Encouraged by the growing enthusiasm of their age for the laws of nature, they added nearly every day to the data of their science something which a few years before had been the stuff of theology.

In 1684, when Increase Mather wrote the Preface to his collection of remarkable providences, he expressed his wish "that the Natural History of New-England might be written and published to the world; the rules and method described by that learned and excellent person Robert Boyle, Esq., being duely observed therein. It would best become some scholar that has been born in this land to do such a service for his countrey." Facts which formerly had been merely points of departure for the imaginative raconteur, or metaphors for sermons to exhort an isolated settlement, were gradually set in order. Now they had become useful knowledge. By the end of the seventeenth century the Puritans' familiarity with their environment, their increasing ability to predict the whims of the weather, and the gifts of the wilderness had seriously dulled—although it had not yet by any means destroyed —their sensitivity to the mysterious and the providential.

The development is nowhere clearer than in the striking change in the Puritan approach to their own history or, more precisely, in the growth of Puritan historical writing. The best early Pilgrim and Puritan accounts of themselves are contemporary chronicles, such as Bradford's history of Plymouth and John Winthrop's journal. These writings, and even lesser ones—like Johnson's *Wonder-working Providence of Sions Saviour in New England*—impress us with the Puritan's sense of his mission, his single-mindedness, his prudence, and his submission to the will of God. They are works of rare seriousness and dignity. But essentially they chronicle the fulfilment of a divine mission rather than the progress of a human enterprise. We are never allowed to forget that the principal protagonist is God, the enemy Satan; each is using men to attain his ends.

By the second or third generation in New England we note a change. It has sometimes been described as the appearance of a "modern" spirit in their historical writing. Now we begin to read works in which *men* are the protagonists: the reader's attention is focused on human successes and failures. Contemporary annals are replaced by retrospective history, dealing with causes and consequences. The discrete judgments of God—his dooms on the good and the evil—intelligible only in the light of cosmic and inscrutable purposes, now give way to the purposes of men.

At this period at the end of the seventeenth century, when the providential glow of the life of earliest New England was still a memory, there appeared the most important work of Puritan historiography, and indeed one of the greatest histories ever written in America. Cotton Mather's *Magnalia Christi Americana*, first published in 1702, was written while Puritan theology was sufficiently alive to give unity to a historical work; yet in its pages we encounter the first full flush of satisfaction at man's accomplishments in the New World. As Mather suggested in his title, he meant to focus on the achievements of Christ rather than on the providences of God. The *Magnalia* seems to tell us that God cannot be better glorified than by a display of the successes of the first two generations of his chosen people in the Wilderness. Here we begin to see the face of Pride.

We have considerable evidence, moreover, that the remarkable combination of piousness and complacency was no peculiarity of Mather, but was a general and growing sentiment. In his Preface to Mather's work, John Higginson writes:

> *The Lord was pleased to grant such a gracious presence of his with them, and such a blessing upon their undertakings, that within a few years a wilderness was subdued before them, and so many Colonies planted, Towns erected, and Churches settled . . . and that the Lord has added so many of the blessings of Heaven and earth for the comfortable subsistence of his people in these ends of the earth. . . . There is also a third generation, who are grown up, and begin to stand thick upon the stage of action, at this day, and these were all born in the country, and may call New-England their native land. Now, in respect of what the Lord hath done for these generations, succeeding one another, we have aboundant cause of Thanksgiving to the Lord*

*our God, who hath so increased and blessed this people, that from a
day of small things, he has brought us to be, what we now are.*

The two heavy volumes of Mather's work seem themselves to
have been intended as a monument to the success which attends the
orthodox. "So mighty was the work to found Christ's empire here," he
boasts in the motto of his first book. Mather's prime interest is in "the
Actors" and "the *Actions*"; his object is to recount "the design where-
on, the manner wherein, and the people whereby, the several colonies of New-England were planted." In no other work of nationalist
history—not even the writings of George Bancroft in the nineteenth
century—can we find greater pride in the fortitude, wisdom, and
ingenuity of particular men. Mather deliberately chooses the form and
even the phrase of epic, which is, after all, a tale of heroic adventure.
He begins with a paraphrase of Virgil, "I write the Wonders of the
Christian Religion, flying from the depravations of Europe, to the
American Strand."

The epic parallel is never forgotten; the role of Aeneas and his
Trojan warriors is played by John Winthrop and his faithful Puritans:

> *Our New-England shall tell and boast of her Winthrop, a lawgiver as
> patient as Lycurgus, but not admitting any of his criminal disorders;
> as devout as Numa, but not liable to any of his heathenish madnesses;
> a governour in whom the excellencies of Christianity made a most
> improving addition unto the virtues, wherein even without those he
> would have made a parallel for the great men of Greece, or of Rome,
> which the pen of a Plutarch has eternized* [Magnalia (*Hartford, 1853*),
> I, 118].

No one would have been more scandalized than Winthrop himself, to
read such idolatry, such preening on the strength of mankind. Winthrop had seen himself as the instrument of God.

Mather is hardly to be blamed for pride in the work of his New
England predecessors. Satisfaction was justified by the firm foundation of the churches and by the heroism of the New England fighters
in "the wars of the Lord," as he called the battles against the Indians.
It would have been surprising had Mather not sung the praises of
Harvard College, which was already well established. He described
his Alma Mater with his customary modesty, as "a river, without the
streams whereof, these regions would have been meer unwatered
places for the devil!" We could hardly ask for better evidence than
Mather has provided us that, even for conservatives, the new security

and prosperity of their community nourished a pride in the works of men. God, the providential guardian, who, for reasons best known to himself, had personally deflected the arrows of the Indians and had led the uncertain traveler by the hand from Boston to Cambridge— this God gradually slipped out of their vision. Instead, they began to see a beneficent Being who blessed their own human undertakings. They were moving from a sense of mystery to a consciousness of mastery; the two spirits could not well live together. . . .

The declining sense of mystery which I have described carried with it an increasing directness in approaching all experience, a willingness to allow experience to give values. As the Puritan in the New World had come to feel that his enemies could be met and overcome, so he had come to feel less vividly the omnipresence of Satan. And as he came to discern and define his obstacles in the wilderness, so he was prepared to believe that even the fate of man's soul, the question of election itself—or at least of title to church membership—might not be entirely hidden from man.

No longer did he feel that he was encircled by enemies; rather he began to think of himself as confronting them. More and more of life seemed predictable, and the Puritan became ready to believe that perhaps the most important facts were intelligible to him, that he might read God's purpose in Nature's design. Once communities had become firmly established and wild men and wild animals had been exterminated from the gaps between the main coastal settlements, the Puritan community began to stand, or to feel that it stood, in a phalanx. With secure and prosperous communities behind them, men felt they could look outward from the larger centers to a definite line of battle in the West. Here, too, circumstances were to define the task.

There is no denying that the Puritan episode was in many ways untypical of later American experience: first, because the intellectual equipment of the earliest Puritans was so thoroughly European and, second, because the America they saw was virginal. By bringing Puritanism to America, they were, of course, starting the long process of importation of ideas from Europe. Their encounter with nature eventually helped disintegrate their original explicit philosophy. Their experience, of course, could not be precisely repeated in other frontier communities which were not equipped with any such explicit philosophy.

The mastery of nature depended on the ability to understand rather than on the ability to persuade. The Big Lie could not help against a snowstorm; it would kill no wolves and grow no corn. Therefore, it was less important to make a grand plan, to make generalities glitter, than to know what was and how to control the forces of nature. In mastering the wilderness, in building institutions and communities, the second and third generation of New England Puritans became somewhat less anxious to dot all the *I*'s and cross all the *T*'s in their theology. They became more and more responsive to the values which seemed to emerge from their daily lives. The Puritan experience thus shows some persistent characteristics of American history which have encouraged belief in the implicitness of values. Already in that earliest age we see a growing sense of "givenness." . . .

GOD PROFIT: "HORRIBLE SNARES AND INFINITE SINS"

12

The Case of Robert Keayne

JOHN WINTHROP

[November, 1639] At a general court holden at Boston, great complaint was made of the oppression used in the country in sale of foreign commodities; and Mr. Robert Keaine, who kept a shop in Boston, was notoriously above others observed and complained of; and, being convented, he was charged with many particulars; in some, for taking above six-pence in the shilling profit; in some above eight-pence; and, in some small things, above two for one; and being hereof convict, (as appears by the records,) he was fined £200, which came thus to pass: The deputies considered, apart, of his fine, and set it at £200; the magistrates agreed but to £100. So, the court being divided, at length it was agreed, that his fine should be £200, but he should pay but £100, and the other should be respited to the further consideration of the next general court. By this means the magistrates and deputies were brought to an accord, which otherwise had not been likely, and so much trouble might have grown, and the offender escaped censure. For the cry of the country was so great against oppression, and some of the elders and magistrates had declared such detestation of the corrupt practice of this man (which was the more observable, because he was wealthy and sold dearer than most other tradesmen, and for that he was of ill report for the like covetous practice in England, that incensed the deputies very much against him). And sure the course was very evil, especial circumstances considered: (1) He being an ancient professor of the gospel: (2) A man

Reprinted from James Savage, ed., *The History of New England from 1630 to 1649. By John Winthrop, Esq.* [Winthrop's Journal] (Boston, 1825), I, 313–17.

of eminent parts: (3) Wealthy, and having but one child:
(4) Having come over for conscience sake, and for the advancement
of the gospel here: (5) Having been formerly dealt with and admon-
ished, both by private friends and also by some of the magistrates and
elders, and having promised reformation; being a member of a church
and commonwealth now in their infancy, and under the curious observation of all churches and civil states in the world. These added
much aggravation to his sin in the judgment of all men of understanding. Yet most of the magistrates (though they discerned of the offence
clothed with all these circumstances) would have been more moderate
in their censure: (1) Because there was no law in force to limit or
direct men in point of profit in their trade. (2) Because it is the
common practice, in all countries, for men to make use of advantages
for raising the prices of their commodities. (3) Because (though he
were chiefly aimed at, yet) he was not alone in this fault. (4) Because
all men through the country, in sale of cattle, corn, labor, etc. were
guilty of the like excess in prices. (5) Because a certain rule could not
be found out for an equal rate between buyer and seller, though much
labour had been bestowed in it, and divers laws had been made,
which, upon experience, were repealed, as being neither safe nor
equal. Lastly, and especially, because the law of God appoints no
other punishment but double restitution; and, in some cases, as where
the offender freely confesseth, and brings his offering, only half added
to the principal. After the court had censured him, the church of
Boston called him also in question, where (as before he had done in
the court) he did, with tears, acknowledge and bewail his covetous
and corrupt heart, yet making some excuse for many of the particulars,
which were charged upon him, as partly by pretence of ignorance of
the true price of some wares, and chiefly by being misled by some
false principles, as (1) That, if a man lost in one commodity, he might
help himself in the price of another. (2) That if, through want of skill
or other occasion, his commodity cost him more than the price of the
market in England, he might then sell it for more than the price of the
market in New England, etc. These things gave occasion to Mr.
Cotton, in his publick exercise the next lecture day, to lay open the
error of such false principles, and to give some rules of direction in the
case. Some false principles were these:

1. That a man might sell as dear as he can, and buy as cheap as he
   can.

2. If a man lose by casualty of sea, etc. in some of his commodities, he may raise the price of the rest.
3. That he may sell as he bought, though he paid too dear, etc. and though the commodity be fallen, etc.
4. That, as a man may take the advantage of his own skill or ability, so he may of another's ignorance or necessity.
5. Where one gives time for payment, he is to take like recompense of one as of another.

The rules for trading were these:

1. A man may not sell above the current price, i.e. such a price as is usual in the time and place, and as another (who knows the worth of the commodity) would give for it, if he had occasion to use it; as that is called current money, which every man will take, etc.
2. When a man loseth in his commodity for want of skill, etc. he must look at it as his own fault or cross, and therefore must not lay it upon another.
3. Where a man loseth by casualty of sea, or, etc. it is a loss cast upon himself by providence, and he may not ease himself of it by casting it upon another; for so a man should seem to provide against all providences, etc. that he should never lose; but where there is a scarcity of the commodity, there men may raise their price; for now it is a hand of God upon the commodity, and not the person.
4. A man may not ask any more for his commodity than his selling price, as Ephron to Abraham, the land is worth thus much.

The cause being debated by the church, some were earnest to have him excommunicated; but the most thought an admonition would be sufficient. Mr. Cotton opened the causes, which required excommunication, out of that in 1 Cor. 5. 11. The point now in question was, whether these actions did declare him to be such a covetous person, etc. Upon which he showed, that it is neither the habit of covetousness, (which is in every man in some degree,) nor simply the act, that declares a man to be such, but when it appears, that a man sins against his conscience, or the very light of nature, and when it appears in a man's whole conversation. But Mr. Keaine did not appear to be such, but rather upon an errour in his judgment, being led by false principles; and, beside, he is otherwise liberal, as in his hospitality, and in church communion, etc. So, in the end, the church consented to an admonition.

13

Last Will and Testament
ROBERT KEAYNE

First and before all things, I commend and commit my precious soul into the hands of Almighty God, who not only as a loving·creator hath given it unto me when He might have made me a brute beast, but also as a most loving father and merciful saviour hath redeemed it with the precious blood of His own dear son and my sweet Jesus from that gulf of misery and ruin that I by original sin and actual transgressions had plunged it into. Therefore, I renounce all manner of known errors, all Popish and prelatical superstitions, all anabaptistical enthusiasms and familistical delusions, with all other feigned devices and all old and new upstart opinions, unsound and blasphemous errors, and other high imaginations that exalt themselves against the honor and truth of God in the way of His worship and ordinances and against the dignity and scepter of the Lord Jesus Christ my Saviour.

I do further desire from my heart to renounce all confidence or expectation of merit or desert in any of the best duties or services that ever I have, shall, or can be able to perform, acknowledging that all my righteousness, sanctification, and close walking with God, if it were or had been a thousand times more exact than ever yet I attained to, is all polluted and corrupt and falls short of commending me to God in point of my justification or helping forward my redemption or salvation. They deserve nothing at God's hand but hell and condemnation if He should enter into judgment with me for them. And though I believe that all my ways of holiness are of no use to me in point of justification, yet I believe they may not be neglected by me without great sin, but are ordained of God for me to walk in them carefully, in love to Him, in obedience to His commandments, as well as for many other good ends. They are good fruits and evidences of justification. Therefore, renouncing though not the acts yet all confidence in those

Reprinted with the permission of The Colonial Society of Massachusetts from Bernard Bailyn, ed., "The Apologia of Robert Keayne," *Publications of The Colonial Society of Massachusetts*, XLII (*Transactions 1952–1956*), Boston, 1964.

acts of holiness and works of sanctification performed by me, I look for my acceptance with God and the salvation of my soul only from the merits or righteousness of the Lord Jesus Christ, and from the free, bountiful, and undeserved grace and love of God in Him. And though this faith in me in respect of application for my own comfort is very weak and feeble, yet I look up to my God in Jesus Christ to strengthen it. And though the sinful failings and weaknesses of my own life have been great and many, and [though] neither myself nor family in respect of close walking with Him hath been so with God as it ought to be (for which I have and shall still desire and endeavor to judge and condemn myself in His sight, and not to allow myself in any ways of evil knowingly), yet I look up to His throne of grace and mercy in the blood of Jesus Christ with some hope and confidence that He will both pardon and subdue them. In this faith alone I desire both to live and die and to continue therein to my life's end.

This faith in the Lord Jesus Christ hath been most plainly and sweetly taught in these churches of New England, in which place, though I met with many and deep sorrows and variety of exercises of spirit and hard measures offered to me, yet with unrepentant thoughts I desire to acknowledge it for a great blessing and undeserved favor of God that He hath brought me hither to enjoy His presence in the beauties of holiness, and to see His walkings in His holy sanctuary. And though there may be failings both in our civil government and churches (for all men have their weaknesses and the best societies of men have their imperfections, so that still there will be some things to be amended and reformed as God shall be pleased to discover new light and means to do it), yet I do unfeignedly approve of the way of the churches of Jesus Christ and the civil government that God hath here set up amongst us, and rejoice therein, as a way that both I pray for and doubt not but God will bless. According to that light that I have received or that which I ever read or heard of, it is one of the best and happiest governments that is this day in the world.

This being premised in respect of my soul and my faith in Jesus Christ, I do next commit my body to the earth (and to comely and decent burial), there to rest till my loving Saviour by His almighty power shall raise it up again, at which time I confidently believe it shall be reunited to my own soul. There it shall receive according to the works that I have done in this life according as they have been good or evil in the sight of God or according to that faith and confidence that I have in the free grace and merits of the Lord Jesus Christ. . . .

But some that shall read or hear of the expressions in this my will will be ready to say [that] if I am and have been of this mind so long, how can it stand with that humble confession that I made both in the Court and in the church, when I endeavored in the one and did in the other give satisfaction, without carrying a great appearance of hypocrisy or at least of repenting my repentings.

I desire in this to clear my conscience both towards God and man and do not think that these things are improper to be mentioned in a will but very natural and suitable to it. Therefore I say, first, if my confession was humble and penitential, as is objected, [then] it did justly call for mercy and clemency and not for advantage and more severity, as some made use of it to that end (but with what equity I leave both them and it to the Lord, to Whom they must give an answer if some of them have not already done it, and to such a time wherein they may stand in need of mercy themselves and shall not find it; for there shall be judgment merciless to them that show no mercy). If my confession was not humble and penitent then the objection is needless. But I am glad the prevailing party at that time so took it, though they look upon it as an act of my guilt and use it as a weapon against me. But I think it will be a witness against them for their perverting of it.

I did not then nor dare not now go about to justify all my actions. I know God is righteous and doth all upon just grounds, though men may mistake in their grounds and proceedings, counsel have erred and courts may err and a faction may be too hard and outvote the better or more discerning part. I know the errors of my life. The failings in my trade and otherwise have been many. Therefore from God [the censure] was most just. Though it had been much more severe I dare not so open my mouth against it, nor never did as I remember, [except to] justify Him. Yet I dare not say nor did I ever think (as far as I can call to mind) that the censure was just and righteous from men. Was the price of a bridle, not for taking but only asking, 2 s. for [what] cost here 20 d. such a heinous sin? [Such bridles] have since been commonly sold and still are for 2 s. 6 d. and 3 s. or more, though worse in kind. Was it such a heinous sin to sell 2 or 3 dozen of great gold buttons for 2 s. 10 d. per dozen that cost 2 s. 2 d. ready money in London, bought at the best hand, as I showed to many by my invoice (though I could not find it at the instant when the Court desired to see it) and since was confirmed by special testimony from London? The buttons [were not even] paid for when the complaint was made, nor I think not yet; neither did the complaint come from him that bought and owed them nor with his knowledge or consent, as he hath since affirmed, but merely from the spleen and envy of another, whom it did nothing concern. Was this so great an offense? Indeed, that it might be made so, some out of their ignorance would needs say that they were copper and not worth 9 d. per dozen. But these were weak grounds to pass heavy censures upon.

Was the selling of 6 d. nails for 8 d. per lb. and 8 d. nails for 10 d. per lb. such a crying and oppressing sin? And as I remember it was above two years before he that bought them paid me for them (and not paid for if I forget not) when he made that quarreling exception and unrighteous complaint in the Court against me, (he then being of the Court himself) that I had altered and corrupted my book in adding more to the price than I had set down for them at first delivery. If I had set down 8 d. after 2 years' forbearance for what I would have sold for 7 d. if he had paid me presently, I think it had been a more honest act in me than it was in him that promised or at least pretended to pay me presently that he might get them at a lower price than a man could well live upon, and when he had got my goods into his hands to keep me 2 or 3 years without my money. All that while there was no fault found at the prices, but when he could for shame keep the money no longer, yet he will requite it with a censure in the Court. For my own part, as I did ever think it an ungodly act in him, so I do think in my conscience that it had been more just in the Court to have censured him than me for this thing, though this was the chiefest crime alleged and most powerfully carried against me. . . .

Now I leave it to the world or to any impartial man or any that hath understanding in trade to judge whether this was a just offense or so crying a sin for which I had such cause to be so penitent (this being the chief [accusation] and pressed on with so great aggravation by my opposers) [or whether] my actions, innocent in themselves, were misconstrued. I knew not how to help myself, especially considering it was no oppressing price but usual with others at that time to sell the like so and since [then] frequently for almost half as much more, as I think all know, and yet both given and taken without exception, or at least without public complaint. Yea, the same gentleman himself, since he hath turned merchant and trader, seems to have lost his former tenderness of conscience that he had when he was a buyer and is not so scrupulous in his own gains. . . .

I confess still as I did then and as I have said before, that the newness and strangeness of the thing, to be brought forth into an open court as a public malefactor, was both a shame and an amazement to me. It was the grief of my soul (and I desire it may ever so be in a greater measure) that any act of mine (though not justly but by misconstruction) should be an occasion of scandal to the Gospel and profession of the Lord Jesus, or that myself should be looked at as one that had brought any just dishonor to God (which I have endeavored long and according to my weak ability desired to prevent), though God hath been pleased for causes best known to Himself to deny me such a blessing. And if it had been in my own power I should rather have chosen to have perished in my cradle than to have lived to such a time. But the good pleasure of God is to keep me low in my own eyes as well as in the eyes of others, and also to make me humble and penitent, lest such mercies should have lifted me up above what is meet. Yet I do say still as I have often done before, that those things for which I was questioned (in the best apprehension, guided by God's word, that I had then or have since attained to) did deserve no such proceedings as was carved out to me, though some blew up those sparks into a great flame. And I am not alone herein, though it was my own case, but many wise and godly servants of the Lord, as well as divers others were and still are of the same mind. Yea, some that were then much against me have confessed since to me that things were carried in a hurry.

14

A Christian at His Calling
COTTON MATHER

. . . There are *Two Callings* to be minded by *All Christians*. Every Christian hath a GENERAL CALLING; which is, to Serve the Lord Jesus Christ, and Save his own Soul, in the Services of *Religion*, that are incumbent on all the Children of men. God hath *called* us, to *Believe* on His *Son*, and *Repent* of our *Sin*, and observe the Sacred Means of our *Communion* with Himself and bear our *Testimony* to His *Truths* and *Wayes* in the World: And every man in the world, should herein conform to the Calls of that God, who *hath called us with this Holy Calling*. But then, every Christian hath also a PERSONAL CALLING; or a certain *Particular Employment*, by which his *Usefulness*, in his Neighborhood, is distinguished. God hath made man a *Sociable* Creature. *We* expect Benefits from *Humane Society*. It is but equal, that *Humane Society* should Receive Benefits from *Us*. We are Beneficial to *Humane Society* by the Works of that Special OCCUPATION, in which we are to be employ'd, according to the Order of God.

A Christian at his *Two Callings*, is a man in a Boat, Rowing for Heaven; the *House* which our Heavenly Father hath intended for us. If he mind but one of his *Callings*, be it which it will, he pulls the *Oar*, but on *one side* of the Boat, and will make but a poor dispatch to the Shoar of Eternal Blessedness.

It is not only necessary, that a Christian should follow his *General Calling*; it is of necessity, that he follow his *Personal Calling* too. The CASE therefore now before us, is,

WHAT IS THAT GOOD ACCOUNT, THAT A CHRISTIAN SHOULD BE ABLE TO GIVE OF HIS OCCUPATION? Or, *How should a Christian be Occupied in the Business of his* PERSONAL CALLING, *that he may give a Good Account of it?* We will thus proceed in our Discourse upon it.

Reprinted from Cotton Mather, *A Christian at His Calling; Two Brief Discourses, one Directing a Christian in his General Calling; Another Directing Him in his Personal* (Boston, 1701).

I. A Christian should be able to give this Account, *that he hath an Occupation.* Every Christian ordinarily should have a *Calling.* That is to say, There should be some *Special Business,* and some *Settled Business,* wherein a Christian should for the most part spend the most of his *Time;* and this, that so he may Glorify God, by doing of *Good* for *others,* and getting of *Good* for *himself.* . . . 'Tis not *Honest,* nor *Christian,* that a *Christian* should have no *Business* to do. There is a variety of *Callings* in the World; even as there are various *Objects,* about which the *Callings* of men are conversant, and various *Designs* unto which the *Callings* of men are Intended. Some *Callings,* are more immediately, to Serve the *Souls* of our *Neighbours;* and some their *Safety,* & some their *Defence;* and some their Bodies; and some their *Estates;* and some their *Delights.* But it is not lawful for a Christian ordinarily to Live without some *Calling* or another, until Infirmities have unhappily disabled him. Indeed a man cannot live without the *Help of other men.* But how can a man Reasonably look for the *Help of other men,* if he be not in some *Calling* Helpful to *other men?* . . . Yea, a *Calling* is not only our *Duty,* but also our *Safety.* Men will ordinarily fall into horrible *Snares,* and infinite *Sins,* if they have not a *Calling,* to be their *preservative.* . . . Tho' it were part of the Curse brought in by *Sin, In the Sweat of thy Face thou shalt eat Bread,* the *Curse* is become a *Blessing,* and our *Sweat* has a tendency to keep us from abundance of *Sin.* Ordinarily no man does *Nothing:* If men have *nothing* to do, they'l soon do *Too much;* do what they *ought not.* The Temptations of the *Devil,* are best Resisted by those that are least at *Liesure* [sic] to Receive them. An *Occupation* is an *Ordinance* of God for our safeguard against the *Temptations* of the Devil. A Bird on the *Wing* is not so soon catch'd by the *Hellish Fowler.* A man is upon the *Wing,* when he is at the *Work,* which God hath set him to do. . . .

II. But upon that Enquiry, *What is your Occupation?* a Christian should be able to give this further Account, *That he hath an Allowable Occupation, yea an Agreeable Occupation; and that he Entered into it with a suitable Disposition.* . . . If our *Calling* be that whereby God will be *Offended,* it cannot be a *Calling* wherein we shall be our selves *Befriended.* What can any man be the better for a *Calling* that will bring him under the *Wrath* of God? But the *Wrath* of God will cleave to all the *Gain* gotten by a *Calling* that shall be Forbidden by the *Word* of God. The man and his Posterity will Gain but little, by a *Calling* whereto God hath not *Called* him. For our *course of Life* then, we must consult the *Word* of God, if we would not fall into a *course of Sin,* when we go to chuse our Occupation. . . . Let this be taken for granted; except a *Calling* have a Tendency to the *Happiness* of Mankind, and except the *Spiritual,* or the *Temporal* Good of other men, be help'd forward by a *Calling,* a man may not meddle with it; the *Calling* is Naught, the Good God *calls* you to let it alone. . . .

But this is not enough. A Christian should have it contrived, That his *Calling* be *Agreeable,* as well as *Allowable.* It is a wonderful Inconvenience for a man to have a *Calling* that won't *Agree* with him. See to it, O *Parents,* that when you chuse *Callings* for your *Children,* you wisely consult their *Capacities,* & their *Inclinations;* lest you Ruine them. And, Oh! cry mightily to God, by *Prayer,* yea with *Fasting* & *Prayer,* for His Direction when you are to resolve upon a matter of such considerable consequence. But, O *Children,* you also should be *Thoughtful* and *Prayerful,* when you are going to fix upon your *Callings;* and above all, propose deliberately *Right Ends* unto your selves in what you do; . . .

III. A Christian should be able to give a Good Account, not only, *What is his Occupation,* but also, *What he is in his Occupation.* It is not enough, That a Christian *have* an *Occupation;* but he must *mind* his *Occupation,* as it becomes a Christian. Well then, That a Christian may be able to give a *Good Account* of his *Occupation,* there are certain Vertues of Christianity with which he is to follow it. Particularly,

1. A Christian should follow his *Occupation* with INDUSTRY. . . . It seems a man *Slothful in Business,* is not a man *Serving the Lord.* By *Slothfulness* men bring upon themselves, What? but Poverty, but Misery, but all sorts of Confusion. . . . On the other Side, a man by *Diligence* in his Business, What may he not come to? A *Diligent* man is very rarely an *Indigent* man. Would a man *Rise* by his Business? I say, then let him *Rise* to his Business. . . . I tell you, With *Diligence* a man may do marvellous things. *Young* man, *Work hard* while you are *Young:* You'll Reap the Effects of it, when you are *Old.* Yea, How can you ordinarily Enjoy any Rest at *Night,* if you have not been well at Work, in the *Day?* Let your *Business* Engross the *most* of Your Time. . . .

Come, come For shame, Away to your *Business:* Lay out your *Strength* in it, put forth your *Skill* for it; Avoid all impertinent *Avoca-*

tions. Laudable *Recreations* may be used now and then: But, I beseech you, Let those *Recreations* be used for *Sawce*, but not for *Meat*.
If *Recreations* go to incroach too far upon your *Business*, give to them
that put off. . . . It may be, there are some, that neglect their *Occupation*, and squander away one *Hour*, and perhaps, one *Day*, after
another, Drinking, and Gaming, & Smoking, & Fooling, at those Drinking *Houses*, that are so Sinful as to Entertain them. Unto you, *O
Miserables*, I must address a Language like that of our Saviour; *Thou
wicked and slothful person*, Reform thy ways, or thou art not far from
Outer Darkness. Is it nothing to thee, that by much *Slothfulness*, thy
Money & Credit, and all is *Decaying*, and by the *Idleness of thy
Hands*, thy *House* is coming to nothing? Is it nothing to thee, that thou
art contracting the character of a *Vagabond*, and a *Prodigal?* . . . If
the Lord Jesus Christ might find thee, in thy *Store House*, in thy
Shop, or in thy *Ship*, or in thy *Field*, or where thy *Business* lies, who
knows, what *Blessings* He might bestow upon thee? . . .

2. A Christian should follow his *Occupation* with DISCRETION. . . . It is
a *Dishonour* to the profession of Religion, if there be no *Discretion*
express'd in the Affairs of its Professors. Every man should with a
praise worthy aemulation strive to get the praise once given to *Joseph*,
There is none so Discreet as thou art.
    More particularly: One *Memorandum* for you, is this: Let every
man have the *Discretion* to be well instructed in, and well acquainted
with, all the Mysteries of his *Occupation*. Be a master of your Trade;
count it a Disgrace to be no *Workman*. And as *Discretion* would bid
you, to have an *Insight* in your *Business* thus it also bids you have a
Foresight in it. . . . Let every man therefore in his *Business*, observe
the most proper *Time* for every thing; For, *There is a Time to every
purpose*: The Wise man says, *There is a Time to Buy, and a time to
Sell*: And, a *Wise man* will do what he can, *to Discern the time*. The
same *Discretion* must show a *man*, how to proportion his *Business*
unto his *Ability*. 'Tis an *Indiscreet* thing, for a man to overcharge
himself in his *Business*: For a man to Distract his *Mind*, to confound
his *Health*, to Lanch [sic] out beyond his *estate* in his *Business*, is a
culpable *Indiscretion*. Be therewithal well advised by the Rules of
Discretion with another *Caveat*: And that is, To suit your *Expenses*
unto your *Revenues*: Take this Advice, O Christians; 'Tis a *Sin*, I say,
'Tis ordinarily a *Sin*, and it will at length be a *Shame*, for a man to

Spend more than he *Gets,* or make his *Layings out* more than his *Comings in.* . . .

3. A Christian should follow his *Occupation* with HONESTY. . . . Truly, *Justice, Justice,* must be Exactly follow'd in that *Calling,* by which we go to get our *Living.* A Christian in all his *Business,* ought so *altogether Justly* to do everything that he should be able to say with him, Act. 23.1. *Men and Brethren, I have lived in all Good Conscience.* A Christian should imitate his Lord; Of Whom 'tis said, *He is Righteous in all His Wayes.* In your *Business,* you have Dealings with other Persons; but a certain Vein of *Honesty,* unspotted and Resolved *Honesty,* should run through all your *Dealings.* You aim at the getting of *Silver* and *Gold,* by your *Occupation;* but you should always act by th[e] *Golden Rule.* . . . Shall I be more particular? I say then; Let a principle of *Honesty* in your *Occupation* cause you to speak the *Truth,* and nothing but the *Truth,* on all Occasions. . . . Well then; Don't conceal from any Customer, that which you ought in *Equity* or *Charity,* to acquaint him withal; and more especially, if your Customer do Rely upon your *Sincerity.* Don't exceed the *Truth,* either in Commendations or Disparagements of Commodities. Don't Assert any thing that is contrary to *Truth,* about the kind or the use, or the price of them. . . . In every *Bargain* that you make in your *Business,* let a principle of *Honesty* keep you from every *Fraudulent,* or *Oppressive* Action. . . . Wherefore, Take no Advantage, either from the *Necessity,* or from the *Unskilfulness,* of those with whom you are concerned: It is *Uncharitable,* it is *Disingenuous,* it is *Inhumane,* for one man to prey upon the *weakness* of another. And therefore also, Never, never make any *Bargain* with such, as you suspect have no just *Propriety,* in what you go to purchase from them. If you fear, that *Stollen* [sic] *Goods* are offered you, never touch those *Burning Coals,* nor incur that Brand, *When thou sawest a Thief, then thou contendest with him.* Are there also any *Manufactures* that you are *to work up* for others? Let them all be *Well wrought.* Give every *Manufacture* its due *perfection.* Cheat no man with any thing, that shall be unserviceable to him. Do nothing *Slightly,* Do nothing *Basely,* Do nothing *Deceitfully.* But I have yet another thing to say: Let a principle of *Honesty,* cause you carefully to pay the *Debts,* which in your *Business* must fall upon you. Run into *Debt,* as *Little* as you may, . . . But being in *Debt,* be as ready to *Get out of it,* as ever you were to *Get in to it.* . . . And, in fine; I have yet one thing more to say; Let a principle of *Honesty*

cause you to keep your *Word*, in all your *Business*. You sometimes give your *Word;* let that *Word* then be as good as your *Bond*.

4. A Christian should follow his *Occupation* with CONTENTMENT. . . . [A] Christian should not be too ready to fall out with his *Calling*. It is the singular Favour of God, unto a man, That he can attend his *Occupation* with *Contentation* and *Satisfaction*. That one man has a Spirit formed & fitted for *One Occupation*, and another man for another, This is from the Operation of that God, who *forms the Spirit of man within him*. . . . Count not your *Business* to be your *Burden or* your *Blemish*. Let not a *proud Heart* make you asham'd of that *Business* wherein you may be a *Blessing*. For my part, I can't see an honest man hard at Work in the way of his Occupation, be it never so mean, (and tho' perhaps driving of a *Wheel barrow*) but I find my Heart sensibly touch'd with Respect for such a man. 'Tis possible, You may see others in some greater and richer *Business;* and you may think, that you might be, your selves Greater and Richer, if you were in some other *Business*. Yea, But hath not the God of Heaven cast you into that Business, which now takes you up? . . . Is your *Business* here clogg'd with any *Difficulties* and *Inconveniences? Contentment* under those *Difficulties*, is no little part of your *Homage* to that God, who hath placed you where you are. Fall not into any fretful *Discontent;* but with *patience* make the conclusion of the Prophet; *Truly, This is a grief, & I must bear it! I must bear it!* . . . And hence, another thing to be press'd upon you, is This; Let all persons take heed of *too suddenly leaving* that *Business*, wherein God has fixed them. When a man is become unfit for his *Business*, or his *Business* becomes unfit for him, unquestionably he may *Leave* it; And a man may be otherwise Invited sometimes justly to *change* his *Business;* I make no question of it. But many a man, meerly from *Covetousness* and from *Discontent* throws up his *Business;* and how many, do you think, *Repent* of their doing so? . . .

5. A Christian should with PIETY follow his *Occupation*. . . . Oh, let every Christian *Walk* with *God*, when he *Works* at his *Calling*, and Act in his *Occupation* with an Eye to *God*, Act as under the Eye of *God*. Syrs, 'Tis a wondrous thing that I am going to say! A poor man, that minds the *Business* of his Calling, and weaves a Threed of *Holines* into all his *Business*, may arrive to some of the highest Glories in Heaven at the last. . . .

15

The Protestant Ethic
PERRY MILLER

When delivering jeremiads, a worried clergy were performing, under compulsions they only half understood, a ritual of confession. Hence these ceremonial discourses do provide, taken in sequence, a chronology of social evolution; in them everything the historian pieces together out of records and documents is faithfully mirrored. They tell the story, and tell it coherently, of a society which was founded by men dedicated, in unity and simplicity, to realizing on earth eternal and immutable principles—and which progressively became involved with fishing, trade, and settlement. They constitute a chapter in the emergence of the capitalist mentality, showing how intelligence copes with—or more cogently, how it fails to cope with—a change it simultaneously desires and abhors.

One remarkable fact emerges: while the ministers were excoriating the behavior of merchants, laborers, and frontiersmen, they never for a moment condemned merchandizing, laboring, or expansion of the frontier. They berated the consequences of progress, but never progress; deplored the effects of trade upon religion, but did not ask men to desist from trading; arraigned men of great estates, but not estates. The temporal welfare of a people, said Jonathan Mitchell in 1667, required safety, honesty, orthodoxy, and also "Prosperity in matters of outward Estate and Liveleyhood."

In fact, in the ecstasy of denunciation, Jeremiahs enthusiastically indorsed those precepts of pious labor which from the beginning had been central in Calvinism. Merchants, farmers, and shipbuilders increased "cent per cent," and the consequence appeared to be a decay of godliness, class struggles, extravagant dress, and contempt for

Reprinted by permission of the publishers from Perry Miller, *The New England Mind: From Colony to Province* (Cambridge, Mass.: Harvard University Press). Copyright, 1953, by the President and Fellows of Harvard College.

learning; New England seemed to be deserting the ideals of its founders, but preachers would have deserted them even more had they not also exhorted diligence in every calling—precisely the virtue bound to increase estates, widen the gulf between rich and poor, and to make usury inevitable.

That every man should have a calling and work hard in it was a first premise of Puritanism. The guidebook for earthly existence, William Ames's *Conscience with the Power and Cases thereof*, confirmed his authoritative summary of theology, *The Marrow of Sacred Divinity*, that even the man who has an income must work. Everyone has a talent for something, given of God, which he must improve. Although poverty is not a sin if it be suffered for causes outside one's control, for any to accept it voluntarily is utterly reprehensible. God has so contrived the world that men must seek the necessities of life in the earth or in the sea, but the objects of their search have been cunningly placed for the finding. Coming to his momentous decision, Winthrop had reflected, "Whatsoever we stand in neede of is treasured in the earth by the Creator, & to be feched thense by the sweate of or Browes." Ames worked it out syllogistically: God is absolute lord of all things; hence private property is only a temporary "dominion"; therefore the temporal possessor must enhance what is entrusted to him. Division of property "is founded, not onely on human, but also on naturall and divine right." The laborer is worthy of his hire, and fidelity in one's occupation, if performed in the fear of God, must lead to reward. Employing an estate so that it should become a larger estate was the inescapable injunction. Even in a jeremiad, William Adams remarked that while of course a believer must be crucified to the world, still he is not to be literally crucified: he "hath much business to do in & about the world which he is vigorously to attend, & he hath that in the world upon which he is to bestow affection." Ames's teaching was repeated in Samuel Willard's *summa:* "Man is made for Labour, and not for Idleness"; ergo, God has not given possessions to be held in common, "but hath appointed that every Man should have his Share in them, wherein he holds a proper Right in them, and they are his own and not anothers." This principle, Willard pointed out—as did all Puritans—has nothing to do with the spiritual condition; a right to property, exercised within civil propriety, is as valid for the pagan or idolater as for the saint.

Max Weber has taught us to call this configuration of ideas the "Protestant ethic." The finest exposition in New England literature occurs in John Cotton's volume of 1641, *The Way of Life;* his is the classic demand that men devote themselves to making profits without succumbing to the temptations of profit, that a believer be drawn by his belief into some warrantable calling, "though it be but of a day-laborer." Here is the ringing and abiding conviction of the Puritan, for whom civil life no less than the religious is lived by faith: "If thou beest a man that lives without a calling, though thou hast two thousands to spend, yet if thou hast no calling, tending to publique good, thou art an uncleane beast."

The peculiarly English note in Cotton's presentation is the strong emphasis upon "publique good." The Puritan's thought was so far from any suggestion of individualism that his exhortation to money makers was, in his mind, not incompatible with enforcing the just price. Furthermore, every laborer must remember that even as his gifts were from God, opportunities for employing them were opened by providence; the rewards of industry were not consequences of industriousness, nor of the state of the market or of rates of exchange. Knowing this, a saint in his counting house would patiently suffer loss as a trial of faith, but would also take good fortune "with moderation" and never be corrupted by success. No matter how much he outstripped his fathers in wealth, he would, by remaining an ascetic in the midst of prosperity, abide by their covenant—especially by the external covenant, within which the management, for public good, of external possessions so largely fell.

The Puritan mind, as we know, found allegory congenial. As Bunyan implores us, "Do thou the substance of my matter see, Put by the curtains . . . Turn up my metaphors." In 1657, twenty-one years before *Pilgrim's Progress,* one "N. D." published in London an allegory for which the curtains require less putting by; it was reprinted at Boston in 1683, and again as late as 1763. According to *A Rich Treasure At an easy Rate: or, The ready Way to true Content,* Poverty lives at one end of town with his wife Sloth, "in a sorry ruinous Cottage; which shortly after falls to the ground, and he is never able to repair it." At the other end dwells Riches, with his servants Pride, Oppression, Covetousness, Luxury, and Prodigality. Of his two sons, Honour died young, Ambition came to an untimely end; one daughter, Delicacy, has a bastard child Infamy, and the other, Avarice, gave birth to Misery. Into town comes Godliness, with a retinue of servants —Humility, Sincerity, Repentance, Experience, Faith, Hope, Charity, Temperance, and Sobriety. He tries to live beside Riches, who insults him; he tries Poverty, who raises a hullabaloo by coming home drunk every night from the ale-house. Godliness is tempted to retreat to the cloister, and then—being a Protestant—bethinks himself, "Man was made for Society." Upon the advice of Gravity, he settles in the middle of town, halfway between Riches and Poverty, beside old Labour, the best housekeeper in the parish, and his wife Prudence. We note—remembering how Riches has been repudiated—that Godliness proves a great help to Labour, assisted by Labour's attendants, Forecast, Diligence, Expedition, Cheerfulnes, and Perseverance, "early Risers and at their work." After Godliness teaches him to pray, Labour's estate increases, until Content comes to live with him, bringing in his train Justification, Adoption, Assurance, and Sanctification. At the end, Labour's happiness knows no bounds: "he had never prayed before, but now Godliness had thoroughly instructed him, and taught him a better Art, and the way of thriving."

John Hull, the greatest Boston merchant of the mid-century and the legendary mintmaster, was no child of Riches; his father was a blacksmith, and he himself had but little "keeping" at school; he hoed corn for seven years, until "by God's good hand" he was apprenticed to a goldsmith. He joined with Godliness at the age of twenty-three, for the Lord made the ministry of John Cotton effectual unto him, whereby he found "room in the hearts of his people," being received in the fellowship of the First Church of Boston. Thereupon the economic virtues waited upon him; he was an early riser and at his work, "and, through God's help, obtained that ability in it, as I was able to get my living by it." He kept his shop so well that shortly it kept him, yielding a surplus to invest in ships and land. But always, whether tradesman, merchant, or banker, he went in the fear of God. When the Dutch got his ships, he knew consolation: "The loss of my estate will be nothing, if the Lord please to join my soul nearer to himself, and loose it more from creature comforts." However, when his foreman at Point Judith Neck stole his horses, a Puritan saint knew what to say: "I would have you know that they are, by God's good providence, mine."

Hull's instructions to his ship-captains mingle piety and business without embarrassment; the Lord should be worshipped in his vessels, Sabbaths sanctified, and all profaneness suppressed. "That the lords prescence may be with you & his blessing upon you," he wrote, and added with the same pen, "Leave noe debts behind you whereever you goe." He told his skippers to follow their judgment, knowing that businessmen must take their chances: "but indeed it is hard to foresee what will be & therefore it is best willing to submit to the great governing hand of the great Governor of all the greater and lesser revolutions that wee the poore sons of men are involved in by the invoyce you see the whole amounteth to £405:16:3." There may be little punctuation, but every threepence is accounted for! Hull died worth over six thousand pounds, but would have been worth twice as much had he not supported the colony's treasury out of his own pocket.

In his old age he declined a venture to the Canaries because he had become desirous only "to be more thoughtfull of Lanching into that vast ocion of Eternity whether we must all shortly bee Carried." Still, it would be stretching the term to call him "otherworldly." To him, religion included seizing the main chance, and sin was synonymous with wasted opportunities. Into his shop he took two apprentices; one of them, Jeremiah Dummer, was a good boy (who became also a wealthy merchant and saint, and the father of—well, not exactly a saint), but the other, Samuel Paddy, was a wastrel. In the heart of John Hull there was little mercy for the Paddys of this world; after he had turned Paddy out of the house, he wrote him: "Had you abode here and followed your calling you might have been worth many hundred pounds of clear estate and you might have enjoyed many more helpes for your sole. Mr. Dummer lives in good fashion hath a wife and three children and like to be very useful in his generation." Was not life itself almost too transparent an allegory?

In 1683 Samuel Willard preached Hull's funeral sermon; taken in conjunction with his jeremiad of the year before, it demonstrates how innocently praise of the merchant and denunciation of commercial sins flourished side by side. Hull "was a Saint upon Earth," and "lived like a Saint here, and died the precious Death of a Saint." But he was no Papist, and so did not flee into desert or cloister: he did live "above the World," and did keep "his heart disentangled," but meanwhile was "in the midst of all outward occasions and urgency of Business." Parson Willard saw nothing incongruous in advancing among Hull's claims to veneration, along with his being a magistrate, church member, father and benefactor, the fact "that Providence had given him a prosperous and Flourishing Portion of this Worlds Goods."

Thanks to this spirit in the covenanted community—there were possibly more Paddys than is generally imagined, but there were several Hulls and Dummers—providence blessed New England with a flourishing portion of worldly goods. As Higginson said, on any rational calculation of the natural resources no one could have expected such success; it had been won despite reason (to the extent that all depended upon the favor of God), and yet in an eminently rational way, to the extent that the hard work of the saints, their leaving no debts behind, had served as "efficient cause." There were occasional bad years, upon which John Hull would moralize; he found in 1664, for instance, a smite upon all employments: "at least in general, all men are rather going backward than increasing their estates." Yet in that year he also noted that about one hundred sail of ships had come into Boston harbor, "and all laden hence." Laden ships meant profits for somebody.

For the first ten years, Massachusetts Bay and Connecticut lived happily off immigrants, who brought in foreign goods and specie, and so furnished a market for local produce. The New England Way, having been established during the "golden age" of 1630–1640 when the economic problem took care of itself, could never thereafter comprehend how economics might dilute religion. The golden age came abruptly to an end when the English Wars stopped immigration. Then New England found itself with little money and no markets; it had to have wares it could not manufacture, but it had little or nothing to peddle in England. Colonists had to find some way of converting their fish, lumber, wheat, flour, and livestock into English cloth and tools. For reasons best known to Himself, God had not laid before His saints the easy opportunity He gave Virginians, who found at their doorsteps a crop marketable at five shillings the pound. New Englanders had to learn commerce or perish.

They learned it. The "sacred cod" became a symbol second only, if that, to the Bible. "When the first way of supply began to be stopped up, God in his merciful providence opened another, by turning us into a way of Trade and Commerce, to further our more comfortable subsistence." But commerce is no half-time occupation. When a man spends all his waking hours amid—as an almanac jingle had it— "Heaps of wheat, pork, bisket, beef and beer; Masts, pipe-staves, fish, should store both far and near, which fetch in wines, cloths, sweets and good tobac," he will hardly have leisure for meditating upon the close distinction between works as a condition of the Covenant of Grace and the conception of works in the Arminian heresy. "Our Maritan Towns began to encrease roundly," the historian of 1650 could already say. The Restoration was a grievous setback for Puritan orthodoxy, and John Hull was most depressed as he saw "the face of things looking sadly toward the letting-in of Popery." Yet economically he had no cause to complain, for the Navigation Acts and the exclusion of the Dutch offered merchants in New England a truly golden opportunity. Through the instrumentality of King Charles, master immoralist of the age, divine providence arranged compensation for the ravages of King Philip.

Whenever preachers of jeremiads answered outside criticism, they put aside denunciation and resolutely boasted of how the people had demonstrated "that Necessity and Freedome could do wonders." Thus wealth did accumulate, which could not be anything but a sign of divine blessing. Men started as millers and were paid in grain; thus providentially invited to find buyers, they grew to be traders. Others started as artisans, took apprentices, and shortly were capitalists. Merchants imported the necessary stocks, advanced them to farmers and frontiersmen on credit, and so became bankers who, in the name of honesty, cracked a whip over their debtors. Was John Hull grinding the faces of the poor when he wrote to a borrower, "I am afraid lest by keepeing a drinkeing House you learn to tipple yor selfe and thereby stifle the voice of yor Conscience that else would call upon you to bee Righteouse me thinks some fruits might have come to mee last winter"? As soon as God made clear the market value of the cod, pious citizens, acting from both necessity and freedom, bought up the fishing fleet, and by the end of the century a few rich men dominated the industry. By then, New England merchants had taken hold of their opportunities with such diligence, expedition, and perseverance that they succeeded the Dutch as the principal competitors of merchants in London and Bristol; at the same time, they were steadily draining the backcountry and Newfoundland of specie, bringing in cargoes from southern Europe, diverting the coinage of the Caribbean into their pockets, earning freight-charges on everything they handled, and then —to cap the climax—selling their very ships at immense profit!

Statesmen who led the migration of 1630 lost so much that if their estates, at their deaths, were a thousand pounds, God had been merciful. But merchant Robert Keayne, even though prevented by theological fiat from charging all he could, left £4,000 in 1656. John Holland, by fitting vessels for the cod-fisheries, had that much by 1653. Though Increase Mather cried that land had become an idol, many church members were accumulating titles. By 1670 there were said to be thirty merchants in Boston worth from ten to thirty thousand pounds. By the end of the century the great names were not only

Winthrop, Dudley, and Mather, but also Lillie, Faneuil, Belcher, Foster, Phillips, Wharton, Clarke, Oliver, Sargent—and Hutchinson. "In the Chief, or high Street," said Ned Ward, "there are stately Edifices, some of which cost the owners two or three Thousand Pounds." He thought that these illustrated the adage of a fool and his money being soon parted, "for the Fathers of these Men were Tinkers and Peddlers," but he did not comprehend Puritan ethics. Few built bigger houses than they could afford; Prudence was still their wife. But that the fathers of many had been tinkers and peddlers was well enough known.

An intellectual historian must detect the workings of change, but no preternatural astuteness is required to decipher the trend when Joshua Moodey in 1685 declared that salvation yields a hundred per cent clear gain and that therefore "It is rational that Men should lay out their Money where they may have the most suitable Commodities and best Pennyworths." Samuel Willard's *Heavenly Merchandize* in 1686 was exactly what the title indicates. Hooker and Shepard often took their illustrations from industry and business: in meditation, said Hooker, a man beats his brains "as the Gouldsmith with his mettal." However, their metaphors did not control their content. (As Jonathan Edwards was later to say, truly spiritual rhetoric mentions these things as illustrations and evidence of the truth of what the preacher says, not of his meaning.) But in Willard's sermon the merchandising metaphor governs the thought; the author never steps out of it: "A prudent buyer will see his wares, & try them before he will buy them." That men naturally try to haggle with God over the terms of salvation is thus conveyed: "He that really intends to buy, will first cheapen; every one hath such a principle, that he could buy at the best rates; to have a thing good, and have it cheap, is most mens ambition." Willard concluded that Christ was a good buy, and that those who can purchase had better pay the price.

Thus we are again confronted with the question of why New England in the second half of the century expressed itself most comprehensively in stylized self-denunciation. Why did spokesmen for a people who triumphed over forest and sea, who were piling up sterling and building more stately mansions on the high street—spokesmen proud of these achievements—call upon their people to abase themselves before the Lord as guilty of the Synod's twelve offenses? Why did they fill their diaries with self-condemnation? Why did a John Hull or a Samuel Sewall accuse himself, even while hastening along the road to wealth? Why, when they assembled together, did they hunger and thirst after a methodical analysis of their imperfection?

Had the jeremiads been directed only at those outside the churches, explanation would be easy. Occasionally we do find an offender galled by his exclusion from the corporation of the saints; modern sympathies instinctively go out to one Peter Bussaker, who in 1648 was whipped in Connecticut because he profanely announced "that hee hoped to meete some of the members of the Church in hell err long and hee did not question but he should." In 1673 Increase Mather intimated that non-members took delight in luring church members into taverns and getting them drunk, and in 1682 Urian Oakes let slip the admission that there were New Englanders weary of "theocracy." . . . In 1691 Joshua Scottow tried to tell himself that most of the enormities were committed by that mixed multitude who had not come with the saints.

All such excuses were in vain. The *Magnalia,* with disarming honesty, confesses that the real issue was the prodigious and astonishing scandals of those "that have made a more than ordinary profession of religion." The heart of the problem was the riddle of Protestant theology: "Why mayn't I, as well as David?" David sinned, to put it mildly, but nevertheless went to heaven . . . . "Perhaps in his fall, and not in his rise again, David has been sometimes too much followed by some eminent professors of religion in this land; and the land has been filled with temptation by so venomous a mischief." No, the declension of New England was not entirely the fault of the vulgar: it was defection among the children of the covenant.

Whereupon a second hypothesis suggests itself: did anybody really believe in the declension? Was there a confession of sinfulness on Sunday, followed on Monday by the foreclosing of a mortgage? The modern temper finds this explanation plausible, and delights to quote, out of the *Magnalia,* the fishermen of Marblehead who announced that they came to America not for religion but for fish. But the problem for our culture is that the weight of the dilemma was felt not by such care-free fishermen, but by orthodox leaders of the community. The mixture of business and piety in Hull's instructions, though to us it seems quaint, is far from a keeping of the left hand in ignorance of the right; the jeremiads came from something deeper than pious fraud, more profound than cant: they were the voice of a community bespeaking its apprehensions about itself.

The cultural and intellectual problem becomes more complex when we ask whether there really was so awful a deterioration. Comparing the Synod's indictment with the recorded facts, Thomas Hutchinson, judging by the standards of an eighteenth-century gentleman, said "we have no evidence of any extraordinary degeneracy." We have heard Cotton Mather admit that the situation was not always so bad as painted. One can indeed cull from the records of the county courts an amusing array of thefts, bastardy, incest, and sheer filthiness, but the mass of the people, whether church members or inhabitants, were hard at work, clearing the land, attending sermons (and taking notes), searching their souls, praying for grace, and humbling themselves for their unworthiness. Above all, following the injunction to increase and multiply, they were begetting children, between-times garnering the rewards, in material recompense, of pious industry. No doubt, Hutchinson was basically correct.

But if, as we measure facts, New England was not declining, it was certainly changing. The orthodox colonies were originally medieval states, based upon a fixed will of God, dedicated to the explicitly just, good, and honest. Men were arranged in hierarchical ranks, the lower obedient to the upper, with magistrates and scholars at the top. Things were right or wrong intrinsically, not relatively, so that the price of a piece of cloth could be determined by theologians. It shall be lawful, said Cotton, for the judges in any town, with the consent of the town officers, to set "reasonable rates" upon commodities; at the end of the century, Willard was still contending for such "Equity," declaring that employers may not take advantage of the laborer "and beat him down so as to enjoy his Labour underfoot, for that which is next to nothing." Gradation in costume according to rank was the visible sign of a social philosophy based upon the law of nature and further sanctioned by revelation. "One end of Apparel is to distinguish and put a difference between persons according to the Places and Conditions." The code resisted change, and therefore changes became declensions; the jeremiads recognized the facts, but refused to accommodate theory to them.

William Hubbard's sermon of 1676, *The Happiness of a People*, is a most interesting memorial to this internal conflict, not only for its eloquence but also for the fact that its author was not in full sympathy with those determined at all costs to make a stand for the charter. On every page, Hubbard betrays his awareness of the changing conditions, and so pleads the more fervently for "unity" and "order." The

Creator made the universe of differing parts, "which necessarily supposes that there must be differing places, for those differing things to be disposed into, which is Order." Especially must this "artificial distribution" be observed in a political structure, and "whoever is for a parity in any Society, will in the issue reduce things into an heap of confusion." Just as the angels in heaven are not all of one rank, and in "the pavement of that glorious mansion place," we shall see one star differ from another in glory, as the eagle surmounts "the little choristers of the valleys," so "it is not then the result of time or chance, that some are mounted on horse-back, while others are left to travell on foot." The Lord appoints her "that sits behind the mill" and "him that ruleth on the throne." The greater portion of mankind are but "tools and instruments for others to work by" rather than "proper agents to effect any thing of themselves"; left to themselves, they "would destroy themselves by slothfulness and security" were they not driven and supervised by their betters. Nothing is more remote from right reason, Hubbard continued—contending with peculiar vehemence against that stubborn egalitarianism which is seldom entirely banished from Christian piety—"than to think that because we were all once equal at our birth, and shall be again at our death, therefore we should be so in the whole course of our lives." Of course, Hubbard delivered this sermon when the war with Philip was still going badly, and it may be read as a covert expression of dissatisfaction with the administration. In any event, he asserted the principle of subordination as resolutely as Winthrop and Cotton. "In fine," he concluded, "a body would not be more monstrous and deformed without an Head, nor a ship more dangerous at Sea without a Pilot, nor a flock of sheep more ready to be devoured without a Shepheard, than would humane Society be without an Head, and Leader in time of danger."

If, as I believe, Hubbard spoke for the band of merchants who had already decided that repeal of the charter was inevitable, it is all the more remarkable that he should invoke the hierarchical conception of society. By this ideal all preachers—whatever their sentiments concerning the charter—were bound to judge the society. The jeremiads therefore testify to a grief that was not merely distress over a failure of reality to conform to theory, but unhappiness about theory itself. Class lines drawn upon the basis of inherited status might have a semblance of eternal order. When new families, such as the Brattles or the Whartons, forged ahead and then availed themselves of the philosophy of social subordination, the metaphysical dilemma became acute. In vain Samuel Willard reminded the new generation of merchants that civil deference ought to be paid to gentlemen, "tho' the Providence of God bring them into Poverty." Cotton Mather could only shake his head: "If some that are now rich were once low in the world, 'tis possible, more that were once rich are now brought very low."

Nor did a family have to rise to the very top of the scale, like the Brattles, in order to upset the hierarchy. It was enough, for instance, if a Robert Turner, admitted as an indentured servant to the church of Boston in 1632, should become master of a tavern, "The Sign of the Anchor," and die in 1664 with an estate of £1,600. Or if a John Kitchin, starting as the servant of Zachery Bicknell, should have a grandson Edward, who in Salem became the equal of Endecotts and Crowninshields. Samuel Shrimpton set up as a brazier, but at his death in 1698 he owned most of Beacon Hill and was inventoried at £1,800. John Harrison bargained for a monopoly of rope-making in Boston, out of which he built a great house on Purchase Street. Thomas Savage, son of an English blacksmith, began as a tailor, erected wharves on Fleet Street, and ended worth £2,500. The social structure refused to stay fixed, and classifications decreed by God Himself dissolved. Pious industry wrecked the city on a hill, in which it had been assumed men would remain forever in the stations to which they were born, and inferiors would eternally bow to gentlemen and scholars.

Had economic development merely recruited a few additions from the commercial classes to the Puritan oligarchy, the ideal would not have been endangered, but it played havoc not only by making some rich but by reducing many to poverty. John Josselyn observed in 1675 that while diligent hands had prospered, those of a "droanish disposition" became wretchedly poor. If there were Shrimptons and Savages, there was also Thomas Turvill of Newbury, whose entire estate consisted of: "An old worne out coat and britches with an old lining £0 6s 0d; A thread bare, tho indifferent close coat and doublet with an old wast coat, 1:00:00; Two shirts and a band, 11s; a pair of shoes, 4s; An old greasy hatt, 6d, a pair of stockings, 1s; An old doublet, an old wast cote and a pair of old sheep skin briches, 0:04:00." There had been a moment when it seemed possible that in New England the poor would not always be with us; by 1700 they were numerous. Had the process brought down only drones, it could have been admired: the problem was that it worked hardship upon yeomen farmers of virtue and industry, whose estates at most never got beyond two or three hundred pounds. They found themselves paying tribute to merchants, millers, and shipbuilders. After their little store of cash had flowed into Boston coffers, they went into debt for imported goods, and even then, since they had to pay with produce, received only the first cost. In rural districts trading was reduced to a commodity basis, wherein what was called "country pay" figured prices at a higher rate than the goods would fetch in sterling; but all this while, merchants tried to collect their debts at the hard money rate.

As the lines became more sharply drawn, even the upper class of inherited position, the sons and daughters of Winthrops, Nortons, Dudleys, Saltonstalls, Bradstreets, became less the dedicated leaders of a religious movement and more a closed corporation of monopolists. They married among themselves—Winthrops with Bradstreets, Dudleys with Saltonstalls—while the ministerial families also intermarried so extensively as to become within three generations a distinct caste, which Dr. Holmes was later to call, not quite realizing the full implications, "Brahmin." The church, it must be said, still did offer an avenue of escape for abler youths of the lower orders, to such as John Wise, son of an indentured servant, or Thomas Barnard, son of a maltster in Hartford; but the exceptions were few, and by 1700 the clergy no less than the merchants were a vested interest—which was not what the founders had envisaged.

New men of wealth came up by a different ladder from that by which Winthrops and Saltonstalls had ascended, and showed the effects of their training. Even in 1650 Edward Johnson was horrified to discover that merchants and vintners "would willingly have had the Commonwealth tolerate divers kinds of sinful opinions" because they wanted more immigrants "that their purses might be filled with coyne." Thirty years later merchants were the most ready of any group to surrender the charter, but whether loyal or disloyal, they and the tradesmen either would not or could not abide by the regulations. Laws fixing wages and prices, prescribing the amounts to be spent on dress and luxury, became dead letters: "Those good orders were not of long continuance, but did expire with the first and golden age in this new world." In 1639 to seek a profit "above 33 per cent" had been to invite condign punishment, but "since that time the common practice of the country hath made double that advance no sin." The records show little prosecution under the sumptuary legislation after about

1675; John Dunton seems again to have spoken truth: "The Laws for Reformation of Manners are very severe, yet but little regarded by the People, so at least as to make 'em better, or cause 'em to mend their manners." Increase Mather had denounced cards and dice in 1674 because, by the original philosophy, "If a man get anothers Goods at under price, this is Injustice, it is Theft, and a Transgression of the Rule of Righteousness." Subsequent jeremiads had to face the fact that not only did cards and dice abound, but that the economic philosophy by which Mather had condemned them became an embarrassment when employed by farmers to make Mather's merchant parishioners pay for produce at the country rate. At every point, economic life set up conflicts with ideology. It was defeat for the plan of New England that frontier towns should be settled without a ministry and a school, but, said Cotton Mather in 1690, the insoluble problem was how "at once we may Advance our Husbandry, and yet Forbear our Dispersion; and moreover at the same time fill the Countrey with a Liberal Education."

The husbandmen and traders were doing nothing but what they had been told to do. They worked in their callings—and brought multiplicity out of unity. There were perceptibly "more divisions in times of prosperity than in times of adversity, and when Satan cant destroy them by outward violence he will endeavour to undo them by Strife and variance." Saints waited upon God for the reward—and became social climbers. The more everybody labored, the more society was transformed. The more diligently the people applied themselves —on the frontier, in the meadows, in the countinghouse or on the Banks of Newfoundland—the more they produced a decay of religion and a corruption of morals, a society they did not want, one that seemed less and less attractive. From the beginning, the city on a hill was to have social classes, but status ordained by God should not become the prize of competition; the jeremiad could not arrest the process in which names rose and fell, but by grieving over the incomprehensible it provided a method of endurance.

Hence we may see in the sermons more than ministerial nagging of worldlings, more than hypocritical show, more than rhetoric. They were releases from a grief and a sickness of soul which otherwise found no surcease. They were professions of a society that knew it was doing wrong, but could not help itself, because the wrong thing was also the right thing. From such ceremonies men arose with new strength and courage: having acknowledged what was amiss, the populace could go back to their fields and benches and ships, trusting that a covenanted Jehovah would remember His bond. When again they grew apprehensive, they could look into their own hearts, find what was festering there, and hasten once more to cleanse their bosoms of poisonous stuff by public confession. Although jeremiads and the Reforming Synod called for an alteration of social habits, the result was only more days of humiliation. Knowing their impotence, the people needed a method for paying tribute to their sense of guilt and yet for moving with the times. Realizing that they had betrayed their fathers, and were still betraying them, they paid the requisite homage in a ritual of humiliation, and by confessing iniquities regained at least a portion of self-respect.

16

Ungodly Puritans
HERBERT W. SCHNEIDER

Not long after the appearance of Cotton Mather's *Essays to Do Good,* the readers of the *New England Courant* were startled by the satirical articles of one Mrs. Silence Dogood. She agreed with the Reverend Mr. Mather that doing good was the most important business of life; but she made it her business to expose evil in high places. She began by attacking college life among the "scollars" at Harvard; then she reprimanded their parents for sending them merely to display their own wealth; then she made fun of the theological debates and pretensions of the professors. The fashionable clergy came in for their share of moral treatment by Mrs. Dogood, and even the magistrates and members of the council were not spared. Such essays to do good were not exactly to the Mathers' taste and, when James Franklin, the editor of the *Courant,* and Silence Dogood, whose real name was Benjamin

From *The Puritan Mind* by Herbert Wallace Schneider. Copyright 1930 by Holt, Rinehart and Winston, Inc., New York. Copyright © 1958 by Herbert Wallace Schneider. Reprinted by permission of Holt, Rinehart and Winston, Inc. and the author.

Franklin, continued in their efforts despite warnings, fines and imprisonment, their journal was finally suppressed.

Removed to Philadelphia, Benjamin continued to "do good." When he organized his Junto Club there, he inserted among the rules of procedure the following paraphrases of Cotton Mather's proposals: "Have you lately observed any encroachment on the just liberties of the people? What new story have you lately heard agreeable for telling in conversation? Have you lately heard of any citizen thriving well, and by what means? Do you think of anything at present, in which the Junto may be serviceable to mankind, to their country, or to themselves?" Between these queries there was a pause "while one might fill and drink a glass of wine," in place of Cotton Mather's pause "that any member may offer what he pleases upon it."

In all this there was evidently an element of sheer wit and playfulness. Franklin had caught the spirit of Addison and Steele's *Spectator*, of Defoe's *Essays*, and in general of the free-thinking, satirical literature of his day. In company with his young deistic friends, first in Boston, then in Philadelphia, and later in London, he enjoyed the free play of radical ideas. During his first sojourn in London he published a tract *On Vice and Virtue*, which proved that on the premises of God's attributes of wisdom, goodness, and power, one is forced to conclude that "vice and virtue are empty distinctions." A few years later he used the same sort of reasoning on prayer and predestination. Franklin's own summary of it appeared in a letter to Vaughan in 1779. "Almost all men, in all ages and countries, have at times made use of prayer. Thence I reasoned, that, if all things were ordained, prayer must among the rest be ordained. But, as prayer can procure no change in things ordained, praying must be useless, and an absurdity. God would therefore, not ordain praying, if everything else was ordained. But praying exists, therefore all things are not ordained, &c."

At first, in his eagerness to be counted one of the clever deistic intellectuals, he concluded from such considerations that morality did not exist. In care-free fashion he exploited the arguments of both Calvinists and Deists. He wrote a *Dissertation on Liberty*, one on *First Principles,* and some *Dialogues Concerning Virtue and Pleasure.* These pieces all reveal a fondness for pushing an argument to its limits; they are not moralistic but sheer free-thinking. Soon, however, Franklin abandoned this speculative and playful tone and emphasized the more serious implications of the business of doing good. He discovered that the arguments in which he and his comrades indulged were merely continuing the bad intellectual habits of the theologians. Here is his own confession and condemnation of his early disputatious habits: "We sometimes disputed, and very fond we were of argument, and were desirous of confuting one another—which disputatious turn is apt to become a very bad habit, making people often disagreeable in company, by the contradiction that is necessary to bring it into practice; and thence, besides souring and spoiling the conversation, it is productive of disgusts, and perhaps enmities, with those who may have occasion for friendship. I had caught this by reading my father's books of dispute on religion. Persons of good sense, I have since observed, seldom fall into it, except lawyers, university men, and generally men of all sorts, who have been bred at Edinburgh."

From this it appears that one reason why Franklin abandoned dialectical and theological disputes was his desire to be well-mannered. He noticed that "positiveness" and "direct contradiction" were not in good taste in polite conversation. Accordingly he disciplined himself and imposed fines on members of the Junto who committed these violations of good manners.

There is a more serious reason, however, for Franklin's so-called conversion from Deism. His own hard experiences and his whole New England training convinced him that vice and virtue were "no empty distinctions" and that the theologies and metaphysics which made them appear such were therefore futile. This discovery he mentions in the *Autobiography* with his characteristic simplicity. "I grew convinced that truth, sincerity, and integrity, in dealings between man and man, were of the utmost importance to the felicity of life." He realized that the liberal theologians and the city churches were relaxing from the gospel of work and discipline which the Puritans had preached during the generations of strenuous building, and were becoming acclimated to the habits of luxury and leisure. The spirit of work was giving way to the theology of having arrived, and the clergy were degenerating into a disputatious crowd of theocrats. Meanwhile more secular workers were exemplifying the strenuous virtues of the early Puritans. In this situation, Benjamin Franklin made the attempt to maintain the Puritan virtues in all their rigor, but to abandon entirely their theological sanctions. He placed the frontier morality on a utilitarian footing, and gave it empirical foundations. The whole issue he put in a few words: "Revelation had indeed no weight with me, as such; but I entertained an opinion, that, though certain actions might not be bad, *because* they were forbidden by it, or good, *because* it commanded them; yet probably these actions might be forbidden *because* they were bad for us, or commanded *because* they were beneficial to us, in their own natures, all the circumstances of things considered." What Franklin said was simply: If you want to achieve anything, these old-fashioned Puritan virtues are the necessary means: temperance, silence, order, resolution, frugality, industry, sincerity, justice, etc. And if you ask for proof, Franklin could point to his own experience and to the colonies themselves as evidence.

What is designated as the Benjamin Franklin morality is probably too familiar to require detailed description. A few of Franklin's own words give its chief outlines. As a young printer in Philadelphia, he wrote the following: "Those who write of the art of poetry teach us that, if we would write what may be worth reading, we ought always, before we begin, to form a regular plan and design of our piece; otherwise we shall be in danger of incongruity. I am apt to think it is the same as to life. I have never fixed a regular design in life, by which means it has been a confused variety of different scenes; I am now entering upon a new one; let me, therefore, make some resolutions, and form some scheme of action, that henceforth I may live in all respects like a rational creature.

"1. It is necessary for me to be extremely frugal for some time, till I have paid what I owe.

"2. To endeavor to speak truth in every instance, to give nobody expectations that are not likely to be answered, but aim at sincerity in every word and action; the most amiable excellence in a rational being.

"3. To apply myself industriously to whatever business I take in hand, and not divert my mind from my business by any foolish project of growing suddenly rich; for industry and patience are the surest means of plenty.

"4. I resolve to speak ill of no man whatever, not even in a matter of truth; but rather by some means excuse the faults I hear charged upon others, and, upon proper occasions, speak all the good I know of everybody."

From his famous chapter on "The Art of Virtue" in the *Autobiography,* I quote the following: "In the various enumerations of the moral virtues I had met with in my reading, I found the catalogue more or less numerous, as different writers included more or less under the same name. Temperance, for example, was by some confined to eating and drinking; while by others it was extended to mean the moderating every other pleasure, appetite, inclination, or passion, bodily or mental, even to avarice and ambition. I proposed to myself, for the sake of clearness, to use rather more names, with fewer ideas attached to each, than a few names with more ideas and I included under thirteen names of virtues, all that at that time occurred to me as necessary or desirable; and annexed to each a short precept, which fully expressed the extent I gave to its meaning.

"These names of virtues, with their precepts, were:

"1. Temperance—Eat not to dulness; drink not to elevation.

"2. Silence—Speak not but what may benefit others or yourself; avoid trifling conversation.

"3. Order—Let all your things have their places; let each part of your business have its time.

"4. Resolution—Resolve to perform what you ought; perform without fail what you resolve.

"5. Frugality—Make no expense but to do good to others or yourself; that is, waste nothing.

"6. Industry—Lose no time; be always employed in something useful; cut off all unnecessary actions.

"7. Sincerity—Use no hurtful deceit; think innocently and justly; and, if you speak, speak accordingly.

"8. Justice—Wrong none by doing injuries, or omitting the benefits that are your duty.

"9. Moderation—Avoid extremes; forbear resenting injuries so much as you think they deserve.

"10. Cleanliness—Tolerate no uncleanliness in body, clothes or habitation.

"11. Tranquility—Be not disturbed at trifles, or at accidents common or unavoidable.

"12. Chastity—Rarely use venery but for health and offspring, never to dulness, weakness, or the injury of your own or another's peace or reputation.

"13. Humility—Imitate Jesus and Socrates.

"My intention being to acquire the habitude of all these virtues, I judged it would be well not to distract my attention by attempting the whole at once, but to fix it on one of them at a time; and when I should be master of that, then to proceed to another; and so on, till I have gone through the thirteen. And, as the previous acquisition of some might facilitate the acquisition of certain others, I arranged them with that view, as they stand above.

"It may be well posterity should be informed, that to this little artifice, with the blessing of God, their ancestor owed the constant felicity of his life. . . . To Temperance he ascribes his long-continued health, and what is still left to him of a good constitution; to Industry and Frugality, the early easiness of his circumstances and acquisition of his fortune, with all the knowledge that enabled him to be a useful citizen, and obtained for him some degree of reputation among the learned; to Sincerity and Justice, the confidence of his country, and the honorable employs it conferred upon him; and to the joint influence of the whole mass of the virtues, even in the imperfect state he was able to acquire them, all that evenness of temper, and that cheerfulness in conversation, which makes his company still sought for, and agreeable even to his young acquaintance."

In *The Way to Wealth,* which is a compilation of the best of his sayings as "Poor Richard," Franklin's moral doctrine takes this more popular form: "It would be thought a hard government that should tax its people one tenth part of their time, to be employed in its service: but idleness taxes many of us much more; sloth, by bringing on diseases, absolutely shortens life. 'Sloth, like rust, consumes faster than labour wears, while the used key is always bright,' as poor Richard says. 'But dost thou love life, then do not squander time, for that is the stuff life is made of,' as poor Richard says. How much more than is necessary do we spend in sleep! forgetting that 'the sleeping fox catches no poultry, and that there will be sleeping enough in the grave,' as poor Richard says.

"If time be of all things the most precious, wasting time must be, as poor Richard says, 'the greatest prodigality'; since, as he elsewhere tells us, 'lost time is never found again, and what we call time enough always proves little enough': let us then up and be doing, and doing to the purpose; so by diligence shall we do more with less perplexity. 'Sloth makes all things difficult, but industry all easy; and he that riseth late, must trot all day, and shall scarce overtake his business at night; while laziness travels so slowly that poverty soon overtakes him. Drive thy business; let not that drive thee; and early to bed, and early to rise, makes a man healthy, wealthy, and wise,' as poor Richard says.

"Methinks I hear some of you say, 'must a man afford himself no leisure?' I will tell thee, my friend, what poor Richard says; 'employ thy time well, if thou meanest to gain leisure; and since thou art not sure of a minute, throw not away an hour.' Leisure is time for doing something useful; this leisure the diligent man will obtain, but the lazy man never; for a life of leisure and a life of laziness are two things. Many, without labour, would live by their wits alone, but they break for want of stock; whereas industry gives comfort and respect. 'Fly pleasures, and they will follow you. The diligent spinner has a large shift; and now I have a sheep and a cow, everybody bids me good-morrow.' "

Philosophers are offended by the simplicity, almost simpleness, of this morality. Surely there can be nothing profound in a doctrine which a Pennsylvania farmer could understand. Though more recent instrumentalists have succeeded in putting this doctrine in language which appeals more to "university men, and generally men of all sorts that have been bred at Edinburgh," any analysis of intelligence usually reveals the validity of Franklin's contentions; and though it may be more systematically developed and more elaborately conceived, the implications for conduct will be substantially the same. Certainly no method of presentation of utilitarian ethics could have been more effective than Franklin's, for he is to this day the patron saint of those who are interested in achievement.

Franklin's mind is typical of an easy, spontaneous hospitality to ends or ideals, and of an intellectual preoccupation with their practical challenge. Pennsylvania needed fortification against the French and Indians; Franklin began at once to work on plans for organizing a militia and buying cannon. In view of their common interests against Great Britain, the colonies wanted some sort of union; Franklin immediately proposed a plan. Throughout his life, he was continually proposing plans—a plan for the promotion of abolition of slavery, a plan for bringing the comforts of civilization to the natives of New Zealand. The "art of virtue" was simply one more plan. Any end, suggested to his mind, immediately raised the problem of its accomplishment. He even told the great evangelist, George Whitefield, how he could most easily convert great numbers of people, advising him to convert a few popular leaders, "grandees," first and then the masses would follow. "For," said he, "men fear less the being in hell than out of fashion." In his scientific researches, too, practical problems seemed to stimulate him most. I do not mean practical applications like the lightning-rod, for these were of minor concern to him, but rather problems of designing apparatus, of experimental conditions for testing hypotheses, and of methods for dealing pragmatically with rival hypotheses. His inventions are further evidence of this habit of mind —an improved harmonica of vibrating glasses, bi-focal spectacles, smokeless fireplaces, to say nothing of his electrical devices. It would be difficult to find a mind more given to free play in the objects of its interests, yet more intent on their practical aspects.

In this preoccupation with instrumental values, Franklin is typical of what Europeans call "Americanism," and the objection usually made to Franklin's moral philosophy, and for that matter to any other utilitarian ethics, is that it is merely instrumental. "You tell us," the criticism runs, "the 'way to wealth,' but you fail to tell us whether or not wealth is a good. You tell us how to succeed in business, but you fail to tell us whether or not our business is worth while." The more superficial critics of Franklin (to say nothing of the critics of utilitarianism and pragmatism) immediately infer that "material prosperity" is the admitted end. To them Franklin is merely a typical American business man who, without stopping to evaluate, simply adopts the business principles of thrift for thrift's sake, money for money's sake, the more the better. That this is not true of Franklin's personal life is easily proved. As soon as he became "free and easy" he quit his business and devoted himself to science, literature, public affairs, and conversation with his friends,—pursuits which from boyhood had been his chief delight. As early as 1748 he wrote to Cadwallader Colden: "I am in a fair way of having no other tasks than such as I shall like to give myself, and of enjoying what I look upon as a great happiness, leisure to read, study, make experiments, and converse at large with such ingenious and worthy men as are pleased to honor me with their friendship or acquaintance, on such points as may produce something for the common benefit of mankind, uninterrupted by the little cares and fatigues of business." And a year later he wrote to his mother: "At present I pass my time agreeably enough. I enjoy, through mercy, a tolerable share of health. I read a great deal, ride a little, do a little business for myself, now and then for others, retire when I can, and go into company when I please; so the years roll round, and the last will come, when I would rather have it said, 'He lived usefully,' than 'He died rich.' " A further example of this attitude is found in his speculations on "raising a United Party for Virtue." The successful demonstration of his "art of virtue" on himself suggested to him the possibilities of its social and political application. Members of this United Party, "good and wise men" of all nations, were to discipline themselves in accordance with the program Franklin had earlier followed himself. They were to be called "The Society of the Free and Easy. Free, as being, by the general practice and habits of the virtues, free from the dominion of vice; and particularly, by the practice of industry and frugality, free from debt, which exposes a man to constraint, and a species of slavery to his creditors."

Mr. D. H. Lawrence's criticism of Franklin's table of virtues rests entirely on his presupposition that they are final, not instrumental virtues. If they are taken as the ends of life, they are easily satirized. Lawrence himself seems to fall into the trap which he lays for Franklin in that he tries to re-define these purely disciplinary virtues in such a way as to give them ideal content. The result is even more ridiculous than it is intended to be. Justice, for example, he re-defines as follows: "The only justice is to follow the sincere intuition of the soul, angry or gentle. Anger is just, and pity is just, but judgment is never just." This is obviously no definition of justice at all. It may be a definition of freedom. Lawrence was so preoccupied with the praise of freedom, of individuality, of mastery, of imagination, of his gods, in short, of the ideal or final values of life, that it never occurred to him that Franklin could be talking about something quite different. Franklin's table of virtues is not a catalogue of his ideals or objects of worship, and to attempt to read ideal content into them is Lawrence's, not Franklin's, mistake. Franklin was just as much interested in being "free and easy" as Lawrence was—more so, in fact, for he was willing to work towards it. No one can blame Lawrence for protesting against the popular confusion of means and ends, and the general tendency to make God an "everlasting Wanamaker," but his reading this into Franklin himself is not excusable. Lawrence seems to have had a fairly keen appreciation of ideals, but none whatsoever of morals; Franklin had some of both. "Early to bed and early to rise, makes a man healthy, wealthy and wise." Health, wealth and wisdom, is not a bad summary of the final goods of human life. But none of them occur in Franklin's table of virtues; it is concerned exclusively with the "early to bed and early to rise" side of life. Lawrence had no room for this instrumental side of life in his philosophy, but one suspects that even he, as a matter of practice, applied considerable "resolution, frugality, industry and sincerity" to the writing of his books, though, as an artist, he had the good taste not to talk about it.

In Franklin's philosophy, as well as in his personal life, therefore, a sense of values is evident, values of which he did not lose sight, and in the service of which his moral philosophy was merely and precisely an instrument. Franklin was not interested in establishing his Puritan discipline as an end in itself. He assumed that people have ends, that they want to be "free and easy," and that they understand wealth as merely the necessary means for enjoying the real ends of leisure society. The reason "wealth" and similar terms figured so largely in Franklin's writings was simply that the people for whom he was writing thought in those terms. Any term which symbolized the ends for which people actually were striving was welcome to Franklin. He made no attempt to prescribe the ends which men should follow.

Franklin's attention was as consistently confined to the concrete analysis of means as the attention of the Greeks to ends. Aristotle made explicit what any Greek would have admitted to be a life well lived. The greatness of his ethics rests on the fact that the Greek virtues,—balance, wisdom, beauty, and the rest,—are commonly admitted ends. Franklin's virtues,—frugality, industry, sincerity, honesty, and the rest,—are not ends. It was the glory of the Greeks that they persisted in painting perfection in the face of practically minded objectors, with their, "But how is this possible in a barbarian world?" It was the greatness of Franklin, on the other hand, that he refused to abandon his Puritan principles because they were disagreeable. The decline of Puritan morals symbolizes less a growing tolerance of natural goods, or a discovery of better methods of attaining them, than an impatience at being obliged to work for them. The freedom, leisure and beauty which we enjoy are obviously the fruit of generations of discipline and even of slavery, and while we do well to point out the slavishness of those Puritans who make discipline an end in itself, we are in danger of the folly of imagining that we can achieve beauty without labor. The Greeks took slavery for granted. We, too, would be nearer the facts of life if we took slavery for granted, than we are when we imagine that Puritan virtues are antiquated. They are as universal in morals as the Greek ideals are in art. Their truth is as old as history and quite proverbial. It was understood long before Franklin, but seldom has it been stated so concretely, so simply, and so empirically. The hypothetic form of these maxims is indicative of their scientific character. They do not dictate, they advise. Franklin does not say, "thou shalt and thou shalt not." He says, "*if* you would be healthy, wealthy and wise, you must go early to bed and be early to rise; *if* you would be free and easy you must cultivate the art of virtue; etc." Judgments in this form are about matters of fact and can be put to empirical tests. Not being bound to a particular set of standards, such an inquiry can discover the physical conditions of any. An ethics of means is, therefore, akin to the sciences, as an ethics of ends is to the arts. Artists are engaged each in his own individual work, but the instruments with which they ply their arts may be common. Or, in Franklin's own terms, the art of virtue may be useful to anyone for whom life is an art.

Franklin's table of virtues, inasmuch as it is not a philosophy of human ideals, is to be regarded neither as a substitute for the Aristotelian ethics, nor as a glorification of bourgeois commercialism in the face of the chivalry of the feudal aristocracy. If the Franklin morality substitutes for anything, it is for the traditional Christian virtues, for they, too, constitute a philosophy of the discipline of life. The Christian life is traditionally portrayed as one of humility, charity, penitence, poverty, self-denial, a forgiving spirit. These are obviously instrumental virtues and not ideal perfections, for they disappear in heaven. This traditional code of the feudal ages proved ill-adapted to the pioneer life of New England. Consequently the Puritan virtues, in spite of the fact that they were sanctioned by a Christian theology, were not traditionally Christian. The contrast between the Yankee and the saint, as types of character, is familiar enough. The two philosophies involved are practical alternatives. Franklin, in the *Autobiography*, explicitly retracts humility, the chief of the Christian virtues, as impractical; he said he found that when he was humble he was proud of his humility, and he admitted that he had hastily inserted humility as the thirteenth virtue in his table on the advice of a Quaker who told him that he "was generally thought proud." Franklin's diagnosis of his own case corresponds fairly well to the historians' diagnosis of Puritans in general. They pretended to live saintly lives, but their actual ideals were pagan. They pursued "health, wealth and wisdom" while they professed election into the Covenant of Grace. Franklin saw clearly the growing incompatibility between the morals practiced and the morals preached, and he changed the preaching.

There was a brief time in Franklin's life when he concerned himself more or less seriously with religious reform. He tried to work out in detail a religious system which would give sincere expression to his moral ideas. He wrote down the rudiments of a theology, composed prayers, and while in England he even undertook, with Lord le

Despencer, to revise the English Prayer Book. For various reasons he soon abandoned this project. To a certain extent Freemasonry and his Junto Club were his substitutes for churches. But above all he dropped religious subjects in order not to stimulate one more theological controversy. He made it a policy to disturb no one in his religious practices and beliefs; he supported various religious institutions and he apparently became a good friend of both Whitefield and Samuel Johnson. Thus he made his peace with all religions and devoted himself to none. And while theologians were struggling, as we have seen, to revise Christian ideas to meet changing American morals, Franklin was free to take the other alternative. He reasserted the stern Puritan morality, but divorced it from the theocratic aims which it originally served.

In his austere moralism, Franklin was undoubtedly a Puritan, however much he may have revolted against Calvinism. His "art of virtue" is in significant contrast to the liberal temper and popular radicalism of his day and it can not be regarded as the product of his contacts with European civilization, nor of his Freemasonry, nor of his admiration for Sir Roger de Coverley. In other ways Franklin was no doubt a typical eighteenth century man of the world, but as a moralist he was a child of the New England frontier. Jonathan Edwards and Benjamin Franklin thus represent the two opposite poles of Puritan thought. It was Edwards who attempted to induce New England to lead a godly, not a sober, life; it was Franklin who succeeded in teaching Americans to lead a sober and not a godly life. . . .

GOD LAND: "THE ALMOST ONLY GARDEN"

17

Planting this Wilderness

EDWARD JOHNSON

*Of the laborious worke Christ's people have in planting this wilder-
nesse, set forth in the building the Towne of Concord, being the first
in-land Towne.*

Now because it is one of the admirable acts of Christ['s] Providence in
leading his people forth into these Westerne Fields, in his providing of
Huts for them, to defend them from the bitter stormes this place is
subject unto, therefore here is a short Epitome of the manner how they
placed downe their dwellings in this Desart Wildernesse, the Lord
being pleased to hide from the Eyes of his people the difficulties they
are to encounter withall in a new Plantation, that they might not
thereby be hindered from taking the worke in hand; upon some
inquiry of the Indians, who lived to the North-west of the Bay, one
Captaine Simon Willard being acquainted with them, by reason of his
Trade, became a chiefe instrument in erecting this Town, the land
they purchase of the Indians, and with much difficulties traveling
through unknowne woods, and through watery scrampes [swamps],
they discover the fitnesse of the place, sometimes passing through the
Thickets, where their hands are forced to make way for their bodies
passage, and their feete clambering over the crossed Trees, which
when they missed they sunke into an uncertaine bottome in water, and
wade up to the knees, tumbling sometimes higher and sometimes
lower, wearied with this toile, they at end of this meete with a
scorching plaine, yet not so plaine, but that the ragged Bushes scratch

Reprinted from Edward Johnson, *The Wonder-Working Providence of Sions
Saviour in New England* (London, 1654).

their legs fouly, even to wearing their stockings to their bare skin in two or three houres; if they be not otherwise well defended with Bootes, or Buskings, their flesh will be torne: (that some being forced to passe on without further provision) have had the bloud trickle downe at every step, and in the time of Summer the Sun casts such a reflecting heate from the sweet Ferne, whose scent is very strong so that some herewith have beene very nere fainting, although very able bodies to undergoe much travell, and this not to be indured for one day, but for many, and verily did not the Lord incourage their naturall parts (with hopes of a new and strange discovery, expecting every houre to see some rare sight never seene before) they were never able to hold out, and breake through: but above all, the thirsting desires these servants of Christ have had to Plant his Churches, among whom . . . Mr. Jones shall not be forgotten.

> *In Desart's depth where Wolves and Beares abide,*
> *There Jones sits down a wary watch to keepe,*
> *O're Christs deare flock, who now are wandered wide;*
> *But not from him, whose eyes ne're close with sleepe.*
> *Surely it sutes thy melancholly minde,*
> *Thus solitary for to spend thy dayes,*
> *Much more thy soule in Christ content doth finde,*
> *To worke for him, who thee to joy will raise.*
> *Leading thy son to Land, yet more remote,*
> *To feede his flock upon this Westerne wast:*
> *Exhort him then Christs Kingdome to promote;*
> *That he with thee of lasting joyes may tast.*

Yet farther to tell of the hard labours this people found in Planting this Wildernesse, after some dayes spent in search, toyling in the day time as formerly is said; like true Jacobites, they rest them one [on] the Rocks where the night takes them, their short repast is some small pittance of Bread, if it hold out, but as for Drinke they have plenty, the Countrey being well watered in all places that yet are found out. Their farther hardship is to travell, sometimes they know not whether, bewildred indeed without sight of Sun, their compasse miscarrying in crouding through the Bushes, they sadly search up and down for a known way, the Indians paths being not above one foot broad, so that a man may travell many dayes and never find one. But to be sure the directing Providence of Christ hath beene better unto them than many paths, as might here be inserted, did not hast call my

Pen away to more waighty matters; yet by the way a touch thus, it befell with a servant maide, who was travelling about three or foure miles from one Towne to another, loosing her selfe in the Woods, had very diligent search made after her for the space of three dayes, and could not possible be found, then being given over as quite lost, after three dayes and nights, the Lord was pleased to bring her feeble body to her own home in safety, to the great admiration of all that heard of it. This intricate worke no whit daunted these resolved servants of Christ to goe on with the worke in hand, but lying in the open aire, while the watery Clouds poure down all the night season, and sometimes the driving Snow dissolving on their backs, they keep their wet cloathes warme with a continued fire, till the renewed morning give fresh opportunity of further travell; after they have thus found out a place of aboad, they burrow themselves in the Earth for their first shelter under some Hill-side, casting the Earth aloft upon Timber; they make a smoaky fire against the Earth at the highest side, and thus these poore servants of Christ provide shelter for themselves, their Wives and little ones, keeping off the short showers from their Lodgings, but the long raines penetrate through, to their great disturbance in the night season: yet in these poore Wigwames they sing Psalmes, pray and praise their God, till they can provide them houses, which ordinarily was not wont to be with many till the Earth, by the Lords blessing, brought forth Bread to feed them, their Wives and little ones, which with sore labours they attaine every one that can lift a hawe [hoe] to strike it into the Earth, standing stoutly to their labours, and teare up the Rootes and Bushes, which the first yeare beares them a very thin crop, till the soard [sward] of the Earth be rotten, and therefore they have been forced to cut their bread very thin for a long season. But the Lord is pleased to provide for them great store of Fish in the spring time, and especially Alewives about the bignesse of a Herring; many thousands of these, they used to put under their Indian Corne, which they plant in Hills five foote asunder, and assuredly when the Lord created this Corne, hee had a speciall eye to supply these his peoples wants with it, for ordinarily five or six graines doth produce six hundred.

As for flesh they looked not for any in those times (although now they have plenty) unlesse they could barter with the Indians for Venison or Rockoons, whose flesh is not much inferiour unto Lambe, the toile of a new Plantation being like the labours of Hercules never at an end, yet are none so barbarously bent (under the Mattacusets especially) but with a new Plantation they ordinarily gather into Church-fellowship, so that Pastors and people suffer the inconveniences together, which is a great meanes to season the sore labours they undergoe, and verily the edge of their appetite was greater to spirituall duties at their first comming in time of wants, than afterward: many in new Plantations have been forced to go barefoot, and bareleg, till these latter dayes, and some in time of Frost and Snow: Yet were they then very healthy more then now they are: in this Wildernesse-worke men of Estates speed no better than others, and some much worse for want of being inured to such hard labour, having laid out their estate upon cattell at five and twenty pound a Cow, when they came to winter them with in-land Hay, and feed upon such wild Fother as was never cut before, they could not hold out the Winter, but ordinarily the first or second yeare after their comming up to a new Plantation, many of their Cattell died, especially if they wanted Saltmarshes: and also those, who supposed they should feed upon Swines flesh were cut short, the Wolves commonly feasting themselves before them, who never leave neither flesh nor bones, if they be not scared away before they have made an end of their meale. As for those who laid out their Estate upon Sheepe, they speed worst of any at the beginning (although some have sped the best of any now) for untill the Land be often fed with other Cattell Sheepe cannot live; And therefore they never thrived till these latter dayes: Horse had then no better successe, which made many an honest Gentleman travell a foot for a long time, and some have even perished with extreame heate in their travells: as also the want of English graine, Wheate, Barly and Rie proved a sore affliction to some stomacks, who could not live upon Indian Bread and water, yet were they compelled to it till Cattell increased, and the Plowes could but goe: instead of Apples and Peares, they had Pomkins and Squashes of divers kinds. Their lonesome condition was very grievous to some, which was much aggravated by continuall feare of the Indians approach, whose cruelties were much spoken of, and more especially during the time of the Peqot wars.

Thus this poore people populate this howling Desart, marching manfully on (the Lord assisting) through the greatest difficulties, and forest labours that ever any with such weak means have done.

18

The Places of Their Acquaintance
SAMUEL SEWALL

As long as *Plum Island* shall faithfully keep the commanded Post; Notwithstanding all the hectoring Words, and hard Blows of the proud and boisterous Ocean; As long as any Salmon, or Sturgeon shall swim in the streams of *Merrimack;* or any Perch, or Pickeril, in *Crane-Pond;* As long as the Sea-Fowl shall know the Time of their coming, and not neglect seasonably to visit the Places of their Acquaintance: As long as any Cattel shall be fed with the Grass growing in the Medows, which do humbly bow down themselves before *Turkie-Hill;* As long as any Sheep shall walk upon *Old Town Hills,* and shall from thence pleasantly look down upon the River *Parker,* and the fruitfull *Marishes* lying beneath; As long as any free and harmless Doves shall find a White Oak, or other Tree within the Township, to perch, or feed, or build a careless Nest upon; and shall voluntarily present themselves to perform the office of Gleaners after Barley-Harvest; As long as Nature shall not grow Old and dote; but shall constantly remember to give the rows of Indian Corn their education, by Pairs: So long shall Christians be born there; and being first made meet, shall from thence be Translated, to be made partakers of the Inheritance of the Saints in Light.

Reprinted from Samuel Sewall, *Phænomena quædam Apocalyptica ad Aspectum Novi Orbis configurata. Or, some few Lines towards a description of the New Heaven As It makes to those who stand upon the New Earth* (Boston, 1697).

19

Paradise in America
JONATHAN EDWARDS

It is not unlikely that this work of God's spirit, that is so extraordinary and wonderful, is the dawning, or at least, a prelude of that glorious work of God, so often foretold in Scripture, which in the progress and issue of it shall renew the world of mankind. If we consider how long since, the things foretold, as what should precede this great event have been accomplished; and how long this event has been expected by the church of God, and thought to be nigh by the most eminent men of God in the church; and withal consider what the state of things now is, and has for a considerable time been, in the church of God, and world of mankind, we cannot reasonably think otherwise, than that the beginning of this great work of God must be near. And there are many things that make it probable that this work will begin in America. It is signified that it shall begin in some very remote part of the world, that the rest of the world will have no communication with but by navigation, in Isa. lx. 9: "Surely the Isles will wait for me, and the ships of Tarshish first, to bring my sons from afar." It is exceeding manifest that this chapter is a prophecy of the prosperity of the church, in its most glorious state on earth, in the latter days; and I cannot think that any thing else can here be intended but America, by the isles that are afar off, from whence the first born sons of that glorious day shall be brought. . . . And what is chiefly intended is not the British Isles, nor any Isles near the other continent; for they are spoken of as at a great distance from that part of the world where the church had till then been. This prophecy therefore seems plainly to point out America, as the first fruits of that glorious day.

God has made as it were two worlds here below, the old and the new (according to the names they are now called by), two great habitable continents, far separated one from the other; the latter is but newly discovered, it was formerly wholly unknown, from age to age,

Reprinted from Jonathan Edwards, *Some Thoughts Concerning the Present Revival of Religion in New England,* in *Works of President Edwards* . . . (New York, 1844), III.

and is as it were now but newly created: it has been, until of late, wholly the possession of Satan, the church of God having never been in it, as it has been in the other continent, from the beginning of the world. This new world is probably now discovered, that the new and most glorious state of God's church on earth might commence there; that God might in it begin a new world in a spiritual respect, when he creates the *new heavens* and *new earth.*

God has already put that honor upon the other continent, that Christ was born there literally, and there made the *purchase of redemption:* so, as Providence observes a kind of equal distribution of things, it is not unlikely that the great spiritual birth of Christ, and the most glorious *application of redemption* is to begin in this. . . .

The other continent hath slain Christ, and has from age to age shed the blood of the saints and martyrs of Jesus, and has often been as it were deluged with the church's blood: God has therefore probably reserved the honor of building the glorious temple to the daughter, that has not shed so much blood, when those times of the peace, and prosperity, and glory of the church shall commence, that were typified by the reign of Solomon. . . .

The old continent has been the source and original of mankind, in several respects. The first parents of mankind dwelt there; and there dwelt Noah and his sons; and there the second Adam was born, and was crucified and rose again: and it is probable that, in some measure to balance these things, the most glorious renovation of the world shall originate from the new continent, and the church of God in that respect be from hence. And so it is probable that that will come to pass in spirituals, that has in temporals, with respect to America; that whereas till of late, the world was supplied with its silver and gold and earthly treasures from the old continent, now it is supplied chiefly from the new, so the course of things in spiritual respects will be in like manner turned.

And it is worthy to be noted that America was discovered about the time of the reformation, or but little before: which reformation was the first thing that God did towards the glorious renovation of the world, after it had sunk into the depths of darkness and ruin, under the great antichristian apostasy. So that as soon as this new world is (as it were) created, and stands forth in view, God presently goes about doing some great thing to make way for the introduction of the church's latter day glory, that is to have its first seat in, and is to take its rise from that new world.

It is agreeable to God's manner of working, when he accomplishes any glorious work in the world, to introduce a new and more excellent state of his church, to begin his work where his church had not been till then, and where was no foundation already laid, that the power of God might be the more conspicuous; that the work might appear to be entirely God's, and be more manifestly a creation out of nothing; agreeably to Hos. i. 10: "And it shall come to pass that in the place where it was said unto them, ye are not my people, there it shall be said unto them, ye are the sons of the living God." When God is about to turn the earth into a Paradise, he does not begin his work where there is some good growth already, but in a wilderness, where nothing grows, and nothing is to be seen but dry sand and barren rocks; that the light may shine out of darkness, and the world be replenished from emptiness, and the earth watered by springs from a droughty desert; agreeably to many prophecies of Scripture. . . .

I observed before, that when God is about to do some great work for his church, his manner is to begin at the lower end; so when he is about to renew the whole habitable earth, it is probable that he will begin in this utmost, meanest, youngest and weakest part of it, where the church of God has been planted last of all; and so the first shall be last, and the last first; and that will be fulfilled in an eminent manner in Isa. xxiv. 16, "From the uttermost part of the earth have we heard songs, even glory to the righteous." . . .

And if we may suppose that this glorious work of God shall begin in any part of America, I think if we consider the circumstances of the settlement of New England, it must needs appear the most likely of all American colonies, to be the place whence this work shall principally take its rise.

And if these things are so, it gives more abundant reason to hope that what is now seen in America, and especially in New England, may prove the dawn of that glorious day: and the very uncommon and wonderful circumstances and events of this work, seem to me strongly to argue that God intends it as the beginning or forerunner of something vastly great. . . .

20

Puritanism, the Wilderness, and the Frontier
ALAN HEIMERT

The notion of subjugating an American wilderness had no place in the aspirations of the English religious dissenters who came to New England in the years after 1620. John Robinson's last letter to the Leyden emigrants charged them to preserve their ecclesiastical polity. Ten years later John Cotton assured Winthrop's company of God's favor for "that which hath beene a maine meane of peopling the world, and is likely to be of propagating the Gospell." But he spoke of no American wilderness; like Thomas Hooker he gathered evidence that the Lord would imminently withdraw from England. Peopling the world and propagating the gospel were parts of the general Protestant purpose of carrying the fruits of the Reformation to the New World. The Massachusetts Bay group left with a more particular aim in mind, that example contained in the "city set on a hill" of Winthrop and Peter Bulkeley. But no one attached significance to their wilderness-destination, certainly nothing comparable to the animism which overcame Puritan thinking about the wilderness in the course of the century. Their concept of the American "wilderness," we must conclude, was not, as it were, carried to America on the *Mayflower* or the *Arbella,* but came out of that wilderness itself.

For the Puritans America was to be "the good Land," as Winthrop put it, a veritable Canaan. The Atlantic, if not the Red, was their "vast Sea," and the successful conclusion of their voyage, the end of their tribulations, their emergence from the "wilderness." In justifying their removal, Cotton drew this same parallel of the Jews leaving Egypt. Even if we discount the promotional aspects of *Mourt's Relation* and Higginson's *New-England's Plantation,* the inference is inescapable that these colonists were not prepared for the "thicke Wood" which they found, for a country "wilde and overgrowne with woods." If this

---

Reprinted with the permission of *The New England Quarterly* and Alan Heimert from Heimert, "Puritanism, the Wilderness, and the Frontier," *The New England Quarterly,* XXVI (1953), pp. 361–82.

were the promised land—and Winthrop could write that "here is sweet air, fair rivers, and plenty of springs, and the water better than in England"—the task of building Zion proved greater than had been foreseen. Very soon Winthrop was writing of "unexpected troubles and difficulties" in "this strange land, where we have met with many troubles and adversities," until he could "discern little difference between it and our own." Plagues, water shortages, famines, miserable climate, and hardships of every kind came between the emigrants and their objectives. By 1643 Roger Williams could write of the American wilderness as a "cleere resemblance of the world; where greedie and furious men persecute and devour the harmlesse and innocent, as the wild beasts pursue and devoure the Hinds and Roes." Whatever is personal to Williams in this passage, enough remains to indicate the distance travelled from the days of Winthrop's "good Land."

Out of these conditions and the various reactions to them was shaped the Puritan conception of the "West." One such response was removal from the original settlements into adjacent areas. Plymouth, "by reason of ye straightnes and ye barrennes of ye same," was, as Bradford complained, especially embarrassed by such withdrawals. Adverse comment and efforts to check this movement on the part of the leadership of the Old Colony and Massachusetts Bay reflect the other (for our purposes) crucial element in New England thought. That part of the New England mind which partook of an inheritance from the Middle Ages, from Aristotle and scholasticism, held that society was an organism and not an aggregate of individuals and that the public good was to be achieved by cohesiveness and coöperation, by being "knitt together in this worke as one man." This conception, doubly significant by virtue of the special form it took in their social thought, dominated the Puritan attitude toward expansion and the frontier. Plymouth sought to hold its people together, to be sure, both for "ye better improvement of ye generall imployments" and "for more saftie and defence." But to Bradford the departures suggested something far more ominous. The prosperity brought with the immigration of the 1630's was as much a "hurte" as a "benefite," for, with an increase in the demand for food:

there was no longer any holding them togeather but now they must of necessitie go to their great lots. . . . By which means they were scattered all over ye bay, quickly, and ye towne, in which they lived compactly till now, was left very thine, and if this had been all, it had been less, though to much: but ye church must also be divided,

*and those yt lived so long togeather in Christian and comfortable
fellowship must now part and suffer many divisions.*

When legislation failed to check these dispersions, Bradford feared
that it meant "ye ruine of New-England, at least of ye churches of God
ther, & will provock ye Lords displeasure against them."

The Bay, though able to regulate such defections, was found
wanting by reason of the "barrenes of the lande, and the coldness of the
ayre in winter." Lord Say and Sele advised Winthrop that Gód had
evidently intended New England as only a way-station to the true new
Canaan of the West Indies. But the great withdrawal was to the
Connecticut valley, its most notable participants being the Cambridge
flock and their leader. This the Bay leaders sought to frustrate, both
with land concessions and with a number of pointed arguments. Their
departure would weaken the economy and expose the settlements to
Indians. "Being knit to us in one body," the group should not depart.
For lastly, though by no means of least importance, "the removing of a
candlestick is a great judgment, which is to be avoided." We should
not interpret this opposition as a mere pious façade hiding an economic reality, if indeed the two realms were thus separable at that
time. As late as 1642, Winthrop was concerned by the dangers brought
on by these splinterings, bewailing the number of those who sought
the "liberty of removing for outward advantages." Those who "confed-
erate together in civil and church estate," he insisted, "implicitly at
least, bind themselves to support each other." This was the social
covenant of the Congregational way, an easy corollary of the whole
federal theology. As Perry Miller has shown, the covenant was the
Puritans' method of infusing static medieval conceptions with a voluntaristic note. Yet the same principle which justified the break with the
established church and society of England appeared through the
century, reflecting, and partially causing, opposition to further separa-
tions within the ranks of American Puritanism. The words of Winthrop and Bradford indicate that, until 1640, the orthodox mind was
unable to equate even tentative penetration of the interior with the
purposes of the Lord.

The migration to the Connecticut valley actually represents the
earliest of the great American land-manias, focussing on one of the
three interior Canaans which so fascinated seventeenth-century New
England, the only one which they were to occupy. The personal
motives of Hooker and Cotton cannot obscure the fact that Connecti-

cut appeared to be the answer to a long-standing hope of the disappointed. At the very moment of landing, Bradford expected to ascend
eventually some "Pisgah, to vew from the wilderness a more goodly
cuntrie," and Higginson, for all his lavish promoting of the Salem
region, betrayed his discomfort with its "thicke Wood" and took final
refuge in a rumor that "about three miles" away "a man may stand on
a little hilly place, and see divers thousands of acres of ground as good
as need be." The petition of Hooker's group posited both the "fruitfulness and commodiousness" of Connecticut and "the strong bent of
their spirits to remove thither." Similarly some men of Plymouth had a
"hankering mind after it," and not much later Davenport was "much
taken with the fruitfulness" of what came to be New Haven. With the
valley's reputation extending to the whole southwest, it is little wonder
that the colonists welcomed an epidemic among the Indians that made
of it the "Lords wast" and undertook a war to prove it so.

Yet, particularly for those who actually observed it, the valley
proved unequal to its assigned role. Both the rascal Underhill and
Thomas Morton agreed that "if you would know the garden of New
England, then you must glance your eye upon the Hudson's river." To
the first arrivals merely one river whose "secrets" they planned to seek
out, the Hudson was, to Nathaniel Morton in 1669, "a place far more
commodious, and the soil more fertile" than the erstwhile Canaan of
Connecticut. In 1680 William Hubbard similarly belittled the Connecticut valley, remarking that the earlier generation had found that
its previous "fame, peradventure, did not a little outdo its real excellency," declaring the Hudson area to be "The most fertile and desirable tract of land in all the southerly part of New England."

If the Hudson valley was coveted, it was hardly a "wast" and not
easy of possession; the region beyond it, however, might profitably
absorb the interest of New England. Winthrop recorded his knowledge of a "great lake," where the Potomac, Connecticut, and Hudson
were supposed to take their rise, the area of the great beaver trade.
Four decades later, Hubbard was still confused as to the precise
geography but wise enough to convert a 1644 trading expedition into
an attempted discovery of the "Great Lakes." For in 1677 Daniel
Gookin had already envisioned the western country to be what Bradford and Higginson had sought and what others had mistaken the
Connecticut valley for. Assuming that "this place is a good climate,
and probably not only very fertile, . . . but . . . otherwise furnished
with furs and other desirable things," he offered a program for "a full

and perfect discovery of this vast lake, or part of the sea." New England's hunger was not thus satisfied until after 1800; but if the notion of a promised land to the westward was, even within the seventeenth century, increasingly divested of its Old Testament framework and the Puritan disposition to identify this earthly Canaan with the country east of the Berkshires, the attitude represented by the Connecticut mania remained in the mind of even the likes of Cotton Mather.

In these early years, the new Connecticut society differed neither ecclesiastically nor in social ideals: "Many of them," wrote Brewster of the Massachusetts group which contended with Plymouth for possession of the valley, "look at that which this river will not afford, excepte it be at this place which we have, namely, to be a great towne, and have a commodious dwelling for many togeather." Indeed in 1654 Edward Johnson stoutly denied any divergence, defending the New England federation. Though the valley was more open to Indian attack, "Yet are the Massachusetts far from deserting them, esteeming them highly so long as their Governments maintain the same purity in religion with themselves." Though the peculiar circumstances of the exodus from Cambridge did leave a somewhat bitter memory, Johnson could publish, as an example to the world, this identity of congregational polity and purpose, though a hundred miles apart, of the New England communities. This conception of a whole people marching as one with each other, and with God, erecting myriad congregational churches throughout New England, supplies the grandeur of Johnson's *Wonder-Working Providence,* an uneven work which has nevertheless inspired one critic to laud it as "the first classical narrative of the American overland trek toward the setting sun." That such could be his major theme suggests that the previous restraints on expansion could be safely relaxed as immigration strengthened the Bay, that the settlement of new towns in the "Inland country" was now a benefit and no longer jeopardized the success of the colony.

But more importantly, it reflected a subtle and crucial change in the purposes of the New England venture. Even Davenport had not erected expansion into a positive virtue of such magnitude, his best offer being a tentative assertion that his New Haven colony might divert "the thoughts and intentions of such in England as intended evil against us, whose designs might be frustrate by our scatterings so far." Hooker's group merely invoked a Dutch menace. But now Winthrop's "city on a hill" had given way to "the service of our Lord Jesus

Christ, to re-build the most glorious Edifice of Mount Sion in a Wilderness." If this was, in major part, a symptom of a changing European scene and the failure and disruption of international Calvinism, the imputation of divine assistance for those who "populate this howling Desart" reflects American experience as well. The new vision was a response to the "greatest difficulties, and sorest labours" which the colony had suffered, subjections which underlay the transition from Higginson's depiction of the wilderness to that of Roger Williams. In 1642 Thomas Shepard, citing the "straits, the wants, the tryalls of God's people," argued that the Lord must have indeed had a great "Worke" in mind "so as to carry out a people of his owne from so flourishing a State, to a wilderness so far distant." This was a minor point in Shepard's defense of New England from charges of weakhearted flight from England. Johnson's work is therefore the first full-dress exposition of the new interpretation given to New England's mission. Instead of the promised land, America had become the wilderness itself through which the generation of Jacob, as he would have it, was forced to pass before entering Canaan, "the Lord being pleased to hide from the Eyes of his people the difficulties they are to encounter withall in a New Plantation, that they might not thereby be hindered from taking the worke in hand." The methods of the Lord, as well as His purposes, of course, had to be reinterpreted in light of experience, and they too were subtly naturalized.

That the subjection of the wilderness was now divinely commissioned did not, however, transform the Puritan into a lonely axe-and-plow pioneer. Even the Indian policy allowed no solitary missionary preceding civilization into the forest; Eliot did not go unto the Indians but brought them into his towns, civilizing them that they might be Christianized. That with which the Puritans sought to replace the wilderness was a "garden." Yet both Fenwick, enjoying "the primitive imployment of dressing a garden," and Bradford, in whose verses roots and herbs, which "in gardens grow," prove the wilderness conquered, intended to limit their meaning to a mere pattern of tillage. The "garden," a sustained metaphor in Samuel Danforth's 1648 poem, was the entire culture which had been transplanted:

> *A skillful Husband-man he was, who brought*
> *This matchless plant from far; & here hath sought*
> *A place to set it in; & for it's sake*
> *The wilderness a pleasant land doth make.*

Johnson's celebration continues in this vein: "This constant penetrating further into this wilderness" meant, for him, not only "Bridges" and "frequented wayes" through "the wild and uncouth woods" but, most importantly, a goodly number of congregational churches and towns. Cotton Mather's representation of New England, late in the century, as "The Almost only *Garden,* which our Lord Jesus has in the vast continent of America," shows how persistently the Puritans refused to identify the garden which they sought or attained with a mere untamed and unchurched paradise, however lush, fertile, or rolling its acres might be.

"The wild boars of the Wilderness" which Mather saw threatening his garden commonwealth still connoted the unsubdued, but he and his generation had come to look on the "wilderness" as something more than the habitat of pagan and papist. Certain obvious sources of this later conception of the wilderness are to be found without, at this point, tracing its elaboration from a merely descriptive term to an intellectual formulation of wider signification. John Higginson's 1663 sermon, in which he credits God for the New England "garden," a "pleasant land" of "towns and fields, . . . habitations and shops," can be read as a mere extension of the logic of Johnson's argument. But the animus of his address betrays the vast difference. Though he was, to be sure, attributing to God's favor the "great increase in blessings" which his contemporaries enjoyed, he, like Michael Wigglesworth, whose narrative poem, *God's Controversy with New England,* was published the preceding year, was reminding a back-sliding people that they who sought the blessings without the favor would soon be without both. In urging a return to the faith which had brought success to their ancestors, this later generation tended to magnify their exemplary achievements. The jeremiad produced the filiopietism of "God sifted a whole nation that he might send choice Grain over into the Wilderness," but it also resulted in an awesome caricature of that wilderness. "The Hazzards they run," intoned Cotton Mather, "and the difficulties they encountered with, in subduing a Wilderness, cannot easily be expressed in a large Tract." They came, went another memorial, to "an *uninhabited Wilderness,* where they had Cause to Fear the *Wild Beasts, and Wilder Men,*" and both Mathers chronicled the Plymouth settlement as a "Flock of sheep amidst a Thousand Wolves." The first generation used neither the Old Testament nor Luther to record their experiences in such extravagant fashion. Perhaps later incidents convinced these writers that their ancestors' wilderness was this frightening, but it is also possible that a belief in the terror of their fathers' predicament colored their perceptions of the contemporary wilderness.

That wilderness suddenly came to life again in the form of King Philip's uprising, which left its mark on New England's thinking. As they saw it, nature itself seemed to contrive with the Indians to work the destruction of the colonists, the Indians withholding from battle until "they should have the leaves of trees and *Swamps* to befriend them," and, when pursued, making their escape "into the deserts." Unfamiliarity with the terrain, together with the Indians' being, so they thought, "so light of Foot that they can run away where they list," through inaccessible "Boggs, rocky Mountains, and Thickets," accounted for some disasters. Even more, however, were consequences of the colonial military methods. Ambushes, of course, were suffered; as was the calamity reported by Increase Mather: "Our Men when in that hideous place, if they did but see a Bush stir, would fire presently, whereby it is verily feared they did sometimes unhappily shoot Men instead of Indians." The Puritan reaction was unvaried; the Indian tactics were denounced as "stealth," cowardice, and withal quite unfair and the Indians as "being like Wolves, and other beasts of Prey." William Hubbard, though knowing the results of the traditional discipline, still branded as a "gross Mistake" one captain's "wrong notion":

> about the best Way and Manner of fighting with the Indians . . . viz. that it were best to deal with the Indians in their own Way, sc. by skulking behind Trees, and taking their Aim at single Persons. . . .

Cotton Mather, in the *Magnalia,* defended that captain for his "successes" but still lauded the others for their "conduct." The new era only fully emerged when Captain Church triumphantly laid his victories to his use of the "Indian custom" of marching "thin and scattered." Meanwhile, that such experiences recurred through the last sorrowful decade of the century explains some of the fury of 1704 despatching of parties "into the Desert, in places almost inaccessible, if possible, to find out those bloody Rebels in their obscure Recesses under covert of a vast hideous Wilderness (their manner of living being much like that of the Wild Beasts of the same)." Yet similar incidents in the Pequot war had only served to attach the adjective "hideous" to swamps; more than this, even together with ancestor-worship, produced this later conception of the wilderness.

In the second half of the century Puritan attention was being drawn to the frontiers, particularly during the war years. Johnson's chants of praise for the "Inland townes," however, gave way to concern for the character of their inhabitants. Orthodox opinion of the outlying settlements, reflecting the dominant social conceptions, was critical of those who appeared to be abandoning the church militant. This was expressed, among other ways, as invective against those who followed the "evil manners of the Indians." The Puritans had their own ideas as to how the wilderness, like the Indians, was to be conquered, and if their criticism of those who became "too like unto the Indians" in neglecting family order or worship now seems ludicrous, perhaps all for which they can be justly condemned is an inability, given their social ideals, to fight two of the good fights at once.

As regards the war itself, however, that the commonwealth was simply guilty of over-expansion was inconceivable to the Puritans; the war was a divine rebuke to New England. That its worst ravages were on the frontiers was not, to them, merely fortuitous. In the "scattering Plantations," Hubbard explained, "many were contented to live without, yea, desirous to shake off all Yoake of Government, both sacred and civil," adopting "the Manners of the Indians they lived amongst." Increase Mather claimed to have foreseen their fate, in having discerned that "they were a scattered people, and such as had many of them Scandalized the Heathen, and lived themselves too like the Heathen, without any *Instituted Ordinances.*" Yet both limited such remarks to "some of the Southern, and all the Eastern Parts" of New England, which had, of course, never been regarded as true members of the union of the Godly.

Though providence was not invoked to account for the disasters in the west, there is reason to believe that the reforming synod of 1679, when, in a list of sinful conditions to be extirpated, it inveighed "against that practice of setling Plantations without any ministry amongst them," was referring to that area directly. In 1642 Winthrop had questioned the worldly ambitions of those who went to the interior, and Johnson observed "an overweaning desire . . . after Medow-land" on their part. But, he quickly added, "though these people are laborious in gaining the goods of this life, they are not unmindful of the chief end of their coming hither." Undoubtedly these settlers were among the first, if not the only ones, who had forgotten that New England was a plantation of religion, not of trade. But a consciousness of something radically amiss in the "Out-Plantations" did not come, as it did by implication in Nicholas Noyes's 1698 demand for "more vigilancy and care" among them, until the end of the century. Then the indictment, compiled under the synodical rubrics by Cotton Mather, quickly comprehended all the sins of Maine: "some woful villages in the skirts of the Colony, beginning to live without the *means of grace* among them," over-weening worldly avarice, and selling liquor to the Indians instead of gospellizing them. "Be sure," was his admonition, "your Sin will find you out, as that of your *Brethren* in the East has done *Them,* and their Trading Houses."

F. J. Turner has characterized Mather's diatribes as little more than the carpings of an orthodox east against a healthily-independent west. Yet Turner himself showed the frontier town's responsibility for implementing the Indian policy, and Mather's position, as we have seen, faithfully engrossed Puritan social ideals. Mather's plea for the west was clearly more complex than Turner saw reason to admit; for, whatever the temperament of Cotton Mather, he was as concerned for these plantations, lest they be damned by an indignant God, as for the remainder of the commonwealth. Nor was this a mask for some seething sectional bitterness; each pamphlet arraigning the frontier in these years can be matched with dozens from the pens of Mather and Benjamin Colman rebuking the dissolute coastal towns in similar terms. Solomon Stoddard, the valley pope, moreover, could both attack the degenerate metropolis and seriously ask if God were not disappointed with the New England frontier. The fact that the frontier was departing from the ranks of the godly was related to New England's sectionalism in a much more subtle manner.

The remarkableness of Mather's arguments cannot, however, be appreciated without returning to the development of the Puritan conception of the "wilderness" in the second half of the century. Neither swamp warfare nor the invocation of ancestral heroism offer the full explanation. This latter, indeed, was merely ancillary to the Puritans' attention to history in their jeremiads. Even in the days of the founders, the covenant theology was commonly buttressed with reference to Jewish history, between which nation and their own the Puritans saw an uncommon similarity. An early use of Biblical imagery pertinent to the American scene was Winthrop's 1642 allusion, in dramatizing the need for social unity, to "such as come together in a wilderness, where there are nothing but wild beasts and beastlike men." The "garden" verses all relied on such a communal covenant, and Bradford's recollections (ca. 1650) of thoughts of "salvage & brutish men, which range up and downe," deterring some in the Leyden deliberations and "a hidious & desolate wilderness, full of wild beasts & willd men" confronting them on arrival indicate his struggle to demonstrate the existence of such a covenant by patterning Plymouth's history after that of Israel. Shepard also wrote in this vein, but the "worthiest Worke" of Johnson was its first successful elaboration.

Just as the social covenant evolved from "a mere adjunct of the Covenant of Grace" into a "self-sufficient principle" and ultimately "a dominant idea in the minds of social leaders in Massachusetts and Connecticut," the comparison with the Jews in the wilderness came to be in part divorced from the national covenant itself and took on a metaphorical existence of its own. The advantage of the covenant was that prosperity could be attributed to God and the over-greedy rebuked without impugning the fruits of their wilderness-labors, yet allowing for God's withdrawal, accounting for His controversy as well as His favor. If Abraham's seed had been consigned to yet another wilderness, so might these latter-day children of Israel. If the God of Higginson and Wigglesworth could say of New England that He had turned "an howling wilderness . . . into a fruitful paradise," and, beginning with Nathaniel Morton, each succeeding memorialist insist that it had indeed been made a "pleasant Land," the post-war synod was not so sure as to the appropriate comparison. "It was a great and high undertaking of our fathers. . . . A parallel instance not to be given, except that," and here they hesitated, "of our Father Abraham from Ur of the Chaldees, or that of his Seed from the land of Egypt." For Hubbard the war was enough proof that his nation was neither, as the first settlers had surmised, the successful occupants of Canaan, nor as Johnson suggested, "Jaacobites," but the generation of Esau:

> *For ever since they forsook their fathers' houses and the pleasant heritage of their ancestors they have by solemn providence been ordered, not into the fields where the mandrakes grew . . . , but rather into the barren wilderness and remote deserts. . . .*

So far as it referred to the actual Indian peril, this extension of the sojourn had substantial meaning. What happened, however, is that crop failures, sea disasters, droughts, and every other ill that New England flesh was heir to were imputed to a "*wilderness*-condition." The partial reality of the Indian wars may have made this myth more credible, but the real wilderness was reclothed in more appalling garments when interpreted through the myth. New England, moreover, was never again certain that it had been brought into the promised land; for all its celebration of the society's achievements, the *Magnalia* frequently questions whether this later wilderness had been overcome. Each new lapse of faith and each succeeding catastrophe strengthened the doubts. A frenzied urgency was given to conquering the wilderness, for on this the ultimate success or failure of the whole society was assumed to depend. Perhaps such fervid imagery as this (from a volume, be it noted, on witchcraft) helped create, in an area for which the reality of a wilderness was no longer immediately relevant, an image so portentous that the popular imagination was never liberated from it:

> *The Wilderness through which we are passing to the Promised Land is all over fill'd with Fiery flying serpents. But, blessed be God, none of them have hitherto so fastened upon us to confound us utterly! All our way to Heaven lies by* Dens of Lions *and the* Mounts of Leopards; *there are incredible droves of Devils in our way.*

The implications of such typological thinking in the realm of social salvation were matched by equally significant ones for the individual in his relation to the wilderness. If calamities were seen as "Thorns" visited by an angry deity, "Why," it was asked, "may not God, as well as Gideon, teach the Men of *Succoth,* and of other places, by the *Briers and Thorns of the Wilderness?*" The wilderness now had a moral purpose, and Cotton Mather, writing of "a continual *temptation* of the *devil,*" explicitly alluded to Christ. Moving, without rigorous logic, among the various Biblical parallels, the piety of Richard Mather was explained by the truth that trials of faith might "be expected" in a wilderness. Cotton Mather contended that New England's faith was the greater because it was more often tried in "*desarts* full of dismal circumstances," and affirmed generally "that a *wilderness* was a place where temptation was to be met withal." This did not, of course, mean that the individual was automatically redeemed or even ennobled by mere contact with the vernal wood, but that its vicissitudes could try his faith and that success in the struggle might be a mark of grace.

Cotton Mather tested this possibility in his commentary on the Indian captives and found the analogies of both Testaments verified by a convenient reality. It is this conception that explains his hope that the frontier inhabitants might, in the threatened war, "get all Possible and *Eternal Good* by the *Evil*" they would meet (a possibility, he insisted, likely only if the proper church ordinances were observed) and accounts for the startling, but neglected, first sentences of his *Frontiers Well-Defended:*

> *An Address is now making to a people, who ought on some Great Accounts, to be the* best People *in the Land. It is unto YOU, O our dear Brethren, who are a people Exposed to inexpressible* Hazards *and* Sorrows *by your being in the Exposed* FRONTIERS *of the Land.*

This hypothesis, by which Mather helped to explain the unique development of New England, thus made virtue a partial function of a "*Wilderness*-condition." If the definition of such virtue had changed in two generations, the Puritan's notion of God's special interest in a wilderness people was thereby reaffirmed.

All the ideas which we have been tracing fed into the apocalyptic visions which possessed many Puritan social leaders near the turn of the century. This chiliasm, yet another effort to revive the faith, depended on the increasingly easy identification with the Jews. If convertability of the Indians was an essential factor, it was, more significantly, to New England's interest "*To be an Habitation of Justice.*" If the Indians were the devil's children, then America would "be the head Quarters of *Gog* and *Magog*" and even "hell itself." "This is worse and worse still," cried Nicholas Noyes, "But may be something alleviated by an opposite Conjecture."

> *For there are others that ask why it may not be the New Jerusalem, or part of it? These Opinions are as wide apart from one another, as Heaven is from Hell. I count it sufficient to set them one against the other; without saying which is the widest from the Truth. Only, Who of an American . . . had not rather (if it may stand with the counsel of God) that it should be the New Jerusalem, then the Old Tophet.*

As early as 1684 Samuel Sewall had asked "why the Heart of America may not be the seat of the New Jerusalem." Assured that the Indians were of Jacob's posterity, he concluded that America *would* be the site, fixing its location somewhere in Mexico, though the beauties of Plum Island gave him final assurance. But Cotton Mather, who could opine that the "last conflict with antichrist" would be to the "westward," based his argument on a more spacious geographical knowledge. Somewhere in "the brave Countries and Gardens, which fill the

American Hemisphere," would be the "HOLY CITY in AMERICA; a *City,* the *Street* whereof will be *Pure* GOLD." Though something of a restatement of the visions of Winthrop and Johnson, this latest and most spectacular western New Jerusulem would lie beyond the confines of New England. The hope of those who now looked for a final divine judgment to rescue them from a darker moral wilderness, their utopia served only to assuage the doubts of a society no longer able to judge itself with any certainty.

The refractions in Puritan thought of their wilderness-experience left one explicit legacy to the eighteenth century. "That the discourse comes forth in such homely dresse and course habit," Thomas Hooker wrote, "the reader must consider, It comes out of the wildernesse." "Wilderness dress" remained an appealing pose for practitioners of the plain style, but a new major theme emerged from the second generation's applying to their ancestors the description of John the Baptist's converts, "They came not into the wilderness to see soft raiment." Said Samuel Danforth of their habit: "Delicate and costly Apparel is to be expected in Princes Courts, and not in wilde Woods and Forrests." Admitting that his own generation had re-entered "pleasant Cities and Habitations," he could still say of "the affection of Courtly Pomp and Gallantry" in his own day, "How much more intolerable and abominable is excess of this kinde in a Wilderness." Though the older Puritan objection was not forgotten—Cotton Mather thought "finery" both "inviting unto *sensualities*" and "disagreeable to a *wilderness*"—these latter-day metaphorical conceptions lent double support to such denunciations as Stoddard's of Boston fashions as "demeanor not becoming a wilderness state" and those of Noyes and Sewall against the wearing of wigs, hastening the process which began with Danforth in 1663 and eventuated in the eighteenth-century apotheosis of American homespun.

Both a century of colonizing experience and the religious nature of New England fed into the Puritan attitudes toward the wilderness. A realistic appraisal dictated the change in identification of the physical setting from a promised land to a wilderness. But only the Judaizing disposition of the Puritan mind accounts for the acceleration of that process and for the dark conclusion that New England was perhaps a permanent and hideous wilderness. Their difficulties in the wilderness served to reinforce the Puritans' belief that they were the chosen of God and to countenance an expectation that the New Jerusalem would lie in America. Subduing the wilderness quickly became an exalted calling for the Puritan; later new graces were imputed to the now-harassed occupants of the frontier. Indeed, only an intense consciousness of covenant obligations kept the Puritan from making the frontiersman the particular avatar of all the American wilderness-virtues. As the belief emerged that those who lived in a wilderness should excel in simplicity, there had appeared by 1700 a large reservoir of concepts and values congenial to later American thinkers.

Part Three

THE PURITAN LEGACY

Introduction

This section consists of reflections by contemporary scholars on the legacy of Puritanism to American culture and character. As Kenneth B. Murdock observes in the concluding essay, "it is pretty generally accepted that somewhere in America's total cultural heritage and the complex of qualities which make up the 'American character' there are traces of Puritanism. It is very difficult, however, to be sure just what these traces are . . . ." The difficulties arise from the general fact that "the continuing influence in intellectual history of any past 'state of mind' is always hard to assess," and from the particular fact that "the special 'state of mind' of the New England colonists has often been misunderstood." How far these difficulties have been overcome the reader will judge from the selections that follow.

The readings are grouped according to the main themes of this collection. In the first part, "The Protestant Ethic," Edmund S. Morgan, Irvin G. Wyllie, and Morton L. Ross comment on the influence of Puritanism on American economic thought and practice from the late eighteenth century to the present. In the second part, "Puritanism and Democracy," H. Richard Niebuhr, Winthrop S. Hudson, and Perry Miller discuss the relations of Puritanism to American political thought and practice, with special reference to the theological and moral underpinnings of the democratic system. Finally, an Englishman, Harold J. Laski, and two Americans, Dixon Wecter and Kenneth B. Murdock, seek answers to the question, as fundamental as it is elusive, of the Puritan trace in the American national character. The reader may wish to refer back to the observations of Richard Schlatter in the essay with which this book began.

Section A

THE PROTESTANT ETHIC

21

The Puritan Ethic and the American Revolution
EDMUND S. MORGAN

The American Revolution, we have been told, was radical and conservative, a movement for home rule and a contest for rule at home, the product of a rising nationality and the cause of that nationality, the work of designing demagogues and a triumph of statesmanship. John Adams said it took place in the minds and hearts of the people before 1776; Benjamin Rush thought it had scarcely begun in 1787. There were evidently many revolutions, many contests, divisions, and developments that deserve to be considered as part of the American Revolution. This paper deals in a preliminary, exploratory way with an aspect of the subject that has hitherto received little attention. Without pretending to explain the whole exciting variety of the Revolution, I should like to suggest that the movement in all its phases, from the resistance against Parliamentary taxation in the 1760's to the establishment of a national government and national policies in the 1790's was affected, not to say guided, by a set of values inherited from the age of Puritanism.

These values or ideas, which I will call collectively the Puritan Ethic,* were not unconscious or subconscious, but were deliberately

Reprinted with the permission of Edmund S. Morgan from Morgan, "The Puritan Ethic and the American Revolution," *William and Mary Quarterly*, 3rd ser., XXIV (January, 1967), with revisions by the author.

* I have chosen this term rather than the familiar "Protestant Ethic" of Max Weber, partly because I mean something slightly different and partly because Weber confined his phrase to attitudes prevailing while the religious impulse was paramount. The attitudes that survived the decline of religion he designated as the "spirit of capitalism." In this essay I have not attempted to distinguish earlier from later, though I am concerned with a period when the attitudes were no longer dictated primarily by religion.

and openly expressed by men of the time. The men who expressed them were not Puritans, and few of the ideas included in the Puritan Ethic were actually new. Many of them had existed in other intellectual contexts before Puritanism was heard of, and many of them continue to exist today, as they did in the Revolutionary period, without the support of Puritanism. But Puritanism wove them together in a single rational pattern, and Puritans planted the pattern in America. It may be instructive, therefore, to identify the ideas as the Puritans defined and explained them before going on to the way in which they were applied in Revolutionary America after they had emerged from the Puritan mesh.

The values, ideas, and attitudes of the Puritan Ethic, as the term will be used here, clustered around the familiar idea of "calling." God, the Puritans believed, called every man to serve Him by serving society and himself in some useful, productive occupation. Before entering on a trade or profession, a man must determine whether he had a calling to undertake it. If he had talents for it, if it was useful to society, if it was appropriate to his station in life, he could feel confident that God called him to it. God called no one to a life of prayer or to a life of ease or to any life that added nothing to the common good. It was a "foul disorder in any Commonwealth that there should be suffered rogues, beggars, vagabonds." The life of a monk or nun was no calling because prayer must be the daily exercise of every man, not a way for particular men to make a living. And perhaps most important, the life of the carefree aristocrat was no calling: "miserable and damnable is the estate of those that being enriched with great livings and revenues, do spend their days in eating and drinking, in sports and pastimes, not employing themselves in service for Church or Commonwealth."

Once called to an occupation, a man's duty to the Maker Who called him demanded that he labor assiduously at it. He must shun both idleness, or neglect of his calling, and sloth, or slackness in it. Recreation was legitimate, because body and mind sometimes needed a release in order to return to work with renewed vigor. But recreation must not become an end in itself. One of the Puritans' objections to the stage was that professional players made recreation an occupation and thereby robbed the commonwealth of productive labor. The emphasis throughout was on productivity for the benefit of society.

In addition to working diligently at productive tasks, a man was supposed to be thrifty and frugal. It was good to produce but bad to consume any more than necessity required. A man was but the steward of the possessions he accumulated. If he indulged himself in luxurious living, he would have that much less with which to support church and society. If he needlessly consumed his substance, either from carelessness or from sensuality, he failed to honor the God who furnished him with it.

In this atmosphere the tolerance accorded to merchants was grudging. The merchant was suspect because he tended to encourage unnecessary consumption and because he did not actually produce anything; he simply moved things about. It was formally recognized that making exchanges could be a useful service, but it was a less essential one than that performed by the farmer, the shoemaker, or the weaver. Moreover, the merchant sometimes demeaned his calling by practicing it to the detriment rather than the benefit of society: he took advantage of his position to collect more than the value of his services, to charge what the market would bear. In short, he sometimes engaged in what a later generation would call speculation.

As the Puritan Ethic induced a suspicion of merchants, it also induced, for different reasons, a suspicion of prosperity. Superficial readers of Max Weber have often leapt to the conclusion that Puritans viewed economic success as a sign of salvation. In fact, Puritans were always uncomfortable in the presence of prosperity. Although they constantly sought it, although hard work combined with frugality could scarcely fail in the New World to bring it, the Puritans always felt more at ease when adversity made them tighten their belts. They knew that they must be thankful for prosperity, that like everything good in the world it came from God. But they also knew that God could use it as a temptation, that it could lead to idleness, sloth, and extravagance. These were vices, not simply because they in turn led to poverty, but because God forbade them. Adversity, on the other hand, though a sign of God's temporary displeasure, and therefore a cause for worry, was also God's means of recalling a people to Him. When God showed anger man knew he must repent and do something about it. In times of drought, disease, and disaster a man could renew his faith by exercising frugality and industry, which were good not simply because they would lead to a restoration of prosperity, but because God demanded them.

The ambivalence of this attitude toward prosperity and adversity was characteristic of the Puritans: it was their lot to be forever improving the world, in full knowledge that every improvement would in the end prove illusory. While rejoicing at the superior purity of the churches they founded in New England, they had to tell themselves that they had often enjoyed more godliness while striving against heavy odds in England. The experience caused Nathaniel Ward, the "simple cobbler of Aggawam," to lament the declension that he was sure would overtake the Puritans in England after they gained the upper hand in the 1640's: "my heart hath mourned, and mine eyes wept in secret, to consider what will become of multitudes of my dear Country-men [in England], when they shall enjoy what they now covet." Human flesh was too proud to stand success; it needed the discipline of adversity to keep it in line. And Puritans accordingly relished every difficulty and worried over every success.

This thirst for adversity found expression in a special kind of sermon, the Jeremiad, which was a lament for the loss of virtue and a warning of divine displeasure and desolation to come. The Jeremiad was a rhetorical substitute for adversity, designed to stiffen the virtue of the prosperous and successful by assuring them that they had failed. Nowhere was the Puritan Ethic more assiduously inculcated than in these laments, and it accordingly became a characteristic of the virtues which that ethic demanded that they were always seen to be expiring, if not already dead. Industry and frugality in their full vigor belonged always to an earlier generation, which the existing one must learn to emulate if it would avoid the wrath of God.

These ideas and attitudes were not peculiar to Puritans. The voluminous critiques of the Weber thesis have shown that similar attitudes prevailed widely among many groups and at many times. But the Puritans did have them, and so did their descendants in the time of the Revolution and indeed for long after it. It matters little by what name we call them or where they came from. "The Puritan Ethic" is used here simply as an appropriate shorthand phrase to designate them, and should not be taken to imply that the American Revolutionists were Puritans.

The Puritan Ethic as it existed among the Revolutionary generation had in fact lost for most men the endorsement of an omnipresent angry God. The element of divinity had not entirely departed, but it was a good deal diluted. The values and precepts derived from it, however, remained intact and were reinforced by a reading of history that attributed the rise and fall of empires to the acquisition and loss of the same virtues that God had demanded of the founders of New England. Rome, it was learned, had risen while its citizens worked at their callings and led lives of simplicity and frugality. Success as usual had resulted in extravagance and luxury. "The ancient, regular, and laborious life was relaxed and sunk in Idleness," and the torrent of vices thus let loose had overwhelmed the empire. In modern times the frugal Dutch had overthrown the extravagant Spanish. The lesson of history carried the same imperatives that were intoned from the pulpit.

Whether they derived their ideas from history thus interpreted or from the Puritan tradition or elsewhere, Americans of the Revolutionary period in every colony and state paid tribute to the Puritan Ethic and repeated its injunctions. Although it was probably strongest among Presbyterians and Congregationalists like Benjamin Rush and Samuel Adams, it is evident enough among Anglicans like Henry Laurens and Richard Henry Lee and even among deists like Franklin and Jefferson. Jefferson's letters to his daughters sometimes sound as though they had been written by Cotton Mather: "It is your future happiness which interests me, and nothing can contribute more to it (moral rectitude always excepted) than the contracting a habit of industry and activity. Of all the cankers of human happiness, none corrodes it with so silent, yet so baneful a tooth, as indolence." "Determine never to be idle. No person will have occasion to complain of the want of time, who never loses any. It is wonderful how much may be done, if we are always doing." And Jefferson of course followed his own injunction: a more methodically industrious man never lived.

The Puritan Ethic whether enjoined by God, by history, or by philosophy, called for diligence in a productive calling, beneficial both to society and to the individual. It encouraged frugality and frowned on extravagance. It viewed the merchant with suspicion and speculation with horror. It distrusted prosperity and gathered strength from adversity. It prevailed widely among Americans of different times and places, but those who urged it most vigorously always believed it to be on the point of expiring and in need of renewal.

The role of these ideas in the American Revolution—during the period, say, roughly from 1764 to 1789—was not explicitly causative. That is, the important events of the time can seldom be seen as the result of these ideas and never as the result solely of these ideas. Yet the major developments, the resistance to Great Britain, independence, the divisions among the successful Revolutionists, and the formulation of policies for the new nation, were all discussed and understood by men of the time in terms derived from the Puritan Ethic. And the way men understood and defined the issues before them frequently influenced their decisions.

In the first phase of the American Revolution, the period of agitation between the passage of the Sugar Act in 1764 and the outbreak of hostilities at Lexington in 1775, Americans were primarily concerned with finding ways to prevent British authority from infringing what they considered to be their rights. The principal point of contention was Parliament's attempt to tax them; and their efforts to prevent taxation, short of outright resistance, took two forms: economic pressure through boycotts and political pressure through the assertion of political and constitutional principles. Neither form of protest required the application of the Puritan Ethic, but both in the end were affected by it.

The boycott movements were a means of getting British merchants to bring their weight to bear on Parliament for the specific purpose of repealing tax laws. In each case the boycotts began with extralegal voluntary agreements among citizens not to consume British goods. In 1764–65, for instance, artisans agreed to wear only leather working clothes. Students forbore imported beer. Fire companies pledged themselves to eat no mutton in order to increase the supply of local wool. Backed by the nonconsumers, merchants of New York, Philadelphia, and Boston agreed to import no British goods until the repeal of the Stamp Act. The pressure had the desired effect: the Stamp Act was repealed and the Sugar Act revised. When the Townshend Acts and later the Coercive Acts were passed, new nonconsumption and nonimportation agreements were launched.

From the outset these colonial boycott movements were more than a means of bringing pressure on Parliament. That is to say, they were not simply negative in intent. They were also a positive end in themselves, a way of reaffirming and rehabilitating the virtues of the Puritan Ethic. Parliamentary taxation offered Americans the prospect of poverty and adversity, and, as of old, adversity provided a spur to virtue. In 1764, when Richard Henry Lee got news of the Sugar Act, he wrote to a friend in London: "Possibly this step of the mother country, though intended to oppress and keep us low, in order to secure our dependence, may be subversive of this end. Poverty and oppression, among those whose minds are filled with ideas of British liberty, may introduce a virtuous industry, with a train of generous and manly sentiments. . . ." And so it proved in the years that followed: as their Puritan forefathers had met providential disasters with a renewal of the virtue that would restore God's favor, the Revolutionary generation met taxation with a self-denial and industry that would hopefully restore their accustomed freedom and simultaneously enable them to identify with their virtuous ancestors.

The advocates of nonconsumption and nonimportation, in urging austerity on their countrymen, made very little of the effect that self-denial would have on the British government. Nonimportation and nonconsumption were preached as means of renewing ancestral virtues. Americans were reminded that they had been "of late years insensibly drawn into too great a degree of *luxury* and *dissipation*." Parliamentary taxation was a blessing in disguise, because it produced the nonimportation and nonconsumption agreements. "Luxury," the people of the colonies were told, "has taken deep root among us, and to cure a people of luxury were an Herculean task indeed; what perhaps no power on earth but a British Parliament, in the very method they are taking with us, could possibly execute." Parliamentary taxation, like an Indian attack in earlier years, was thus both a danger to be resisted and an act of providence to recall Americans from declension: "The Americans have plentifully enjoyed the delights and comforts, as well as the necessaries of life, and it is well known that an increase of wealth and affluence paves the way to an increase of luxury, immorality and profaneness, and here kind providence interposes; and as it were, obliges them to forsake the use of one of their delights, to preserve their liberty." The principal object of this last homily was tea, which, upon being subjected to a Parliamentary duty, became luxurious and enervating. Physicians even discovered that it was bad for the health. Importations, it now appeared, were mainly luxuries, "Baubles of Britain," "foreign trifles."

In these appeals for self-denial, the Puritan Ethic acquired a value that had been only loosely associated with it hitherto: it became an essential condition of political liberty. Americans, like Englishmen, had long associated liberty with property. They now concluded that both rested on virtue. An author who signed himself "Frugality" advised the readers of the *Newport Mercury* that "We may talk and boast of liberty; but after all, the industrious and frugal only will be free," free not merely because their self-denial would secure repeal of Parliamentary taxes, but because freedom was inseparable from virtue, and frugality and industry were the most conspicuous public virtues. Bostonians were told that "by consuming *less* of what we are not really in want of, and by industriously cultivating and improving the natural advantages of our own country, we might save our *sub-stance, even our lands,* from becoming the property of others, and we might effectually preserve our *virtue* and our *liberty,* to the latest posterity." Liberty, virtue, and property offered a powerful rallying call to Americans. Each supported the others; but virtue was the sine qua non of the trio, for while liberty would expire without the support of property, property itself could not exist without industry and frugality. Expounding this point, the *Pennsylvania Journal* assured its readers that "Our enemies very well know that dominion and property are closely 'connected; and that to impoverish us, is the surest way to enslave us. Therefore, if we mean still to be free, let us unanimously lay aside foreign superfluities, and encourage our own manufacture. SAVE YOUR MONEY AND YOU WILL SAVE YOUR COUNTRY!"

There was one class of Americans who could take no comfort in this motto. The merchants, on whom nonimportation depended, stood to lose by the campaign for austerity, and it is not surprising that they showed less enthusiasm for it than the rest of the population. Their lukewarmness only served to heighten the suspicion with which their calling was still viewed. "Merchants have no country," Jefferson once remarked. "The mere spot they stand on does not constitute so strong an attachment as that from which they draw their gains." And John Adams at the Continental Congress was warned by his wife's uncle that merchants "have no Object but their own particular Interest and they must be Contrould or they will ruin any State under Heaven."

Such attitudes had been nourished by the merchants' behavior in the 1760's and 1770's. After repeal of the Stamp Act, Silas Downer, secretary of the Sons of Liberty in Providence, Rhode Island, wrote to the New York Sons of Liberty that "From many observations when the Stamp Act was new, I found that the Merchants in general would have quietly submitted, and many were zealous for it, always reciting the Difficulties their Trade would be cast into on Non Compliance, and never regarding the Interest of the whole Community. . . ." When the Townshend Acts were passed, it was not the merchants but the Boston town meeting that took the lead in promoting nonimportation, and after the repeal of the Acts the merchants broke down and began importing while the duty on tea still remained. Samuel Adams had expected their defection to come much sooner for he recognized that the nonimportation agreements had "pressed hard upon their private Interest" while the majority of consumers could participate under the "happy Consideration that while they are most effectually serving their Country they are adding to their private fortunes."

The merchants actually had more than a short-range interest at stake in their reluctance to undertake nonimportation. The movement, as we have seen, was not simply a means of securing repeal of the taxes to which merchants along with other colonists were opposed. The movement was in fact anticommercial, a repudiation of the merchant's calling. Merchants, it was said, encouraged men to go into debt. Merchants pandered to luxury. Since they made more on the sale of superfluous baubles than on necessities, they therefore pressed the sale of them to a weak and gullible public. What the advocates of nonimportation demanded was not merely an interruption of commerce but a permanent reduction, not to say elimination, of it. In its place they called for manufacturing, a palpably productive, useful calling.

The encouragement of manufacturing was an accompaniment to all the nonimportation, nonconsumption movements. New Yorkers organized a society specifically for that purpose, which offered bounties for the production of native textiles and other necessaries. The nonconsumption of mutton provided new supplies of wool, which housewives turned into thread in spinning matches (wheelwrights did a land-office business in spinning wheels). Stores began selling American cloth, and college students appeared at commencement in home spun. Tories ridiculed these efforts, and the total production was doubtless small, but it would be difficult to underestimate the importance of the attitude toward manufacturing that originated at this time. In a letter of Abigail Adams can be seen the way in which the Puritan Ethic was creating out of a Revolutionary protest movement the conception of a self-sufficient American economy. Abigail was writing to her husband, who was at the First Continental Congress, helping to frame the Continental Association for nonimportation, nonexportation, and nonconsumption:

> *If we expect to inherit the blessings of our Fathers, we should return a little more to their primitive Simplicity of Manners, and not sink into inglorious ease. We have too many high sounding words, and too few actions that correspond with them. I have spent one Sabbeth in Town since you left me. I saw no difference in respect to ornaments, etc. etc. but in the Country you must look for that virtue, of which you find but small Glimerings in the Metropolis. Indeed they have not the advantages, nor the resolution to encourage their own Manufactories which people in the country have. To the Mercantile part, tis considerd as throwing away their own Bread; but they must retrench their expenses and be content with a small share of gain for they will*

find but few who will wear their Livery. As for me I will seek wool and flax and work willingly with my Hands, and indeed their is occasion for all our industry and economy.

In 1774 manufacture retained its primitive meaning of something made by hand, and making things by hand seemed a fitting occupation for frugal country people who had always exhibited more of the Puritan Ethic than high-living city folk. Abigail's espousal of manufactures, with its defiant rejection of dependence on the merchants of the city, marks a step away from the traditional notion that America because of its empty lands and scarcity of people was unsuited to manufactures and must therefore obtain them from the Old World. Through the nonimportation movements the colonists discovered that manufacturing was a calling not beyond the capacities of a frugal, industrious people, however few in number, and that importation of British manufactures actually menaced frugality and industry. The result of the discovery was to make a connection with Britain seem neither wholly necessary nor wholly desirable, so that when the thought of independence at last came, it was greeted with less apprehension than it might otherwise have been.

Nonimportation had produced in effect a trial run in economic self-sufficiency. The trial was inconclusive as a demonstration of American economic capacity, but it carried immense significance intellectually, for it obliged the colonists to think about the possibility of an economy that would not be colonial. At the same time it confirmed them in the notion that liberty was the companion not only of property but of frugality and industry, two virtues that in turn fostered manufactures. By invoking the Puritan Ethic in behalf of a protest movement Americans had led themselves into affirmations of value in which can be seen the glimmerings of a future national economic policy.

While engaged in their campaign of patriotic frugality, Americans were also articulating the political principles that they thought should govern free countries and that should bar Parliament from taxing them. The front line of defense against Parliament was the ancient maxim that a man could not be taxed except by his own consent given in person or by his representative. The colonists believed this to be an acknowledged principle of free government, indelibly stamped on the British Constitution, and they wrote hundreds of pages affirming it. In those pages the Puritan Ethic was revealed at the very root of the constitutional principle when taxation without representation was condemned as an assault on every man's calling. To tax a man without his consent, Samuel Adams said, was "against the plain and obvious rule of equity, whereby the industrious man is intitled to the fruits of his industry." And the New York Assembly referred to the Puritan Ethic when it told Parliament that the effect of the sugar and stamp taxes would be to "dispirit the People, abate their Industry, discourage Trade, introduce Discord, Poverty, and Slavery." Slavery, of course, meant no liberty and no property, and without these, men had no motive for frugality and industry. In other words, the New York protest was pointing out that uncontrolled Parliamentary taxation, like luxury and extravagance, was an attack not merely on property but on industry and frugality, for which liberty and property must be the expected rewards. With every protest that British taxation was reducing them to slavery, Americans reaffirmed their devotion to industry and frugality and their readiness to defy the British threat to them. Students of the American Revolution have often found it difficult to believe that the colonists were willing to fight about an abstract principle and have sometimes dismissed the constitutional arguments of the time as mere rhetoric. But the constitutional principle on which the colonists rested their case was not the product either of abstract political philosophy or of the needs of the moment. In the colonists' view, the principle of no taxation without representation was a means, hallowed by history, of protecting property and of maintaining those virtues, associated with property, without which no people could be free. Through the rhetoric, if it may be called that, of the Puritan Ethic, the colonists reached behind the constitutional principle to the enduring human needs that had brought the principle into being.

We may perhaps understand better the urgency both of the constitutional argument and of the drive toward independence that it ultimately generated, if we observe the growing suspicion among the colonists that the British government had betrayed its own constitution and the values which that constitution protected. In an earlier generation the colonists had vied with one another in praising the government of England. Englishmen, they believed, had suffered again and again from invasion and tyranny, had each time recovered control of their government, and in the course of centuries had developed unparalleled constitutional safeguards to keep rulers true to their callings. The calling of a ruler, as the colonists and their Puritan forbears saw it, was like any other calling: it must serve the common good; it must be useful, productive; and it must be assiduously pursued. After the Glorious Revolution of 1688, Englishmen had fashioned what seemed a nearly perfect instrument of government, a constitution that blended monarchy, aristocracy, and democracy in a mixture designed to avoid the defects and secure the benefits of each. But something had gone wrong. The human capacity for corruption had transformed the balanced government of King, Lords, and Commons into a single-minded body of rulers bent on their own enrichment and heedless of the public good.

A principal means of corruption had been the multiplication of officeholders who served no useful purpose but fattened on the labors of those who did the country's work. Even before the dispute over taxation began, few colonists who undertook trips to England failed to make unflattering comparisons between the simplicity, frugality, and industry that prevailed in the colonies and the extravagance, luxury, idleness, drunkenness, poverty, and crime that they saw in the mother country. To Americans bred on the values of the Puritan Ethic, England seemed to have fallen prey to her own opulence, and the government shared heavily in the corruption. In England, the most powerful country in the world, the visitors found the people laboring under a heavy load of taxes, levied by a government that swarmed with functionless placeholders and pensioners. The cost of government in the colonies, as Professor Gipson has shown, was vastly lower than in England, with the per capita burden of taxation only a fraction of that which Englishmen bore. And whatever the costs of maintaining the empire may have contributed to the British burden, it was clear that the English taxpayers supported a large band of men who lived well from offices that existed only to pay their holders. Even an American like George Croghan, who journeyed to London to promote dubious speculative schemes of his own, felt uncomfortable in the presence of English corruption: "I am Nott Sorry I Came hear," he wrote, "as it will Larn Me to be Contented on a Litle farm in amerrica. . . . I am Sick of London and harttily Tierd of the pride and pompe. . . ."

In the 1760's Americans were given the opportunity to gain the perspective of a Croghan without the need for a trip abroad. The Townshend Acts called for a reorganization of the customs service with a new set of higher officials, who would perforce be paid out of the duties they extracted from the colonists. In the establishment of this American Board of Customs Commissioners, Americans saw the extension of England's corrupt system of officeholding to America. As

Professor Dickerson has shown, the Commissioners were indeed corrupt. They engaged in extensive "customs racketeering" and they were involved in many of the episodes that heightened the tension between England and the colonies: it was on their request that troops were sent to Boston; the Boston Massacre took place before their headquarters; the *Gaspée* was operating under their orders. But it was not merely the official actions of the Commissioners that offended Americans. Their very existence seemed to pose a threat both to the Puritan Ethic and to the conscientious, frugal kind of government that went with it. Hitherto colonial governments had been relatively free of the evils that had overtaken England. But now the horde of placeholders was descending on America.

From the time the Commissioners arrived in Boston in November 1767, the newspapers were filled with complaints that "there can be no such thing as common good or common cause where mens estates are ravaged at pleasure to lavish on parasitical minions." Samuel Adams remarked that the commissioners were "a useless and very expensive set of officers" and that they had power to appoint "as many officers under them as they please, for whose Support it is said they may sink the whole revenue." American writers protested against the "legions of idle, lazy, and to say no worse, altogether useless customs house locusts, catterpillars, flies and lice." They were "a parcel of dependant tools of arbitrary power, sent hither to enrich themselves and their Masters, on the Spoil of the honest and industrious of these colonies." By 1774, when the debate between colonies and Parliament was moving into its final stages, town meetings could state it as an intolerable grievance "that so many unnecessary officers are supported by the earnings of honest industry, in a life of dissipation and ease; who, by being *properly* employed, might be useful members of society."

The coming of the Customs Commissioners showed the colonists that the ocean barrier which had hitherto isolated them from the corruption of Britain was no longer adequate. Eventually, perhaps, Englishmen would again arise, turn out the scoundrels, and recall their government to its proper tasks. And Americans did not fail to support Englishmen like John Wilkes whom they thought to be working toward this end. But meanwhile they could not ignore the dangers on their own shores. There would henceforth be in their midst a growing enclave of men whose lives and values denied the Puritan Ethic; and there would be an increasing number of lucrative offices to tempt Americans to desert ancestral standards and join the ranks of the "parasitical minions." No American was sure that his countrymen would be able to resist the temptation. In 1766, after repeal of the Stamp Act, George Mason had advised the merchants of London that Americans were "not yet debauched by wealth, luxury, venality and corruption." But who could say how long their virtue would withstand the closer subjection to British control that Whitehall seemed to be designing? Some Americans believed that the British were deliberately attempting to undermine the Puritan Ethic. In Boston Samuel Adams observed in 1771 that "the Conspirators against our Liberties are employing all their Influence to divide the people, . . . introducing Levity Luxury and Indolence and assuring them that if they are quiet the Ministry will alter their Measures." And in 1772 Henry Marchant, a Rhode Island traveler in England wrote to his friend Ezra Stiles: "You will often hear the following Language—Damn those Fellows we shall never do any Thing with Them till we root out that cursed puritanick Spirit—How is this to be done?—keep Soldiers amongst Them, not so much to awe Them, as to debauch their Morals—Toss off to them all the Toies and Baubles that genius can invent to weaken their Minds, fill Them with Pride and Vanity, and beget in them all possible Extravagance in Dress and Living, that They may be kept poor and made wretched. . . ."

By the time the First Continental Congress came together in 1774, large numbers of leading Americans had come to identify Great Britain with vice and America with virtue, yet with the fearful recognition that virtue stands in perennial danger from the onslaughts of vice. Patrick Henry gave voice to the feeling when he denounced Galloway's plan for an intercolonial American legislature that would stand between the colonies and Parliament. "We shall liberate our Constituents," he warned, "from a corrupt House of Commons, but thro[w] them into the Arms of an American Legislature that may be bribed by that Nation which avows in the Face of the World, that Bribery is a Part of her System of Government." A government that had succeeded in taxing seven million Englishmen (with the consent of their supposed representatives), to support an army of placeholders, would have no hesitation in using every means to corrupt the representatives of two and one half million Americans.

When the Second Congress met in 1775, Benjamin Franklin, fresh from London, could assure the members that their contrast of England and America was justified. Writing back to Joseph Priestley, he said it would "scarce be credited in Britain, that men can be as diligent with us from zeal for the public good, as with you for thousands per annum. Such is the difference between uncorrupted new states, and corrupted old ones." Thomas Jefferson drew the contrast even more bluntly in an answer rejecting Lord North's Conciliatory Proposal of February 20, 1775, which had suggested that Parliament could make provisions for the government of the colonies. "'The provisions we have made," said Jefferson, "are such as please our selves, and are agreeable to our own circumstances; they answer the substantial purposes of government and of justice, and other purposes than these should not be answered. We do not mean that our people shall be burthened with oppressive taxes to provide sinecures for the idle or the wicked. . . .'"

When Congress finally dissolved the political bands that had connected America with England, the act was rendered less painful by the colonial conviction that America and England were already separated as virtue is from vice. The British Constitution had foundered, and the British government had fallen into the hands of a luxurious and corrupt ruling class. There remained no way of preserving American virtue unless the connection with Britain was severed. The meaning of virtue in this context embraced somewhat more than the values of the Puritan Ethic, but those values were pre-eminent in it. In the eyes of many Americans the Revolution was a defense of industry and frugality, whether in rulers or people, from the assaults of British vice. It is unnecessary to assess the weight of the Puritan Ethic among the many factors that contributed to the Revolution. It is enough simply to recognize that the Puritan Ethic prepared the colonists, in their political as in their economic thinking, to consider the idea of independence.

22

God and Mammon

IRVIN G. WYLLIE

Matthew H. Smith, who had a double career as a clergyman and a Wall Street journalist, spoke wisely in the year 1878 when he predicted that whoever wrote the history of American business would also have to write the history of religion. Having served both God and Mammon, Smith was conscious of their relationship and sensed that justice could not be done to one if the other were ignored. As it turned out, European not American investigators first explored the connection between capitalism and Protestantism. Thanks to Max Weber, Ernst Troeltsch, Richard Tawney and others, the complex relation of religion to the spirit of business enterprise has been carefully and critically examined. Thanks also to fruitless debates on whether Protestantism caused capitalism, or *vice versa*, the fact of their historic congeniality has too often been lost to view.

In nineteenth-century America religion and business were no less partners in common enterprise than they had been in seventeenth-century England. Both Weber and Tawney erred in assuming that in the eighteenth century religious and moral foundations of the get-ahead gospel had been swept away by secular currents. Weber, for example, looked upon Benjamin Franklin as a classic symbol of the secularization of the Protestant ethic, an ethic "without the religious basis, which by Franklin's time had died away." Tawney contended that by the nineteenth century the church possessed no independent standards to which economic practice was expected to conform, and that the church's customary warnings against materialism "wore more and more the air of afterthoughts." If this means that Russell Conwell had less power to enforce fair business practices in Philadelphia than John Calvin had in Geneva, the point must be conceded without debate.

Reprinted with the permission of Rutgers University Press from Irvin G. Wyllie, *The Self-Made Man in America* (Brunswick, N. J.: Rutgers University Press, 1954). Copyright 1954 by the Trustees of Rutgers College in New Jersey.

But if it means that Conwell and his clerical associates had no serious interest in the morality of success, and had nothing to teach in this sphere, the contention must be emphatically denied. Throughout the nineteenth century religious and moral precepts provided the foundation for the self-help creed, and clergymen who preached the gospel of success encouraged their business allies to behave in a conscionable manner. Their counsel was often ignored, but the fact of failure should not obscure the extent and vigor of the effort.

One of the impressive facts about the American cult of self-help is that many of its leading proponents were clergymen. The names of Henry Ward Beecher, Lyman Abbott, William Lawrence, Russell Conwell, and Horatio Alger were as familiar to readers of success tracts as to those who worshipped in the leading Protestant churches on the Sabbath. By teaching that godliness was in league with riches such spokesmen put the sanction of the church on the get-ahead values of the business community. And by so teaching they encouraged each rising generation to believe that it was possible to serve both God and Mammon.

Like the businessmen whose careers they glorified, these clergy were of the Protestant faith. Fully 90 percent of of the leading American businessmen of the early twentieth century were Protestant, and of the well-known clergy who pointed the way to wealth, none was a Roman Catholic. Despite Catholicism's numerical strength in the urban centers where the great fortunes were made, no eminent prelate wrote books or preached sermons urging young men to seek salvation along the road to wealth. The reasons for this negative performance are obvious. Since there were relatively few Catholics in the American business elite, probably never more than 7 percent prior to 1900, the Church had no special interest in glorifying this group. Furthermore, less than 10 percent of the nation's business leaders were foreign born. In ministering to immigrants in the years after the Civil War, and especially to those from southern and eastern Europe, the Catholic Church was working with men who had very little chance of achieving outstanding financial success. In addition, by standing aloof from the glorification of wealth, Catholic spokesmen upheld their church's traditional indictment of materialism.

Virtually all the leading Protestant denominations, with the exception of the Lutheran, produced at least one nationally known clergyman who honored the wealth-through-virtue theme. Most of these ministers, like the business leaders of the time, were natives of the New England and the Middle Atlantic states. Almost without exception they had pulpits in the financial and industrial centers of the North and East, and by virtue of their location, and the economic status of their congregations, they had easy contact with businessmen and business values. A substantial number were Calvinists: the Congregational church produced more prominent self-help publicists than any other denomination. How much this was due to theology, and how much to the church's dominant position in industrial New England no one can say, but there is a suggestion in the fact that rural clergymen did little to glorify the cult of self-help, while their urban brethren, Calvinists and non-Calvinists alike, preached it as true gospel.

Consider some of the nineteenth-century Congregational clergy who, by their utterances on success, proved themselves worthy successors to Cotton Mather. One of the earliest of these was John Todd, who lectured on *The Foundations of Success* in 1843, and subsequently wrote two self-help handbooks, *The Young Man* (1845) and *Nuts for Boys to Crack* (1866). Todd was no back-country preacher, though his pulpit was at Pittsfield, Massachusetts, in the extreme western portion of the state. The fact that Todd preached at Pittsfield when it was developing as an important shoe and textile manufacturing center probably had something to do with his interest in worldly success. Matthew H. Smith began his career as a Congregational clergyman in 1842 at Malden, Massachusetts, a boot and shoe center not far removed from Boston. After eight years in Malden Smith moved to New York where he began a new career as a Wall Street journalist. In addition to his address, *The Elements of Success* (1854), Smith wrote *Twenty Years Among the Bulls and Bears of Wall Street* (1870), and *Successful Folks* (1878). Francis E. Clark, nationally famous as the founder of the Christian Endeavor Society, was a Congregational minister in Portland, Maine, the commercial metropolis of that state. His two self-help books, *Our Business Boys* (1884), and *Danger Signals, the Enemies of Youth from the Business Man's Standpoint* (1885), were based on ideas and information provided by Portland businessmen. Wilbur F. Crafts, who published *Successful Men of Today and What They Say of Success* (1883), occupied a pulpit in New Bedford, Massachusetts, a cotton manufacturing center, before moving to larger pastorates in Chicago and Brooklyn. Through *Seven Lectures to Young Men* (1844) Henry Ward Beecher had established himself as an expert on self-help long before he began to preach industry, frugality, and sobriety to the wealthy congregation of Brooklyn's Plymouth Church. Lyman Abbott followed in Beecher's footsteps, taking over the pastorate of Plymouth Church in 1887. His book, *How to Succeed* (1882), established him as a true prophet of the success cult.

Though Congregational ministers were most prominent in this line they had considerable competition from leaders of other faiths. The principal Episcopal self-help spokesman was William Lawrence, Bishop of Massachusetts and son of the industrialist Amos A. Lawrence. He memorialized success values in his *Life of Amos A. Lawrence* (1888) and in a famous essay on the "Relation of Wealth to Morals," published in *The World's Work* in 1901. William Van Doren, author of *Mercantile Morals* (1852) occupied a pulpit of the Dutch Reformed Church at Piermont, New York, the town that served as the first eastern terminus of the Erie Railroad. The leading Baptist spokesman was Russell Conwell, a self-made Yankee who built the Baptist Temple in Philadelphia, founded Temple University, and created a popular sensation with his success sermon, *Acres of Diamonds*. Methodism was represented by Daniel Wise, a one-time grocer's apprentice who filled many pulpits in the commercial and industrial towns of New England and New Jersey, and glorified the self-made man in his book, *Uncrowned Kings* (1875).

Of all the popularizers of self-help values none was better known to the post–Civil-War generation than Horatio Alger, who got his start as a Unitarian minister at Brewster, Massachusetts, in 1864. Like Matthew H. Smith before him, Alger abandoned both the pulpit and New England for a literary career in New York. He found his inspirations in the city, as did others who played upon the rags-to-riches theme. Unlike Smith, who reported the doings of Wall Street operators, Alger concentrated on boys who had not yet arrived. He invested his heroes with all the moral virtues honored by the cult of self-help, but even in this he was different, in that Ragged Dick and Tattered Tom won success by some sudden stroke, rather than by steady application to business. These features, together with his preference for the fictional form, set Alger apart from other leading writers in this field.

Even without Alger the success-minded clergy represented a numerous host, and one of great influence in the cult of self-help. They wrote many of the books of its bible, preached its gospel, tried to restrain its excesses, and protected it against the charge of godlessness and materialism. In nineteenth-century America, where the mass of men respected business and religion, the partnership organized by the clergy proved profitable to both.

The doctrine of the secular calling provided the foundation for the religious defense of worldly success. In proclaiming this doctrine American clergymen, like their European predecessors, argued that God required every man to lead a successful and useful temporal life as well as an acceptable spiritual life. Under this conception the calling was an exacting worldly enterprise in which man could conquer his own base nature and overcome the limitations of his social environment. The man who succeeded in his vocation proved that he deserved a high station in this life as well as salvation in the next. Since every man won salvation in his profession, and not outside it, God provided a suitable calling for all. As one authority explained, "The principle is, that however poor, ignorant, or prone to evil we are born, God gives to each a glorious opportunity. If true to him, and if rightly alive to our great advantages, we may make our fortune."

Throughout the nineteenth century clergymen and laymen alike insisted that business stood high on God's list of approved callings. Matthew H. Smith, writing for *Hunt's Merchants' Magazine* in 1854, asserted that God had ordained business as the great purpose in life. "The race were [sic] made for employment," Smith said. "Adam was created and placed in the Garden of Eden for business purposes; it would have been better for the race if he had attended closely to the occupation for which he was made." The man who chose business as a career did not have to fear that he would be cut off from opportunities for spiritual improvement, for the spiritual and the material were united in business. Theodore Parker emphasized this point when he described the merchant as "a moral educator, a church of Christ gone into business—a saint in trade . . . the Saint of the nineteenth century is the Good Merchant; he is wisdom for the foolish, strength for the weak, warning to the wicked, and a blessing to all. Build him a shrine in Bank and Church, in the Market and the Exchange . . . no Saint stands higher than this Saint of Trade." Despite the secularization of American thought in the latter part of the century, the theme of the God-appointed business calling did not lose its popularity with either clerical or lay writers. As the century closed, Orison Marden warned his readers against the "fatal error" of regarding the church as sacred and the warehouse as secular, for both were sacred and uplifting. In the year 1898, Charles P. Masden, a Methodist clergyman in Milwaukee, told a group of business college students that business was not just an occupation but a divine calling. "It is sacred," Masden declared. "It is a means of grace. It is a stewardship. It is building up for eternity, and laying up treasures in heaven."

This did not mean that God disapproved the laying up of treasures on earth. Far from it, for in the American cult of success, as in the Calvinist ethic, the pursuit of wealth became a positive religious duty. Reverend Thomas P. Hunt, one of the earliest writers on this subject, summarized the case for riches in the title of his work: *The Book of Wealth; in Which It Is Proved from the Bible that It Is the Duty of Every Man to Become Rich* (1836). Lyman Abbott rejoiced in the parable of the talents, and used it to justify his claim that Jesus approved the building of great fortunes. "He did not condemn wealth," Abbott declared. "On the contrary, he approved of the use of accumulated wealth to accumulate more wealth." Russell Conwell agreed, for in *Acres of Diamonds* he asserted that it was man's "Christian and godly duty" to seek wealth. Secular writers were especially pleased to have such friendly assurances from the clergy. Edwin T. Freedley, for one, argued that as long as religion sanctioned accumulation, no other sanction was needed.

If religion blessed business by approving the pursuit of wealth it doubled the blessing by sanctifying all the economic virtues essential to its accumulation. Of the virtues dear to the business community, religion exalted industry above all others. God required hard, continuous labor of rich and poor alike, not only as punishment for original sin, but as a constructive means of personal discipline. Labor kept man from sensuality, intemperance, and moral degeneration. It offered an opportunity to worship and glorify God through imitation of his creative labors. When combined with other virtues it allowed man to lay up treasures on earth as well as in heaven, and helped him win an earthly success which served as a measure of his heavenly salvation. Protestant clergy of all denominations agreed that labor had special honor in the sight of God, and that it formed an integral part of true religion. Daniel Wise, a Methodist minister, spoke for all religious prophets of success when he advised a group of young men that "Religion will teach you that industry is a SOLEMN DUTY you owe to God, whose command is, 'BE DILIGENT IN BUSINESS!' " The religious aspect of labor was emphasized so much in the nineteenth century that even secular-minded men sometimes talked of labor in religious terms. Andrew Carnegie, for example, once remarked that an honest day's work was "not a bad sort of prayer."

Frugality also had special honor in the sight of God, and was considered like labor, a positive religious duty. In the tradition of the Protestant ethic the man who aspired to success and salvation was supposed to live simply and frugally, avoiding luxury and ostentation. This tradition carried over into the American ethic of self-help, whose clerical prophets advertised frugality as "the good genius whose presence guides the footsteps of every prosperous and successful man." Through frugality God provided a way to wealth which was open to all, and one which all were supposed to travel. The great exemplar of frugality was none other than Jesus of Nazareth, who, after he had fed the multitude with loaves and fishes, "commanded his disciples to gather up the fragments, lest anything should be wasted." Frugality led inevitably to sobriety, for the man who husbanded his means had nothing left to spend on the vices. "Drinking habits," Henry Ward Beecher observed, "take hold indirectly upon the whole framework of a man's prosperity. They lead to very many expenses besides the daily expenses of the cup."

According to the theology of success God always rewarded the industrious, the frugal, and the sober with wealth. One Episcopal clergyman argued that it would have been surprising indeed if God had not provided material rewards for the faithful practice of his appointed virtues. These rewards, said the cleric, "like all the profit of godliness, are to be gathered in this life as well as in that which is to come." According to this logic the possession of wealth made the possessor one of the elect. Wealth was a gift from God, an evidence of his favor, and a reward for faithfulness—comforting doctrine to substantial pew-holders in urban churches. Apologists who turned to the Scriptures noted that Abraham, Solomon and other Old Testament heroes received wealth from the Lord in token of his approval. "The Old Testament doctrine of wealth is frank and unmistakable," a Unitarian minister told his congregation in 1885. "It is a *blessing from the Lord*. It is a sign of the divine approval. . . ." Little wonder, in view of such assurances, that John D. Rockefeller brushed off his critics with the simple assertion that it was God who had given him his money.

In accounting for the superior prosperity of the well-to-do, clergymen invariably pointed to their superior morality. Russell Conwell insisted that ninety-eight out of every hundred rich Americans stood above their fellowmen in honesty. "That is why they are rich," he said. "That is why they are trusted with money. That is why they carry on great enterprises and find plenty of people to work with them. It is because they are honest men." If one were to accept the gospel of success at face value he would believe that virtually every rich man was a paragon of moral virtue. William Lawrence, Episcopal Bishop of Massachusetts, summarized the clerical point of view when he observed that "in the long run, it is only to the man of morality that wealth comes. . . . We, like the Psalmist, occasionally see the wicked prosper, but only occasionally. . . . Godliness is in league with riches."

Turned around, this doctrine meant that wickedness was in league with poverty. Those who were poor had no reason to reproach the Giver of Gifts, for they had been tested and found deficient in virtue. "It is no respect for persons that causes the Lord to make some rich and some poor," said one authority, "but it comes of His infinite love to all, and His effort to save all from the evils and corruptions of their own hearts." The man who complained against God's wise way of distributing wealth had the root of evil in him. "And is the young man aware, when repining at his penury, that he is reproaching his Maker, and charging Him indirectly with being stingy?" another clergyman asked.

By identifying the rich with the elect and the poor with the damned, clergymen provided strong religious and moral defenses for the well-to-do. He who attacked the rich, or urged a system of distribution favorable to the poor, automatically advertised himself as an enemy of God and of the moral order. Thanks to the religious defense of money-making, wealthy Americans of the nineteenth century knew the meaning of the assurance offered by one popular success handbook: "Heaven taketh notes of thy career, and the angels are guardian watchers and abettors of thy prosperity."

No one-way system of advantages characterized the partnership of God and Mammon. In return for the sanction of religion, businessmen were supposed to be sincerely religious, identifying themselves with the doctrines and activities of the church. Clergymen and laymen alike agreed that the way to wealth passed through the church. A Methodist minister, Daniel Wise, insisted that the qualities necessary for success appeared most often in those who embraced and faithfully followed the teachings of Christ. And William Speer, a lay writer, claimed it was more important for the young man to begin his business career with proper religious perceptions than with a diploma "certifying that he is master of all the 'ologies' of all the colleges." Since Bible-reading developed proper religious perceptions, business-men were constantly advised to seek inspiration in the Scriptures, especially in Solomon's Proverbs. By the same token they were sup-posed to shun those intellectual influences which undermined faith. In the 1890s, after Darwinism, the higher criticism, and the social gospel had made inroads on traditional religion, Edward Bok warned pro-spective businessmen that one of the keys to success was strict adher-ence to the ancient creeds. The man who rejected the faith of his fathers invited disaster. "Without that faith, without that absolute conviction," Bok declared, "he will be hindered and crippled in what-ever he undertakes." Except for Andrew Carnegie, the major post–Civil-War titans did not cripple themselves by straying off the paths of orthodoxy. And at the turn of the twentieth century the vast majority of American business leaders still identified themselves with the Episcopal, Presbyterian, Methodist, Baptist, and other respectable Protestant churches.

Mere affiliation was not enough, however. The responsible man of affairs attended church regularly, after the manner of J. P. Morgan, Jay Cooke, John D. Rockefeller, Peter Cooper, and a host of others. Even on week-days periods of formal worship had their uses. J. P. Morgan sometimes left his office in mid-afternoon to go to St. George's Church, to pray and sing hymns, hour after hour. In the years after the Civil War, Wall Street capitalists paused on their way to the Exchange to seek the Lord's blessing in Trinity Church or stopped there at the end of the day to offer thanks for victories won. Nearby, at the old Dutch church, every day many of the most prominent men on the Street dropped their worldly cares at noon to commune with God through prayer. These worshippers probably agreed with another famous churchgoer, Daniel Drew, who observed that "When a man goes to prayer meeting and class meeting two nights of the week, and to church twice on Sunday, and on week days works at his office from morning till night, his life is made up of about two things—work and worship."

Sometimes these men also played an active role in the work of the church. In addition to attending Episcopal conventions as a deputy from New York, J. P. Morgan usually transported the leading church dignitaries to the convention city. Peter Cooper fulfilled his obliga-tions to the Lord by serving as a Sunday School superintendent, while

John D. Rockefeller taught industry, frugality, and sobriety to young men in a Baptist Bible class. Nor were these exceptional cases. Two close observers of the New York business community testified that the most prominent merchants and financiers could usually be found on Sabbath mornings in the churches interpreting the Scriptures. Making money was important but saving souls appeared to go along with it hand in hand.

If a man had no talents as an evangelist he could at least pay the way for those who did. Men of wealth were expected to support the local work of the church and to underwrite missionary activity in distant vineyards. Methodist ministers encouraged Daniel Drew to endow a theological seminary which would send men out to preach the gospel to a sinful world. The more common tactic was to ask for more magnificent houses of worship; the Astors, Vanderbilts, Rockefellers, Wanamakers, Morgans, Armours, Pullmans, and Mellons were all builders of churches.

Even in the conduct of business affairs there were opportunities to promote religion. In hiring clerks employers could give preference to those with religious connections; self-interest suggested such a policy anyway. They might also coerce clerks into participating in religious observances. Arthur Tappan was exceptional, no doubt, but he showed what could be done. Tappan required his clerks to attend prayer meetings twice a week and regular services twice on Sunday. Every Monday morning his employees had to report what church they had attended, the name of the clergyman, and the texts used as the basis of the sermon. Those employers who had no desire to police the religious activities of their employees could still promote religion by not requiring them to work on the Sabbath and by not asking them to perform deeds that violated their religious scruples. The wise businessman respected evidence of Christian living at all times. "Don't scoff at those . . . who are trying to lead Christian lives," one adviser warned, "and don't for a moment belittle the importance of their competition in the struggle for supremacy. The quiet, easy, smooth-spoken man who is looked upon as a milk-sop, may have in him all the elements of business success." William Van Doren, a Dutch Reformed minister, claimed that he knew one hard-hearted employer who rescinded a Sabbath working order when he discovered that his clerk was ready to sacrifice his job rather than violate the Lord's day. The employer "cared neither for God, heaven, hell, or worse, but he did care for a trusty clerk," Van Doren said. "He knew not the value of an interest in the Redeemer, but he did most accurately understand the value of one, whom nothing of pecuniary interest could tempt." The clerk who advertised that he had lost his job by refusing to work on the Sabbath was bound to receive many offers of employment, for according to the cult of success, church-attending employers always sought Sabbath-observing employees. Creditors also took notice of who went to church. This led one success tract to advise that "A good advertisement for a working man, is a seat in church."

By attending church, participating in its work, underwriting its expenses, and honoring its teachings, the businessman put his stamp of approval on religion. In so doing he reciprocated the application of religious sanctions to business, and sealed the partnership of God and Mammon.

The application of these religious sanctions, however, was by no means automatic. Clergymen who identified themselves with the success cult did not hesitate to pass moral judgment on men and methods in business. Like other authorities on self-help they did not attempt to glorify notorious men like Jay Gould, Jim Fisk, or Daniel Drew, for they generally held that "No amount of money can make a highway robber or any other kind successful. . . . Even millions of plunder does not constitute success, which must include a good name." P. T. Barnum was denounced by Matthew H. Smith who claimed that in his race for wealth Barnum had operated on the principle that any tactic was legitimate so long as it was not criminal. "Humbug, tricks, deceit, low cunning, false stories, were stock in trade," Smith declared. And Henry Ward Beecher pointed from his Plymouth pulpit to "an old obese abomination of money" operating in Wall Street, and warned his congregation against worshipping such a man. "He has utterly defiled and destroyed his manhood in the manufacturing of wealth," Beecher charged; "he is a great epitomized, circulating hell on earth, and when he dies, hell will groan—one more woe."

In order to enjoy the approval of the church wealth had to be earned in an honorable calling, one that contributed to the social welfare. Saloon-keepers, speculators, gamblers, and others who rendered no useful service could not qualify. Merchants, manufacturers, and bankers were honored by the clergy as long as they kept in touch with the needs of mankind and provided the necessary capital, goods, and services. "When will you manufacturers learn that you must know the changing needs of humanity if you would succeed in life?" Russell

Conwell asked. "Apply yourselves, all you Christian people, as manufacturers or merchants or workmen to supply that human need. It is a
great principle as broad as humanity and as deep as the Scripture
itself."

The clergy knew that an honorable calling was not enough,
however, for there were many dishonorable men in reputable voca-
tions. Too many businessmen agreed with the sentiment attributed to
Daniel Drew. "A business man has got to get along somehow," he said.
"Better that my hog should come dirty home, than no hog at all." Such
men, even if they acquired wealth, did not have any honor among
clerical writers of success tracts. "Riches got by fraud, are dug out of
one's own heart and destroy the mine," said Henry Ward Beecher.
"Unjust riches curse the owner in getting, in keeping, in transmitting."
William Van Doren, who was aware of the questionable tactics of
many New York businessmen, insisted that in all fortunes dishonestly
acquired there was a curse which "sooner or later will break forth like
a leprosy." To a widespread belief in the business community that the
completely honest man was at a disadvantage in the quest for wealth,
the clergy answered that whatever the short-term disadvantages, honesty brought the long-term gains. Though the wicked might enjoy a
temporary prosperity, the laws of moral retribution would deprive
them of permanent fortune.

Ministers constantly warned moneymakers of the moral dangers
inherent in their quest. These warnings were not inspired by religious
objections to wealth, but rather by the fear that the passion for money
would lead men into sin. The only man who could seek wealth and
remain morally upright was the one who was capable of the most
rigorous personal discipline. "If you have entered this shining way,
begin to look for snares and traps," warned Henry Ward Beecher. "Go
not careless of your danger, and provoking it." While one rich man
climbed into heaven, ten sank into the bottomless pit of hell. "You seek
a land pleasant to the sight, but dangerous to the feet," Beecher
declared, "a land of fragrant winds, which lull to security; of golden
fruits, which are poisonous; of glorious hues, which dazzle and mis-
lead."

All wealth-seekers ran the risk of making accumulation an end in
itself. Religion warned her business partner against this deadly sin. "It
is folly supreme, nay madness," said William Van Doren, "to make the
acquiring riches, and enjoying them, the chief end of life." The man
who coveted wealth for its own sake was a mere beast of burden, who

would go "toiling beneath his load, with gold on his back, and hell in his heart, down to destruction." Clergymen who taught that Jesus approved the quest for wealth also taught that Jesus scorned the man who loved the quest for its own sake. He who did not think beyond the problems of accumulation was hell-bent. "The man that worships the dollar instead of thinking of the purposes for which it ought to be used, the man who idolizes simply money, the miser that hordes his money in the cellar, or hides it in his stocking, or refuses to invest it where it will do the world good, that man who hugs the dollar until the eagle squeals," Russell Conwell warned, "has in him the root of all evil."

Since the twin of miserliness was prodigality, clergymen had to remind their business associates that God had not given them wealth just to live merrily and without care. In the eyes of the church it was a sin for the wealthy to waste their substance on luxurious clothing, lavish entertainment, great mansions, and other forms of ostentatious display. The rich man was meant to live simply and frugally, spending no more than necessary for his subsistence. Here, as elsewhere, moderation should characterize his actions; he should be neither miserly nor prodigal but follow instead a middle course.

The doctrine of the stewardship of wealth provided the clue to the right use of wealth. Since it was God who had made the rich man's lot different from that of his poor brother, his money was simply held in trust to be used in doing God's work. Thus it could not be used exclusively for his own benefit, but must be applied primarily to the benefit of others. In practice this meant support of schools, libraries, museums, orphanages, hospitals, churches, and similar beneficent institutions. As a one-time Unitarian minister, Ralph Waldo Emerson, explained, "They should own who can administer, not they who hoard and conceal; not they who, the great proprietors they are, are only the great beggars, but they whose work carves out the work for more, opens a path for all. For he is the rich man in whom the people are rich, and he is the poor man in whom the people are poor. . . ." By this reasoning the good steward could be considered as much a saint as any saint of the church and as deserving of religious honor.

The church's teachings on the subject of wealth provided the foundation on which secular writers built an elaborate body of doctrine concerning the ethics of success, but they also provided the businessman with a convenient rationale by which he could justify his superior position in society. It would be a mistake, however, to assume that all those who used the rationale either lived by its precepts or gave them a respectful hearing. Occasionally God and Mammon exchanged harsh words. In 1891 an English Methodist minister, Hugh Price Hughes, condemned Andrew Carnegie for piling up a fortune at the expense of his fellowmen. Carnegie, who never took the partnership of business and religion seriously, was so nettled by the attack that he hurled back into the minister's teeth the parable of the talents and the teaching of John Wesley, founder of the Methodist faith: "Gain all you can by honest industry." Clergymen, in time, grew weary of businessmen who quoted the Scriptures to suit their own purposes. It was no accident that the Episcopal and Congregational churches, which had led all others in providing spokesmen for the self-help cult before 1890, became the most productive of clergymen of the social gospel after that date. With the rise of the social gospel, ministers like Washington Gladden, George D. Herron, W. D. P. Bliss, Bouck White, and Walter Rauschenbusch tried to dissolve the partnership of God and Mammon.

23

Poor Richard and Playboy

MORTON L. ROSS

Mr. Hugh Hefner, editor-publisher of *Playboy* magazine, is now famous and affluent enough to have been explained by a number of interesting names. The less pejorative include "moral benefactor," "liberator," "theologian," "oracle," and "prophet." Even this small collection of wowsers means that whatever Mr. Hefner *qua* Hefner really is, he has become, like kosher pizza and the late Clara Bow, a cultural phenomenon. Whether Mr. Hefner welcomes this status is

Reprinted by permission of *The Colorado Quarterly* from Morton L. Ross, "Poor Richard and *Playboy*: brothers under the flesh," *The Colorado Quarterly*, XV (Spring, 1967). Copyright, 1967, by the University of Colorado, Boulder, Colorado.

literally, of course, his business; whether it can be here and properly explained is mine. And the way to begin is to insist that labels like the above are shamefully inadequate. The truth is simply that Hefner as cultural phenomenon is the twentieth century avatar of Benjamin Franklin. To know Hefner, then, we must begin with Ben.

Dr. Franklin's attendance at the birth of so many other American institutions may obscure his services as obstetrician for the nation's capitalism, but it's true that even before Hamilton and his colleagues could deliver infant capitalism to the new Republic, Franklin had provided prenatal care by creating necessary habits in the public mind. The problem of a people seeking economic as well as political independence is to create its own capital, and the least dependent method is simple abstinence. Franklin was the colonies' most vocal champion of the abstemious, or squirrel, virtues, industry and frugality. By practicing industry, he tirelessly insisted, the amount produced could be increased. By practicing frugality, one could refrain from consuming some of the increased production, thereby creating even more capital.

Franklin did not, of course, invent the Protestant Ethic; his unique contribution to this lovely marriage of money and morals was to publish its banns. His media were those snappy maxims, now part of folklore, spread to the tradesmen and farmers of his day in the pages of *Poor Richard's Almanack* appearing between 1733 and 1758. Franklin described the *Almanack* in his *Autobiography* as "a proper vehicle for conveying instruction among the common people, who bought scarcely any other books," and explained his choice of proverbial sentences as "chiefly such as inculcated industry and frugality, as a means of procuring wealth and thereby securing virtue."

The economic essence of Poor Richard was distilled in Franklin's famous sermon *The Way to Wealth*, so enduringly popular that it has since appeared in more than seventy English editions and has been translated into at least sixteen languages, including such exotic script as Catalan and phonetic writing. Father Abraham, another of Ben's avatars, there delivers himself of some choice Poor Richardisms: "We may make the times better, if we bestir ourselves. There are no gains without pains, then help hands for I have no land. . . . A fat kitchen makes a lean will, as Poor Richard says. If you would be wealthy, think of saving as well as getting." Such is the stuff of capitalism's folklore; for us the verbal vestiges of the institution's past.

But the infant institution nursed by Franklin has aged, and its mature needs are far different from, indeed the reverse of, those of its swaddling days. The change has made Ben's once good advice at worst obsolete, at best embarrassing. Franklin had to assume an economy of scarcity; we must assume an economy of abundance. Franklin demanded abstention from consumption in order to create capital; we must consume mightily in order to further multiply capital. In short Franklin's ethics of production served an infant capitalism; we now need an ethics of consumption to maintain a mature one. And it is just here, of course, that Mr. Hefner, as cultural phenomenon, was born; or rather it is just here that Dr. Franklin refreshes himself with an avatar.

This simple fact would have been recognized long ago had not the dazzling flesh of Hefner's *Playboy* hidden the Poor Richard within. Hefner himself has been coy as a belly dancer's navel about acknowledging his debt, allowing only the slyest confessions as on the occasion when his editors finally granted Franklin the title of "that respected playboy of the past." But usually two hundred years of improvements in the arts of making magazines amply enfold the old gentleman in the new fashions.

Properly exposed, however, the Franklin pit in Hefner's peach is revealing in more ways than one. For instance, it tends to exonerate Hefner from one of the more frivolous charges brought against him. Those who fulminate against the naked cuties in his magazine must understand that the girl on the gatefold is only the shill to get the marks into the tent. Once here the citizen is subject to a proselytizing much more severe than easy invitations to lust. A new, now swinging Father Abraham takes over and his message—the essence of *Playboy* —is simply Franklin's prudential ethics, differing from the original only because of a slight temporal adjustment. As a *Playboy* editor once mused: "Every time we're told that a penny saved is a penny earned, we find ourselves wishing there were some governmental bureau to adjust proverbs—like price supports or vital statistics—to take into account the advance of civilization." The man was badly misled; no need to look to the government when his own free-enterprising employer has done the job. Ben urges us to be frugal; Hefner implores us to be prodigal. Ben counsels us to productive industry; Hefner enjoins us to strenuous leisure. As *Playboy* says, "chaste makes waste." And while it's true that the original maxims for active abstinence have given way to those for active indulgence because the institution their preacher serves has matured, all else is the same. The economic moralist is in business at the same old stance. As Marx inverted Hegel, so Hefner has turned Franklin outside in, but in the process of reëmbodying the old essence, he has retained enough of Franklin's manner to make it a dead giveaway.

Hefner repeatedly describes himself as a man with a deep sense of mission, on one occasion as "a rather dedicated and one-way kind of guy." And he has been candid about the mission, carefully explaining that "our editorial emphasis is on entertainment and leisure-time activity rather than on the ways in which man earns his daily bread and yet the articles, on the creature comforts and the infinite variety of man's more elegant, leisure-time possessions, clearly stress that these are the prizes available in our society in return for honest endeavor and hard work." The prudential virtues recommended by Franklin are, then, by no means their own reward. Once they have accomplished the accumulation of capital, they quite naturally become their opposites, indulgence and prodigality, now enjoying the prizes which Franklin implicitly promised and which Hefner graphically displays.

The essential identity of these two economic moralists is further established by certain shared habits. There is, for example, their aggressive candor in discussing the uses of venery, or the fact that both, having early arrived at fame and fortune, devote their declining years to good works, then the Philadelphia charities, now the newly chartered, nonprofit Playboy Foundation. Note also the emphatic protest of Franklin-Hefner against harsh and repressive sex laws. It was in the course of such a protest, as a matter of fact, that Franklin anticipated his modern avatar by inventing the playmate bunny. Striking at the law of Puritan Massachusetts, Franklin imagined the plea of one Polly Baker, early swinger, to her judge. She argues that it is wrong to punish her for doing her duty, "the duty of the first and great command of nature, and of nature's God, *encrease and multiply*. A duty, from the steady performance of which, nothing has been able to deter me; but for its sake, I have hazarded the loss of the publick esteem, . . . and therefore ought, in my humble opinion, instead of a whipping, to have a statue erected to my memory." In at least a symbolic sense, Hefner's cottontail legions are Polly's true memorial.

Such parallels are, however, minor when compared with the rather startling truth that Hefner was seemingly compelled to adapt the entire format of his magazine from that of *Poor Richard's Alma-*

nack. Compare, for example, this advertisement for the first issue of the *Almanack* with the table of contents in any *Playboy.* In addition to Lunations and Eclipses, retained by Hefner as the Bunny Calendar, Richard Saunders' first offering included "many pleasant and witty verses, jests and sayings, author's motive of writing, Moon no Cuckold, Batchelor's Folly, New Fashions, Games for Kisses, Katherine's Love, Conjugal Debate, Men and Melons, Breakfast in Bed." *Playboy's* gustatory adventures find models in Poor Richard's often exotic receipts, one for "Dauphiny Soup, which in Turkey is call [sic] Trouble." "International Datebook" is the economy jet set's version of Poor Richard's listings of the annual fairs and Quaker general meetings. Poor Richard's homely counsels on when to plant "pease" are extended by the *Playboy* advisor who is knowledgeable on such anxiety-producing matters as whether the pleats of the cummerbund should be worn opening upward or downward or who should mount the tandem bicycle first, boy or girl. The point is simply that despite the gaudy new exterior, the old American come-on and know-how remain unmistakably the same.

Perhaps the most direct hints that we are in the presence of Poor Richard when we read *Playboy* are the ruminations of J. Paul Getty, self-made billionaire and the magazine's contributing editor for finance and business. Getty frequently out-Franklins Franklin. For instance, in an essay in the April, 1965, issue called 'Force of Habit," Getty perhaps unwittingly illustrates his title as he revives one of Ben's maxims: "That ancient adage 'Time is money' has always been valid and it is more valid today than ever before." Getty continues at some length to make the familiar case for the habit of thrift and its related virtues, the old prudential ethics thus nesting comfortably amid its modern brothers in *Playboy.* Getty's essays for the magazine have now been collected and published by the Playboy Press as *How to be Rich,* a title making it the obvious sequel for those generations who have arrived via Franklin's *The Way to Wealth.*

For those who remain unconvinced that Hefner is Franklin's avatar, the final argument is of course that neither of these economic moralists quite practices what he preaches. In Franklin's career, this discrepancy is revealed in his *Autobiography,* justly celebrated as the first American success story. In form the work is a classic comedy, charting the protagonist's rise in fortune "from the poverty and obscurity in which I was born and bred, to a state of affluence and some degree of reputation in the world." This ascending curve displays his career as an exemplum demonstrating that the assiduous practice of the prudential virtues would, in fact, lead to capitalistic success.

Yet read the story carefully and it reveals Ben as being less interested in being industrious and frugal than in appearing so. The reason is simply that the money which gave him his start did *not* come from capital accumulated through personal industry and frugality; it came instead from wealthy patrons who saw him as a good risk, amiably conned by their protégé's skill in projecting the image of industry and frugality. "In order to secure my credit and character as a tradesman, I took care not only to be in *reality* industrious and frugal, but to avoid all *appearances* of the contrary."

The record is rich in further evidence of Franklin's skill with appearances. For example, "to show that I was not above my business, I sometimes brought home the paper I purchas'd at the stores, thro' the streets on a wheelbarrow. Thus being esteemed an industrious thriving young man, . . . I went on swimmingly." Even Franklin's lapses from prudence are done with an eye to public response. "A book, indeed, sometimes debauch'd me from my work; but that was seldom, snug, and gave no scandal." As Franklin later says of his attempt to practice humility: "I cannot boast of much success in acquiring the *reality* of this virtue; but I had a good deal with regard to the *appearance* of it." Much the same can be said for his performance of the capital-producing virtues he so ardently thrusts upon us.

Mr. Hefner has not yet written his autobiography, although the cinema version has been long announced, but his technicolor rise to affluence and celebrity, a curve repeating Franklin's, has prompted several reportorial glimpses into his private life, among them Bill Davidson in *Saturday Evening Post*, Diana Lurie in *Life*, and Richard Gehman in *Fact*. Their approach, by now seemingly definitive, has been to offer two Hefners, the public Playboy and the one I now must insist is the private Franklin. Out front, of course, Hefner is suave, urbane, London tailored, Escoffier fed, potable loaded, and given to tasting every delight from Abelard to Zucchini-Flambeau. The insiders tell us he is driven, boyish, habitually pajamaed, short-order fed, Pepsi-filled, and happiest when consumed by his enterprise—in short a most careless consumer.

In fact recent probings of Hefner's private life have given the impression that he lives in a cork-lined closet in the bowels of his mansion, spinning the gaudy world of *Playboy* out of the constantly strained resources of his personal industry and frugality. This tension between public and private Hefner displays the man as what a longer-lived Franklin might have been. In the old days, Franklin took pains to be publicly industrious and frugal, debauching only in the snugness of his closet where it gave no scandal. Today Hefner must spectacularly debauch in public, and only in the snugness of *his* closet can he be, without scandal, industrious and abstemious.

It would be base to accuse these economic moralists of deliberate hypocrisy. That the demands of their role force them into behavior at variance with their personal inclinations might, for all we know, be the price of success. Their common inability, however, to meet the demands of the virtuous life which they lay on others does suggest that while the prophetic spirit of capitalist morality that sustains them both is forever willing, the flesh they share with us is weak.

PURITANISM AND DEMOCRACY

24

The Idea of the Covenant and American Democracy
H. RICHARD NIEBUHR

. . . One of the great common patterns that guided men in the period when American democracy was formed, that was present both in their understanding and in their action, and was used in psychology, sociology and metaphysics as in ethics, politics and religion, was the pattern of the covenant or of federal society.

It is not meant that this was the exclusive pattern in the minds of all men or exclusively present in the minds of any man. None of our symbols, save in fanaticism, is likely to be exclusively employed and there are few periods, if any, in human history when a dominant pattern of interpretation does not have its rivals. What is suggested is that a *fundamental* pattern in American minds in the seventeenth, eighteenth and early nineteenth centuries was the covenant idea, competing with the mechanical pattern and displacing the organic and hierarchical ideas.

Reprinted by permission from *Church History*, XXIII (June, 1954), pp. 129–35. The article from which this selection is taken advances two hypotheses respecting the moral and intellectual character of American democracy. "The first of these hypotheses," writes Professor Niebuhr, "is general; it does not apply to America only but to men, to Western men at least, in their various cultures. It reads: There is at all times a close correspondence and a dialectical relationship among the general ideas men hold about their own constitution, that of the societies and of the world in which they live; their efforts at self-control (ethics), at social construction (politics), and their attitudes toward their ultimate environment (religion) are in consequence influenced by similar ideas." The second hypothesis, the subject of this selection, "is a special application of the first one." It has to do with the relation of the idea of the covenant to American democracy.

The significance of the covenant idea for Puritan thought in the seventeenth and early eighteenth centuries has been called to our attention, after a long period of neglect, by Professor Perry Miller in his *Orthodoxy in Massachusetts, The New England Mind* and *From Colony to Province.* As the religious thought of the seventeenth and eighteenth centuries is being more adequately explored other studies are beginning to contribute to our knowledge of this idea. At the same time new studies in the ideas of the Scriptures, such as Pedersen's *Israel* and Eichrodt's *Theology of the Old Testament,* illuminate this aspect of that view of human life in its world which is native to the book that was more widely and thoroughly read than any other by the small and great founders of America. It is often pointed out and as frequently forgotten by those who seek to understand the minds of Englishmen and Americans in the seventeenth, eighteenth and nineteenth centuries, that, in Trevelyan's words, "The effect of the continual domestic study of the book (i. e. the Bible) upon the national character, imagination and intelligence for three centuries—was greater than that of any literary movement in our annals, or any religious movement since St. Augustine." The idea of covenant had many proximate sources as it was developed in the Netherlands, in England, and in America during the seventeenth century. It had roots in Calvin; it was suggested and influenced, no doubt, by the development of contract law and of commercial companies; it was raised to special significance in religious circles by the reaction against a mechanical version of Calvinistic determinism. But its chief source in the Scriptures was available to all men and not only available but pervasively present.

If the dialectical theory of the development of the great patterns is true then the covenant idea may be thought of as something which, originating in the experience of social compacts by early Israelites, was extended to the understanding of the cosmos and, as reunderstood in its application to divine-human and divine-natural relations, was then reapplied to social life and to personal existence in society and the cosmos. In the seventeenth century there seems to be a kind of re-enactment of this earlier history, though in dependence on it, with variations due to the new experiences of the time.

We may begin to define the covenant idea by noting its application to the ultimate environment, in the effort to understand the cosmic scene of human life in history. This ultimate environment, it is affirmed, is one, integrated, unified. We live neither in a world of dualistic principles at war with each other nor in a pluralistic environment of many gods or other forces. If there is chance in this world, even chance is under control, subject therefore to a kind of prediction. This unity is not to be conceived after the pattern of a logical system of thought, not as similar to a mathematical system, nor after the idea of a machine, though logical, mathematical and mechanical relations are present in it. Its unity is much more like that of human society than like that of human mind or human technique. Hence such phrases as kingdom of God, *Civitas Dei*, Divine Commonwealth are to be employed in referring to it; and when speaking of natural phenomena, the behavior of stars and gases, the political symbol of law is preferred to the symbols of automatic action.

This ultimate world, however, is not like a family, though the phrases Father and Son and children can be significantly employed with reference to certain features in it. Nor is it a company, nor a democracy in which there is a certain equality among the members. The will of the members of this society is never sovereign. They neither elect themselves into being, nor can they choose under what ultimate laws they shall live. They are the objects of action before they are its subjects. There is a thus-and-so-ness about their existence, about the conditions under which they live and die, with their bodies, given constitutions and the inescapable demands made upon them so that if the social image is to be employed at all it must be the image of an absolute kingship.

But the image of absolute despotism does not fit. There is a tie between monarch and subjects and a relationship among the subjects not compatible with the idea of absolute monarchy. The world is a peculiar kind of society in which all parts are bound to each other by *promises*. Promise or covenant is the ordering principle. There is nothing arbitrary about the king, for he is above all faithful and has bound himself to govern in accordance with purposes and the laws that he has promulgated. Though there seems to be something arbitrary about his original promulgation of the laws, there is nothing arbitrary in his administration. He does not change them because he has favorites; he is not subject to whims and caprices; his unity is like the unity of the loyal man who though he has sworn even to his own hurt does not change. Furthermore, the laws by which the king has promised to govern, in the freedom of his sovereign decision, are not unknown. Some are indeed beyond present understanding, but the processes of nature, the reason of man and the revelation of the divine will make the content of much of the fundamental law of the universe known to man. The administration of the world is reliable; the laws can be known by means of patient inquiry; their execution can be counted upon. The fundamental characteristic of the powerful One is that he is faithful, keeping his promise.

Again, this ultimate society in which men live is one in which as subjects they are invited and ultimately required to achieve the maturity of full citizenship, to accept the laws as their own, to enter into a kind of reciprocal relationship with the king and each other, engaging by promise to maintain and support a commonwealth they did not create but in whose administration they are privileged to participate. The significance of all the special covenants into which God enters with man under the fundamental covenant is this, that by their means a free and responsible citizenry is to be brought forth out of what, as a result of the great perversion, had become a mass of slaves, partly supine in the acceptance of fate, partly in insurrection against the rule they can not escape. But it is the design of the ultimate ruler and the ultimate commonwealth that government should be not only by consent of the governed but with their participation in it.

The idea of the macrocosm as a covenant society had been derived in part from the experience of human societies of a more than "natural" sort in which men entered into relationship with each other not on the basis of feeling or of blood-kinship only but of mutual compact and promise. The covenant idea, so developed, was applied in turn to all human societies. Even when their basis was in nature, as in the case of the relationship of the sexes, they now were seen to become truly human societies only when promise or covenant was added to and transformed the natural. The question was not whether society has a natural or a contract origin but to what extent every society becomes truly human and truly a society within the cosmic society by having the moral dimension, or the covenant character, added to it. Religious society so regarded could no longer be merely a community of those who had similar interests in the supernatural or a society of those who held the same religious beliefs, though it was that. It did not become complete society until interest was disciplined by promise, obedience to external laws internalized by the oath of fealty, duties to God associated with freely accepted, promised duties to one another and, in general, belief supplemented and transformed by the will to be loyal. The covenant theory of relationships did not necessarily mean that the religious society should be made up of *individuals* without previous common relationships. But it meant that even a natural religious society did not become true church until it became a covenanted church based on promises. One must not read into the seventeenth century, for instance, the individualism that characterized the later revival periods and then regard the half-way covenant as a great distortion of original doctrine. It was probably quite in line with the original idea of covenant.

Covenant meant that political society was neither purely natural nor merely contractual, based on common interest. Covenant was the binding together in one body politic of persons who assumed through unlimited promise responsibility to and for each other and for the common laws, under God. It was government of the people, for the people and by the people but always under God, and it was not natural birth into natural society that made one a complete member of the people but always the moral act of taking upon oneself, through promise, the responsibilities of a citizenship that bound itself in the very act of exercising its freedom. For in the covenant conception the essence of freedom does not lie in the liberty of choice among goods, but in the ability to commit oneself for the future to a cause and in the terrible liberty of being able to become a breaker of the promise, a traitor to the cause. (I use these terms in dependence on Josiah Royce who alone among American modern philosophers has seen and explored in his philosophy of loyalty the meaning of this kind of liberty and this dimension of common life.)

The view of man associated with these ideas about the world and about society was one that set his will, in the sense of his ability to commit himself by means of promise, at the center of his being. To be sure man was a rational being; he was a being with many interests; he was a happiness-seeker; but above all his distinguishing characteristic was moral. As moral man he was a being who could be trusted or ought to be trustworthy because he had given his word, pledged himself to be faithful to the cause and the fellow-servants of the cause. All the perversion which has entered into man's relationships to God and to his fellow-men through his distrust of divine faithfulness and his breaking of his own promises cannot change the fundamental fact that the moral requirement and ability of promise-keeping is central to human existence.

The conception of the covenant in the macrocosm, the mesocosm and the microcosm has been confused in the beginning and throughout subsequent history with other patterns. It was mixed in Calvin and in the Westminster Puritans and, I believe, in Jonathan Edwards with the idea of the machine. Thus ideas of *pre*determination (not ideas of election) were connected with the thought of design and of mechanical construction rather than of covenant. In Deism the mechanical image prevailed so far as the macrocosm was concerned and tended to be carried over into the political realm. From this point of view civil society was largely a self-regulating mechanism that required very little government, very little assertion of human moral freedom, since liberty to pursue one's interests was the motive spring that had been supplied while inherent laws such as those of sympathy regulated the moving parts so that harmony resulted.

On the other hand the covenant idea was confused with the idea of contract from which it had been in part derived. But contract meant something rather different from covenant. In religion it meant that God was a being who had contracted to do certain things for men in case they performed certain reciprocal duties toward him, not that he had obligated himself to maintain his realm and its laws and to liberate its citizens no matter what the cost to them or him might be. Marriage also could be regarded as a contract, entered into for the sake of gaining certain common advantages, not a covenant of unlimited commitment. Civil or political society too could be interpreted as based on limited contract into which men entered with parts of themselves, as it were, for limited purposes and which they might reject if they did not gain from it the benefits they had been promised in the contract. Contract always implies limited, covenant unlimited commitment; contract is entered into for the sake of mutual advantages; covenant implies the presence of a cause to which all advantages may need to be sacrificed. The tendency of the covenant idea to degenerate into the limited contract idea is evident in all the later religious and social history.

To what extent the covenant idea forms the chief unconscious background of American democracy as we know it, I will not venture to assess. Our democracy contains various and disparate elements in it from beginning to end. The mechanistic idea of the world and of human life with *laissez faire* as the consequent policy and freedom to pursue one's own happiness as the motive force; the contract idea of limited obligations and of mutual aid organization—these have always been with us. But one may raise the question whether our common life could have been established, could have been maintained and whether it can endure without the presence of the conviction that we live in a world that has the moral structure of a covenant and without the presence in it of men who have achieved responsible citizenship by exercising the kind of freedom that appears in their taking upon themselves the obligations of unlimited loyalty, under God, to principles of truth-telling, of justice, of loyalty to one another, of indissoluble union. Can freedom of religion be maintained on a contract basis, i.e. on the basis of tolerating one another? Or does it presuppose the presence in men of a sense of responsibility to a cause that goes beyond all limited causes and their acceptance of explicit loyalty to a community of faithfulness that is eternal and inclusive? Is freedom of speech a right that could have been maintained in society where there was no prior implicit and unlimited promise among the members that they would be loyal to truth as they saw it and not bear false witness against their neighbor?

Perhaps the problem of democracy is never soluble in historical terms but only in terms of contemporary action. All the forces that have contended in our common life from the beginning are with us today and some new ones have been added. In our situation some men are making their decisions in democracy on the basis of the conception that the world at large is a field of forces, that man himself is a similar complex of powers and that social life is something that must be engineered as a system of pressures and counter-pressures. Others may be making their decisions with the conviction that a great machine is operative and seek their small freedoms within a large determinism. But the conviction that the world is fundamentally a moral society, that those who are bound to each other by nature and interest must bind themselves to each other by unlimited promises to be loyal to one another in common loyalty to universal principles is a conviction that is also present. Whatever the influences of Christianity on the development of American democracy have been in the past, there is no small number of men in this society today who participate in its actions, exercise their pressures, use their freedom, as those who believe that the world has this fundamental moral structure of a covenant society and that what is possible and required in the political realm is the affirmation and reaffirmation of man's responsibility as a promise-maker, promise-keeper, a covenanter in universal community. I know no way by which their influence can be measured. But they and their principles are and have been an element in our democracy. It is safe to say that without Christianity, so broadly defined, our democracy would be something quite different from what it is.

25

Theological Convictions and Democratic Government
WINTHROP S. HUDSON

It is sometimes suggested that democracy arose quite independently of any religious roots or presuppositions, either as a result of pressures exerted by a rising middle class or as a consequence of forces generated by a frontier society. It is maintained by others that religion in general—any religion and all religion—provides the indispensable moral and spiritual foundations for a democratic society. Both contentions are equally false. Democracy, as it is understood in America, is the product of religious convictions and rests upon certain very definite theological assumptions. But this is not to say that religion in general does provide or will provide the necessary undergirding of our democratic way of life.

A belief in God is no guarantee that a person will be a good "democrat," just as a belief in God is no guarantee that a person will be kindly, compassionate, humble, and forgiving. Arthur Schlesinger, Jr., has asserted . . . that "the whole record of history . . . gives proof that a belief in God has created . . . (overweening) vanity . . . and (intolerable) arrogance." Schlesinger, of course, was simply stating what all great religious leaders have asserted—that it makes a difference *what* God one believes in. Religion may be responsible for all that is noblest in human life, but religion also has written many of the bloodiest and most tragic chapters of human history. A deeply religious man, a zealot and fanatic who has lost any sense of human limitation and human fallibility and who finds in his faith no reason for humility, is a most dangerous person. If it is true that it makes a difference what kind of a God we believe in, the scope of our inquiry must be to identify that type of faith which has nurtured democratic institutions and whose theological assumptions have provided the structural support for a democratic society.

Reprinted with the permission of *Theology Today* from Winthrop S. Hudson, "Theological Convictions and Democratic Government," *Theology Today*, X (July, 1953).

André Siegfried, a French observer of the American scene, has said: "If we wish to understand the real sources of American inspiration, we must go back to the English Puritanism of the seventeenth century." And Lord Bryce, in his *American Commonwealth,* which is perhaps the most perceptive account of American institutions and mores that has yet been written, made this point more explicit in terms of our political structure:

> *There is a hearty Puritanism in the view of human nature which pervades the instrument of 1787. . . . It is the work of men who believed in original sin, and were resolved to leave open for transgressors no door which they could possibly shut. Comparo this spirit with the enthusiastic optimism of the Frenchman of 1789. It is not merely a difference of race and temperaments; it is a difference of fundamental ideas.*

It would seem to be no mere coincidence that modern democracy— with its checks and balances and its insistence upon minority rights— arose and put down its deepest roots in lands most deeply influenced by the Reformed faith—in England, Scotland, Holland, Switzerland, the United States, and the British Dominions. It would also seem to be no mere coincidence that it is largely only within these lands that democracy has been able to offer effective resistance to the totalitarian revolutions of the twentieth century.

In assessing the role of religion in a democracy, we must first inquire as to what are the indispensable theological bases of democratic government which have been contributed by the Churches of the Puritan-Calvinist-Reformed tradition. Far from being derived from any abstract philosophical ideas as to human freedom and equality, democracy as we understand it in America was derived from the three theological doctrines of the sovereignty of God, human bondage to sin, and a particular understanding of the way in which the implications of revelation are made known and confirmed. From these three doctrines, in turn, were derived an insistence upon fundamental law, limitation of power, and the efficacy of discussion and persuasion.

The first postulate was *the absolute sovereignty of God.* In the realm of politics, this meant that God, as Calvin said, is the "King of kings" to whose will the desires of earthly princes must be forever subject, to whose decrees their commands must yield, to whose majesty their sceptres must submit (*Institutes,* IV, xx, 32). In other words, a king, a prince, a magistrate is limited in the exercise of his power by the superior authority of God, and consequently the rule of all civil government must always be in subjection to the precepts of the moral law. The king can do no wrong. He must abide by the dictates of the fundamental law—a higher law than any statutory enactments.

The moral law to which all governments are subject, said Calvin, is no mere arbitrary divine requirement. Its purpose is to secure the well-being of mankind, and the purpose of civil government is to make the moral law effective in the life of the world. The vocation of magistrates, therefore, is "not to rule for their own interest but for the public good." Magistrates are "ordained by God for the well-being of mankind." Consequently, they are not "endued with unbridled power, but what is restricted to the well-being of their subjects; in short they are responsible to God and to men in the exercise of their power" (*Commentary on Romans*, 13: 3–4). It is the moral law, then, which serves as a "bridle" to the governing power, and Calvin suggested that the judicial law which implements the moral law should be reduced to writing so that "recourse may be had to the written law" and thus "the mutual obligation of head and members" may be made apparent to all (cf. Herbert D. Foster, *Collected Papers*, pp. 81–82). It was quite in keeping with this point of view that the founding fathers drafted a written constitution to "establish justice, insure domestic tranquility, provide for the common defense, promote the general welfare, and secure the blessings of liberty to ourselves and our posterity," and it was equally in keeping with this point of view that the Bill of Rights should begin with the phrase: "Congress shall make no law respecting . . . ."

The concept of fundamental law led not only to constitutionalism. It had as its corollary the right of resistance. When a king fails to abide by the moral law, he ceases to be a king and becomes a tyrant whom the people are duty-bound to resist and against whom, if he persists in his tyranny, they are obligated to rebel. Nowhere is this principle stated more clearly than in the American *Declaration of Independence:*

> *We hold these truths to be self-evident, that all men are created equal, that they are endowed by their Creator with certain unalienable rights, that among these are life, liberty, and the pursuit of happiness—that to secure these rights, governments are instituted among men . . . that whenever any form of government becomes destructive of these*

ends, it is the right of the people to alter or abolish it. . . . Prudence, indeed, will dictate that governments long established should not be changed for light and transient causes. . . . But when a long train of abuses and usurpations . . . evinces a design to reduce them under absolute despotism, it is their right, it is their duty, to throw off such government, and to provide new guards for their future security.

To provide guards for their security is a key phrase. It leads us to the second proposition that *all earthly power must be limited, because earthly power is forever subject to the temptation to exalt itself in rebellion against God and the common good.* If recourse to the ultimate expedient of revolution is to be avoided, the exercise of power must be subjected to constitutional restraints. The basic postulate here is that all men, without exception, are in bondage to sin. As Robert Barclay, the great Quaker theologian, put it: "All Adam's posterity, or mankind . . . is fallen, degenerated, and dead . . . and is subject unto the power, nature, and seed of the Serpent." Therefore, short of the harmonization of all powers in God's final act of redemption, the only possible procedure in dealing with the universal tendency of all human power to absolutize itself was to surround it with limitations. Human nature being what it is, all unchecked power could lead only to a defiance of God and a contemptuous indifference to the common good.

Let all the world learn to give mortal man no greater power than they are content they shall use, for use it they will. . . . It is necessary that all power that is on earth be limited, church-power or other. . . . It is counted a matter of danger to the state to limit prerogatives, but it is a further danger not to have them limited.

This was a warning voiced by John Cotton, but it reflects the common conviction of all who had gone to school to John Calvin. The fundamental assumption, as it applies to political life, was phrased by Calvin with characteristic irony in these words: "It very rarely happens that kings regulate themselves so that their will is never at variance with justice and rectitude," nor are they "endowed with such penetration and prudence as in all cases to discover what is best" (*Institutes*, IV, xx, 8).

How is political power to be limited so that the common good—which is the principal end of the moral law—may be made secure? Calvin suggested that this would be accomplished in part by the extension of the franchise, so that the self-interest of the one or of the few may be checked by the self-interest of the many. "It is safer and more tolerable for the government to be in the hands of the many, that they may afford each other mutual assistance and admonition, and that if any one arrogate to himself more than is right, the many may act as censors and masters to restrain his ambition." "No kind of government is more happy than this . . . and I consider those most happy people who are permitted to enjoy such a condition" in which they have the right and the duty to "exert their strenuous and constant efforts" to preserve their liberties. This is "the best condition of the people, when they can choose by common consent their own shepherds; for when any one by force usurps the supreme power, it is tyranny, and when men become kings by hereditary right, it seems not consistent with liberty" (*Institutes,* IV, xx, 8; *Commentary on Micah,* 5: 5).

It must not be supposed that Calvin was an advocate of democracy in the Greek or classical sense of the word. John Winthrop was later to declare, "A democracy is, among most civil nations, accounted the meanest and worst of all forms of government"; and Calvin would have agreed. While "the transition," said Calvin, "is easy from monarchy to despotism," and "not much more difficult from aristocracy to oligarchy . . . it is most easy of all from democracy to sedition" (*Institutes,* IV, xx, 8). Even a majority, Calvin well knew, could become tyrannical and seek to subvert the rights of the minority. Hence any system of government needed to be equipped with checks and limitations designed to prevent the exercise of arbitrary power. It was for this reason that he advocated what he called a "mixed state" embracing elements both of democracy and aristocracy, which is precisely what we in America have traditionally understood by the word democracy.

A "mixture of aristocracy and democracy" was the form of government advocated by the leaders of the American Revolution, and it was this form of government which was adopted in the Federal Constitution. Instead of a "mixed state," we call it a representative democracy, but it possesses all the features of that mixture of aristocracy and democracy which Calvin regarded as essential in an ideal commonwealth. The separation of powers in the American Constitution, as well as the reservation of a large portion of the powers to local government, reveals a typically Calvinistic distrust of the concentration of authority. These "checks and balances" of our system of government are familiar enough, but the aristocratic features of the system are not always so generally recognized. In the federal government, the judges—the guardians of the liberties of the people—are appointed for life. The Executive originally was intended to be (and still is theoretically) chosen by a council of the "wisest heads" of the nation, and the Executive, in turn, with the advice and consent of the Senate, appoints the chief officers of the state. The legislative power does not rest with the people but is exercised in a bi-cameral body, the upper portion of which was not elected originally by a direct vote of the people. No provision was made for popular initiative and referendum. And, finally, both the Executive and the legislators were to be elected for definite terms and not subject to recall.

In the post-Revolutionary period, Alexander Hamilton laid more stress on the aristocratic element in the federal government, while Jefferson emphasized the democratic element, but neither denied its essential mixed character. Even the term "democratic republican," which Jefferson adopted as his party label, was an affirmation of the "mixed state" ideal. John Adams, who certainly ought to have known what was in the minds of the early leaders, explicitly acknowledged the debt which the "founding fathers" owed to Calvin and the political theorists of Calvinism.

If the checks and balances, the reservation of powers, and the separation of powers are being by-passed today, and if there is what may seem to some people a dangerous concentration of power in the hands of the Executive which threatens the independence of both the judiciary and the Congress, this would seem to be evidence of a weakening of those theological convictions which caused these constitutional provisions to be adopted in the first place. It may be that the Churches are less effective today in inculcating that suspicion of human deceit and skepticism of human motives which springs from a lively sense of man's proneness to sin and to exalt himself at the expense of his fellows. As a result, the necessity for the limitation of power may not be so apparent, and the fear that a majority or an individual upon whom power is conferred will abuse that power may be less keen. A romantic and sentimental confidence in the essential goodness of man and in the purity of his motives would seem to be one of the major perils to the maintenance of a democratic society.

The sovereignty of God, we have said, implies the idea of fundamental law which is of the essence of constitutionalism. The conviction of human bondage to sin necessitates the limitation of power. The third, and perhaps the most important, structural support of our democratic way of life is grounded upon *a particular doctrine of revelation,* a particular understanding of the way in which the will of God is made known and the implications of the moral law become apparent.

In the Protestant understanding of the divine economy, no mortal man and no earthly institution is infallible, and any attempt to absolutize the fallible can only be interpreted as idolatry. Since the human mind is darkened and the human affections are corrupted, Calvin had insisted that the self-disclosure of God could not be regarded as self-explanatory. The understanding of divine truth was dependent upon the gift of the Holy Spirit. This introduced both an element of humility and of tentativeness. "We doubt not what we practice," declared Thomas Hooker, "but it's beyond all doubt that all men are liars and we are in the number of those poor feeble men; either we do or may err, though we do not know it; what we have learned we do profess, and yet profess still to live that we may learn." This, of course, was no mere relativism or subjectivism. The possibility that the human apprehension of the divine self-disclosure might be imperfect must be affirmed, but the objective reality of the revelation of God was not questioned.

The only way in which divine truth, either in Scripture or in nature, could be confirmed and its implications for the common life could be ascertained was through unfettered discussion. "We have a proverb," declared one of the early Puritan manifestoes, "that they that will find must as well seek where a thing is not, as where it is."

> Let us look upon the truth as God's and not ours, and let us look upon ourselves in all our discourses as hunting after it; every one acknowledging that God must lead every man. . . . And this liberty of free disquisition is as great a means to keep the truth as to find it. The running water keeps pure and clear, when the standing pool corrupts. . . . The true temper and proper employment of a Christian is always to be working like the sea, and purging ignorance out of his understanding, and exchanging notions and apprehensions imperfect for more perfect.

Such a free and unconstrained recognition of truth—the exchange of the imperfect for the more perfect—through discussion, could be realized only if the Spirit remained unbound. And the Spirit was no respecter of persons. Even the humblest layman might be its instrument. Light might break forth "from the meanest of the brethren."

Truth might be perceived by any man. Every man, therefore, must be free to be convinced and in turn to convince. Even the Church must submit its claims in the forum of public discussion. For as H. Richard Niebuhr has said, "the great usurpation of the kingdom which belonged only to God had taken place," so all the early Americans believed, "in the Church." Ecclesiastical pretensions were more to be feared than anything else. "Magistrates," said John Cotton, "must not take things *ipso facto* from the Church." That would be to make the Church a "monster." And Calvin, a century earlier, had insisted that the power of the Church was limited to the influence which could be exerted by persuasion.

It was because they were convinced that honest inquiry and discussion were indispensable to the determination of God's will that the architects of the American system of government insisted that minority rights must be guaranteed so that the channels of discussion might be kept open. Freedom of speech, freedom of assembly, freedom of religion, the right to trial by jury, all that is implied in the "due process of law" clause are basic necessities. They are part of the God-given rights of man which supersede all but a most critically clear and present danger to the common good. Our government, then, is a government by discussion, with a minimum of coercion. It rests on a dependence upon the efficacy of persuasion. Said Jefferson: "If the channels of discussion are kept open, truth and right will ultimately prevail." Or, in Abraham Lincoln's more vivid words: "You can fool some of the people all of the time, and all of the people some of the time, but you can't fool all of the people all of the time."

The most unique feature of the democracies of Calvinist lands is that differences of opinion and belief are not merely tolerated, they are encouraged. "This new principle of government," Lord Lindsay has said, "is far-reaching." It implies that "it is a good thing when people disagree but a bad thing when they are unanimous." It implies "an attitude of mind which finds expression in the common phrase, 'It takes all sorts of people to make a world,' or theological expression in the words that, because God is incomprehensible, it takes all believers to express the mind of Christ." And it implies, finally, that for practical purposes most of the differences between men are capable of reconciliation and that the necessary minimum of agreement can be reached through discussion. "What matters in this view of democracy is the quality of the discussion, that all different points of view should contribute to it, that the discussion should be thorough, that therefore

minorities should play and should be encouraged to play their part."
Without every one speaking his mind freely, without fear or embarrassment, something less than an approximation of truth, justice, and
wisdom will be achieved and something less than the full consent of
the governed will have been obtained. Indispensable in the whole
process is the acknowledgment that we may be wrong, the conviction
that "what we believe is not the last word on the subject" and that "we
may learn something from other people" (A. D. Lindsay, in R. P.
McKeon, *Democracy in a World of Tensions,* pp. 174–181). "I beseech
you, by the bowels of Christ," said Oliver Cromwell to men who
entertained pretensions to the possession of absolute and final truth,
"to consider that you may be mistaken." It is only as religion engenders this necessary humility of spirit and openness of mind that
democracy and the democratic way of life are secure.

What, then, is the role of religion in a democracy? It is to win an
acknowledgment of the sovereignty of God as the solid ground upon
which the concept of a fundamental moral law rests. It is to win a
recognition of the universal human bondage to sin and the consequent
necessity for the limitation of power. It is to secure the admission that,
since God cannot be captured and fenced in and manipulated by the
human mind, all apprehensions of truth are at best partial and imperfect, and need the correction provided by free and open discussion. If
it is true, as Judge Learned Hand has suggested, that our democracy
has begun to slip into that "process of dissolution where each man
begins to eye his neighbor as a possible enemy; where nonconformity
with the accepted creed, political as well as religious, is a mark of
disaffection; where denunciation, without specification or backing,
takes the place of evidence; where orthodoxy chokes freedom of
dissent; where faith in the eventual supremacy of reason has become
so timid that we dare not enter our convictions in the open lists to win
or lose"—then it is apparent that a renewal of the religious foundations of our society is desperately needed.

Unfortunately, too many of those who talk the loudest about the
present dangers to our democratic institutions have no real awareness
what the real dangers are. The pressure for conformity, the inhospital-
ity to new ideas, the impatience with criticism, the attempts to bottle
up and suppress unpopular opinions and independent thought—these
are the real dangers to a nation whose great word has been "freedom."
Of this we may be sure. "What the Constitution or laws provide about

free speech and free press and free conscience is not so important as what the spirit of the people provides." Much more important than having principles in a written Constitution is to have them written in the hearts and souls of men.

26

The Resolution of Nonconformity
PERRY MILLER

Students are constantly coming to me with this question: "If the Puritans believed that everything was predestined, not only their salvation but the moment of their death, why did they ever exert themselves? Why did they ever *do* anything?" . . . what is hard to get moderns to comprehend about the founders of New England is, first, that for them the doctrine of predestination did not have as a psychological consequence the surrender of all volition but rather that it was a powerful stimulus to activity; second and more important, this tremendous exertion being made in a social context, the incentive was therefore strengthened by an awful realization that without it the whole enterprise might fail. Hence they could not work out their particular salvations in a fear and trembling about only themselves; redemption of the soul was inextricably tied up with the question of whether the remnant of virtue and piety was enough, and could be kept enough, to save the community. . . .

. . . the question . . . has become our question: How can a society save itself? History is assuredly strewn with wreckages of societies; hence we have a superfluity of lessons as to the ways in which a community can go to pieces. We have none as to how it can escape, once a collapse appears inevitable. And it would seem, as I

Reprinted from Perry Miller, "The Social Context of the Covenant," *Bulletin of the Congregational Library*, VI (January, 1955), by permission of the Congregational Library of the American Congregational Association, Boston, Massachusetts.

have remarked, that from one angle, Puritan thinking would teach
that there is nothing at all the citizens of a foredoomed state can do
about the inevitable. A volume of John Cotton's—I think the most
readable of his publications—was printed in London in 1641 as *The
Way of Life*. In a preface, the editor announced in conventional
language what he supposed was the theme of the collected discourses:

> *What small power have we over our owne spirits! how little are we
> able to turne them, or to keep them so when they are well; but let
> the heart bee brought into never so gracious and sweet a frame, let
> grace be accompanied with peace, and peace with joy; yet how little
> can we doe with our grace, if God leave us to work in the strength
> of it! now how soone will our graces die, and our comforts wither?*

This would certainly seem to inculcate an extreme inability, a passiv-
ity so absolute that even when men have received an influx of divine
grace they are still powerless to accomplish anything by and of themselves, that they are incapable of keeping up even their hope and
comfort. . . .

In this same *The Way of Life* Cotton discusses, without resorting
to the technicalities of the Federal Theology, the problem of Christian
sociology. In ordinary situations, he says—as he continues, it becomes
clear that the theory of the normal situation is hardly ever exemplified
in actual fact—God regards the society as one with the people. "If
they be innocent, so is the whole Nation before him; if they be
humble, reformed, and upright, such is the whole Nation." In other
words, sanctification is not only a condition achieved or attained by
this, that, or the other individual; it is also corporate; or as Cotton puts
it, "the whole lumpe is sanctified." Hence if a nation of righteous men
seek God, no matter where they live, "he will heare in Heaven and all
the country shall fare the better for their sakes."

But unfortunately, in all too many cases—indeed in most cases—
the circle of righteousness is not identical with the national frontier.
When the discrepancy becomes too great, then the minority of good
men can no longer save the majority. There are, Cotton specifies, two
ways in which they fail. When they offer themselves as substitutes for
the others, when they try to take the affliction upon themselves, God
. . . will inflict His vengeance despite them. But the other, and the
more fatal, way in which the saints lose their usefulness is when they
themselves become "wrapt up in the contagions of the sinners of the

times and places they live in." Here let us stop for a moment and marvel at what an intolerable dilemma Cotton presents to the chosen of God. Unless they happen to be members of a society where holiness is virtually universal, they have the alternatives of recognizing that their virtue is too little to save the community, or else, by complying with the national ethos, of so acquiring the sins of the time and place as justly to be included in the national condemnation! In the one you must resign yourself to unpopularity and ineffectiveness, in the other to conformity and destruction.

If then the "mourning of Gods people," to use Cotton's phrase— by which he means their spiritual resolution—be the mourning of the whole land, then "as the people of God shall behave themselves in times of publick danger, so will the state of things stand." And now, when this is not the case, what do we do? Do we despair, do we say that the catastrophe, the declension, the collapse is fated, that nothing we perform can arrest it? Have we no social ability whatsoever? No, says Cotton, there is one thing we can achieve: "Bee well acquainted, not onely with your own sins, but be not strangers to the sinnes of the Town and Country you live in." I think it not too rough a modernization of Cotton's injunction to say that in times of public crisis we are not to submit or to sit apart, we are to become active critics of our society. The best patriotism in such emergencies is not conformity; it is speaking out against those abuses which have brought us into the dire predicament.

> *Complain not therefore of any declension of times, or decayes of things that are good, or breaking in of things that are kinde (though they ought unfainedly to exercise us) but follow close to wise and faithfull preservation of our selves from fellowship in these evils, and as much as in us lies, reforme what is amisse in our selves and ours; and let it be a strong motive to us to fall faithfully to this work, because if we shall so doe, such a mourning of a few will be counted the mourning of a whole Land.*

I think it likely that this sermon was delivered in England, before 1633 when Cotton fled to New England; the manuscript had probably been left behind, and so could be published there in 1641. In that case, John Cotton was really talking to his people about the attitude they should hold toward a state that was imposing upon the saints a corrupt and destructive, as they believed, church system. The whole passage is a kind of double talk about Nonconformity; I suppose those who do not love the Puritans can see in it only another piece of casuistry and hypocrisy. Why doesn't he come out in the open and say what he means?

Well, he does say what he means. Cotton is not a radical, a revolutionary. Actually, as he later was to show, in political philosophy he is, by the standards of his day, a conservative. But he is a decent, conscientious citizen faced with the spectacle of his country, which he dearly loves, embarking on a policy, maintaining a line of conduct, employing methods, which he is certain will lead to disaster. What then does a man do, we ask? By virtue of that very concern for the health and reputation of the nation, he refuses to conform. And this logic, let us remember, was possible in a universe conceived as conforming to Calvinist principles. Nay, more than that, this resolution not to conform, this courage to stand by the resolution of Nonconformity, was not at war with the theology; it was in fact a direct consequence of it. This is the fruit of Christian freedom. Thus the righteous man stands for his freedom, when politicians and majorities demand that he comply with a system and a discipline he knows is wrong.

PURITANISM AND THE AMERICAN CHARACTER

27

The Spirit of America
HAROLD J. LASKI

Americans are optimistic, friendly, inquisitive, practical-minded. They find it difficult to believe that progress is not inevitable. They do not easily accept the right to reserve and privacy; they assume that if two men meet the natural thing is for them to exchange experiences. They have a distrust of theory. What interests them is the ability to apply an idea to the solution of a problem; and they reserve their supreme respect for men of the type of Ford . . . This is why there is an important sense in which the supreme symbol of the American spirit is Benjamin Franklin, for he made a success of all that he attempted. He met kings and statesmen, merchants and workmen, on equal terms. He always wanted to know the how and, if possible, the why of anything he encountered; and if he is a great figure in the history of physics, his invention of the cooking stove enabled him greatly to improve the domestic amenities of his time. There was nothing in him of that remoteness which is characteristic of George Washington, nothing, either, of that inner and ultimate melancholy which makes Lincoln so untypical an American. In his shrewdness, his sagacity, his devotion to making this world the thing that a kindly and benevolent soul would wish it to be, Franklin seems to summarize in a remarkable way the American idea of a good citizen.

From the outset, almost, of his history, the American has been accustomed to scan a vast horizon, and this has tempted him to equate bigness with grandeur. It has made him a restless person, anxious rather to do than to be. For, until quite recent times, there has always been, for him, the frontier beyond the frontier, and his amazing vitality has been the secret by which he has conquered the continent. And the very fact of that immense space to which, once Jefferson had completed the Louisiana purchase, he has been in fact the unchallenged heir, has made him approach the issues of life very differently than did his European ancestors. He never needed to assume, as the Englishmen did, that there was some allotted station in life that was his, and others that were, almost *a priori,* beyond his reach. He never accepted the Frenchman's ideal of achieving an adequate competence as early as possible that he might devote his time, preferably in some provincial countryside, to cultivating his garden. History never imposed upon him the tragedy of the German citizen who was not of noble birth—the need to realize that the great careers, whether of politics or of the army, were only too likely to be closed to him. Nor did he suffer from the human contradiction of being either a nobleman without the means to live the noble life, or being a merchant or a peasant, and finding, even if he was successful, that these circles of social life to which he might aspire were beyond his hope of entry.

There is a real sense in which every American belongs to a self-made generation; he is full of the consciousness that he may both begin anew and climb upwards without the fear that he will encounter some barrier laid by history in his road. It is even, I think, broadly true to say that the Americans most certain to fail in satisfying their needs of the spirit are those who expect the past they have inherited to determine the future upon which they can enter. It is difficult to think of a more complete example of this truth than Henry Adams. He had a mind of the first order, he was a man of profound cultivation, he knew almost everyone in the America of his time whom it was worth while to know, and he had an intimate experience of the forces by which the civilization of his time was shaped. Yet no one can read his autobiography without the conviction that, from the time he returned to America with his father after the Civil War, he was a profoundly unhappy man. And that unhappiness was not the outcome merely of the personal tragedy of his married life. Some of the things he achieved might well have left him with the conviction of a fulfilled personality. In his academic days at Harvard University, it is clear that he swiftly conquered a significant place among scholars. The books that he wrote before he had passed the milestone of middle age secured for him the admiring recognition of all who were capable of judging. He had friends of outstanding quality who gave him instant and abiding affection. Wherever he heard of beauty, in nature, in art, in architecture, he would travel to see it. When he settled in Washington, few visitors of distinction but sought the chance of his acquaintance. Yet not all the quasi-scientific alibis by which he sought to ward off despair can conceal the fact that there was in his most intimate self a black sense of frustration.

Henry Adams yearned, like the three generations of his family before him, to play a pivotal part on the political stage. But he could not stoop to conquer. There was something in his disposition which made him seek the palm without the dust. And since he chose to mask his passionate ambition in the role of a spectator to whom descent into the arena was unthinkable, no one thought of asking him to enter the battle. He spent the crucial years of his life preparing to be the general of an army in which some quality of his nature prevented him from enlisting. He saw far smaller men than himself, Henry Cabot Lodge, for example, and John Hay, move to the forefront of the political stage. He could not bring himself to take the steps which might have organized for him the opportunities he desired. It was not that his nature was too precious for him to do so. Partly, I think, he was weighed down by the fear of failure if he made the attempt; partly he assumed that a man of his position and connections would be sought after; an Adams in the United States was the moral equivalent of a Cecil or a Stanley in England. What he did not see, and what, I suspect, he never understood, was that the American spirit compelled the citizen to build for himself the ladder on which he could mount in politics. So that when he became conscious of a failure for which, mainly, great historian though he was, his own lack of historical insight was largely responsible, he spent almost a generation of his life in building himself, as compensation, into a legend, and writing those books of his later years in which, behind the appearance of an historical cosmology, there is in reality an apologia for his failure, large parts of which are no more than a method of concealing his angry contempt for an age which did not call upon him to lead it.

It would be interesting to compare the symbols of the American spirit which Franklin epitomized in the eighteenth century with the judgment implicitly passed upon them by Henry Adams in the nineteenth. But that would sacrifice the larger issues of this theme to a single variation upon it. I can only summarize the argument by saying that what emerges, as the United States emerges from the thirteen colonies, is the conviction that the successful man is the happy man,

and that the criterion of success is either the utilitarian one of power
—most easily measured by wealth and the influence it commands—or
the judgment of one's fellows that one has achieved significance. John
Jacob Astor and Abbott Lawrence are happy because their success in
material terms is beyond denial, just as Henry Wadsworth Longfellow
and Bronson Alcott are happy because the world about them accords
them the crown of that genius for which they longed. The happy
American is thus, on my view, the American who is deemed successful
in the relevant environment in which he moves. So that, when one
reads the history of New England in the early part of the nineteenth
century, Miss Peabody may be happy in her little bookshop because
her friends regard her judgment as important in the same way as the
textile manufacturers of New England regard the judgment of Abbott
Lawrence as important. The vital roots of the American spirit are
either the building of a fortune or the building of a reputation which
makes you held in esteem by your neighbours. And for either of these
things it is important to be doing something, until some such epoch as
the presidency of General Grant, to be doing something oneself. It is
not easy, therefore, for most of his contemporaries to understand why
Thoreau can be happy; they almost need the assurance of Emerson,
who is at once successful and a seer, that the queer contemplative
spirit of Walden finds ecstasy so great in the observation of nature that
his massive acquiescence is itself a form of action. And if practically
nothing material that Bronson Alcott undertakes seems able to keep
poverty from his door, he is yet successful because he is so incredibly
energetic in discovering, almost every other week, the inner secret of
the universe.

No attempt to grasp the nature of the American spirit can be
complete which does not emphasize the degree to which action is of
its essence. Americans are always doing things or trying things; more,
they are always seeking a shorter way of getting things done. And
with that search there goes the desire, first, to discover the shorter road
for oneself, and, second, so to discover it that others want to follow
where the pioneer has led. It is, I think, significant that, until that
remarkable springtime of New England in the first half of the nineteenth century, what is important in American life is related either to
the amenities of practical living, architecture for example, or to the
writings of jurists and political pamphleteers. Early American theology is sometimes persuasive, and even, as with Jonathan Edwards, of
amazing logical power, but it is rarely an innovating literature. And

polite letters, until this New England springtime, are rarely much more than what the scholar is driven to read to see how the winter burgeoned into that spring. Law and politics, and, to some degree, economics also, are from the outset different. There the writer is conscious that the word is the deed. He is writing, whether it be Thomas Hooker or Cotton Mather in one century, or John Wise or Thomas Jefferson in the next, to make people act one way rather than another way. His aim is not to fill an idle hour, but to push his generation in a direction of which he approves.

It thus becomes tempting to argue that the American spirit, in its main outlines, has been until quite recent times the quintessence of a secularized puritanism. The regard for effort, the belief that success attends upon it, the suspicion that failure is due to some defect of character, the justification of wealth as a stewardship the obligations of which the public may expect to see fulfilled, the dislike of radical doctrines as a social form of antinomianism, the fear of any ideas which may bring into jeopardy the unity of the commonwealth, all of these seem little more than an adaptation of the religious principles with which the seventeenth century was familiar. And because the Puritan gospel was operative in a society which almost until our own day was still engaged in pioneering, it is natural enough that, as it became secularized, it should regard with praise the qualities that enable the pioneer to succeed. To take a risk, to show courage, to display the capacity to organize, even more, to show that talent for leadership which imposes law and order in a community fighting primitive conditions, whether physical or social, all of these are elements in the character of man which shape the American spirit. It is not a spirit which easily accepts the notion of a social hierarchy. It is not the spirit of a civilization which emphasizes either perfection of technique or refinement of manner. It is more concerned with getting the thing done, with shaping the tools which can do the job, with saying bluntly what needs to be said, than with method or with convention, whether of craftsmanship or speech.

Since the American spirit works in an environment that is constantly changing, it lays great stress on the power to innovate and adapt. It has a veneration for the past; there are few countries in the world where the past is so religiously commemorated as in the United States. But this veneration is wholly compatible not only with the right of each generation to experiment with itself, but, more, with the right of each individual to make his own bargain with fate. Because America has been a land of adventurers, its spirit has put a high value on self-reliance. This high value, in its turn, has begotten an impatience with constraint, an assumption, accordingly, that the less the interference with the individual's action, the more fully he will be a whole man. It is not wholly fanciful to argue that American individualism is the secularized form of American puritanism, that it leaves the individual face to face with his fate, as the chief forms of puritanism left the individual face to face with his God. The American, moreover, as he watched the toughening of fibre, the assurance of success, the inventiveness developed, by this kind of experience, came almost unconsciously to think that a state power which did more than organ ize external defence and internal police was going beyond its proper function. The "rugged individualism" of Mr. Herbert Hoover has deep links with the foundations of the American spirit. It assumes the validity of that social order which, violence apart, permits a man to make the best of himself that he can.

28

The Pilgrim Fathers and the American Way
DIXON WECTER

It is plain that the founders of New England have had an immense effect upon our concept of Americanism—that collective symbol which means those things for which the Pilgrims settled this country, for which the Revolutionary fathers bled, for which the Civil War was fought and Abraham Lincoln suffered, and possibly for which our boys in France offered their lives. It is a vague but important concept, which always grows more dear to us in times of crisis. For all its vagueness, nobody will deny that Americanism has a rich kernel of truth and reality we all prize. But, on the other hand, all will agree that this emblem has been abused by generations of doctrinaires with axes to grind. Walter Lippmann some years ago compared collective symbols, like "Americanism," to strategic railroad centers, where many roads meet regardless of their point of origin or where they are going. A political strategist claiming these junction centers successfully enough to convince the public of his right to be there, controls the highroads of mass policy. He may attack or defend proposed legislation, call for more or less taxes, urge or decry government control of business, win support for war or peace, because his platform is "American." With such a fulcrum he can move a hundred million people. It is useful, therefore, to sift some of the myths and the truths concerning the Pilgrims and the Puritans as guides to the American way.

First, for the myths. . . . the Pilgrims and Puritans have passed so far beyond the Lethe of legend that we have lost touch with their reality. Some moderns have charged them with greater dourness than they actually had—forgetting, for example, their abundant use of rum and wine even at the ordination of ministers, and their still shocking practice of "bundling"—while other moderns have praised them for liberal virtues which they heartily detested. Between the common picture of Pilgrims in sugar-loaf hats and kerchiefs, with angel faces, trudging to church through the snow, and the equally familiar caricature of the blue-nosed, lank-haired hypocrite labelled "Bigotry" or "Prohibition" by Rollin Kirby and other cartoonists a couple of decades ago, runs the whole span from white to black.

Various attempts have been made to solve this paradox. A century ago, growing hostility to the memory of the Puritans—in some circles a synonym for "demure rogues" or "formal hypocrites," as John Foster noted in 1826—led to a feeling that the Puritan builders of the Bay Colony should be divorced from the Pilgrim Fathers who arrived ten years earlier. A piece of fiction like Harriet Cheney's *A peep at the Pilgrims* in 1824 shows the Plymouth settlers as kindly, hospitable, tender-hearted, while their neighbors to the north are stern bigots. But the distinction was not altogether common: another novel of the time, Lydia Maria Child's *The first settlers of New England*, in 1829, draws them all as cruel and bloodthirsty toward the Indians, on account of the Jewish strain in their religion! The label "Pilgrim Fathers," which suggests the spiritual patriarch and takes away the odor of priggishness attached to "Puritan," is one which the original settlers at Plymouth did not use about themselves. Surcharged with its present sentiments, it was first used by Cotton Mather and other divines three generations later in seeking to recall the good old days. These later

Puritans were eager enough to identify themselves with the traditions of Plymouth. Of course there were some initial differences between Plymouth and Massachusetts Bay, in social rank, education, and ideas of church government. But soon they drew together, Boston swelling to a metropolis while Plymouth with its stony acres and poor trading-ground shrank to a village. "It was in Massachusetts Bay, not Plymouth," as Samuel Eliot Morison has written, "that were worked out those characteristic forms of state, church, and school, which have set off New England as a province apart." The Puritan of the Bay is, therefore, the effective moulder of "the American way," while the Pilgrim fades into sentimental legend. Today the average American is prone to lump them together.

Both have been appealed to as founders of democracy in America. Timothy Dwight, president of Yale from 1795 to 1817, was one who (although a foe of Jeffersonian democracy, as befitted a kinsman of New England's first industrial families) extolled the Puritans for giving us a pattern of equality. Unlike the Virginians, said Dwight, the fathers of New England had banned primogeniture and entail, thus fostering

> *The noblest institutions man has seen*
> *Since time his reign began. In little farms*
> *They measured all their realms, to every child*
> *In equal shares descending.*

Many Northern orators in Daniel Webster's generation said the same thing. This, however, is not the complete picture. Though the plantation covenant of Plymouth was more democratic than the charter of Massachusetts Bay, neither fits the modern American concept. The Pilgrim Fathers began as communists—laboring jointly upon the common land, and feeding from a communal store of supplies, to each according to his needs—but like the early communists of Jamestown they found that the experiment soon collapsed, thus proving, as William Bradford admits, "the vanitie of that conceite of Platos." On the other hand, the Puritans of the Bay emphatically were not democrats. Birth, breeding, education, wealth, and religious orthodoxy gave prestige that was both social and political. Governor Winthrop in 1642, when litigation between rich Captain Robert Keayne and poor Mistress Sherman over the ownership of a sow roused some popular sympathy for the widow, rebuked such meddling as tending toward a

democracy, and of course "there was no such Governm! in Israel."
Likewise this haughty governor, in a famous letter to Thomas Hooker,
expressed his conviction that "the best is always the least, & of that
best part the wiser part is always the lesser." Puritanism itself, beginning in England in the fiery furnace of minority loyalties, when
dominant quickly cooled into the clinkers of authoritarianism. Pride,
among all the seven deadly sins, was the one to which the Puritan was
most susceptible—and this flaw left its mark upon the ruling caste.
Many recent scholars have agreed with the late Frederick J. Turner,
who said that American democracy as we now know it "was not
carried in the *Susan Constant* to Virginia nor in the *Mayflower* to
Plymouth. It came out of the American forest, and it gained strength
each time it touched a new frontier."

These early settlers are often praised, also, as pioneers of religious
liberty. Freedom of thought and speech and worship we rightly regard
as precious to Americanism. Do we owe them to the Puritans? Mrs.
Felicia Hemans, who loved the sentimental heroic, . . . wrote a poem
that used to be found in every school reader. The stern and rock-
bound coast, a nobler frame for arduousness than the mild shores of the
James River, she thus rhapsodized:

> *Aye, call it holy ground,*
>   *The soil where first they trod!*
> *They have left unstained what there they found—*
>   *Freedom to worship God!*

But it is plain that neither Plymouth nor Boston, but rather Rhode
Island and Connecticut, were the nurseries of New England liberalism. Such a jolly dissenter from Calvinism as Morton of Merrymount
was suppressed twice—first by the Pilgrim Fathers under Miles Standish, and later by the Puritans of the Bay under Endecott. Orthodoxy
in Massachusetts, as is well known, agreed to whip Quakers and
Baptists; to banish Anne Hutchinson, who in her friendless state was
slain by the Indians; and to expel saintly Roger Williams, who wrote
back to the elders: "Yourselves pretend liberty of conscience, but
alas! it is but self, the great god self, only to yourselves." The spirit of
John Calvin—who had burned Servetus for disagreeing with him—did
not foster much true charity. Too many of the first settlers came, not to
set up an asylum of religious liberty for all men, but to establish their
own brand of intolerance. Later, after Puritanism in evaporating left

behind such crystals as Unitarian intellectualism, easy-going Congregationalism, and democratic evangelism, it became easier to read into the early spirit of Massachusetts the liberal virtues admired by modern times. But they were hardly there in the beginning. Of political and religious liberalism, as understood by the Republic of Jefferson and Madison, these Forefathers had few traces.

On the other hand, the Puritans have often been praised as the epitome of rugged individualism and free competition. Old guard Republicans frequently appeal to them in this way. Yet evidence shows that the Puritans favored government regulation of business, price-fixing for the common good, and curbing of excess profits made by an individual at the public expense. In some respects they were convinced New Dealers. This same Captain Keayne was fined £200 by the General Court for making a profit of sixpence or more in the shilling; while the Reverend John Cotton in 1639 condemned the thesis "that a man might sell as dear as he can, and buy as cheap as he can." This aspect of the Puritan has been forgotten, probably because it ran against the grain of later mythologies in New England. Within a few generations after the first settlers, with the heroic age of Puritanism waning fast, more and more attention came to be paid to the gospel of business enterprise. Weber, Tawney, and others have suggested that Calvinist ethics was the seed-plot from which modern capitalist philosophy sprang. Unlike Luther, who taught that work in the sweat of one's brow was the original curse God laid upon Adam, Calvin held that work is man's holy duty. Idleness is shameful. "Work, for the night is coming," exhorted a later Protestant hymn. The first Puritans believed that good works—including thrift, soberness, and the making of money to be used wisely—were a badge of God's favor. Prosperity was important only because it showed that God was on one's side. John Cotton wrote of the "mystery" of Puritanism, namely "diligence in worldly business and yet deadnesse to the world." His grandson Cotton Mather described the two callings of man as his eternal salvation and his daily business: "If he mind but one of his callings, he pulls the oar but on one side of the boat, and it will make but a poor dispatch to the shoar of Eternal Blessedness." In his book of hero-worshipping biographies called *Magnalia Christi Americana*, Mather wrote his longest and most enthusiastic life about a self-made man, Sir William Phips, who from poverty rose to riches and knighthood—"Behold one raised by God!" cried Mather, defying "pale Envy" to "fly-blow the Hero." That Phips had burnt his fingers at piracy did not seem to matter. The Puritan, in fact, was an idealist tinged with cynicism—cherishing dreams of utopia but knowing that on account of corrupt human nature they could never be realized on earth. The Yankee could skin a stranger at a horse-trade because he was convinced that his fellow-man was a bottomless well of original sin.

Soon, in the waning moon of Puritanism, Poor Richard after his Boston boyhood would help to secularize the gospel of wealth—preaching, in a hundred proverbs, diligence in business, thrift, and that self-improvement which was a Yankee passion. The sign of God's grace, prosperity, in time came to seem more important than the grace itself. When Irving came to write with the pen of Diedrich Knickerbocker, "the ingenious Yankee" was already a stock type, hard-fisted and God-fearing, sprung from "such a squatting, bundling, guessing, shingle-splitting, pumpkin-eating, molasses-daubing, cider-watering, horse-jockeying, notion-peddling crew." His clipper ships rounded the Horn with argosies of the Indies; his outposts of the fur trade rose along the Columbia River; his tall chimneys at Lowell and Taunton belched forth the smoke of a new industrialism. Doctrines took shape concerning the holy stewardship of business, preached by President Porter of Yale and President McCosh of Princeton. "Acres of Diamonds," a lecture given six thousand times by the Reverend Russell H. Conwell, declared:

> *Money is power. Every good man and woman ought to strive for power, to do good with it when obtained. Tens of thousands of men and women get rich honestly. But they are often accused by an envious, lazy crowd of unsuccessful persons of being dishonest and oppressive. I say, Get rich! get rich! but get money honestly, or it will be a withering curse! . . .*

John D. Rockefeller said to the first graduating class at his new university, "The good Lord gave me my money, and how could I withhold it from the University of Chicago?" while Bishop Lawrence of Massachusetts in 1900 asserted that "Godliness is in league with riches." Indeed, the old Calvinist link between religion and business returns in many guises. In 1920, for example, post-war Puritanism began a spirited campaign against Sabbath movies and golf—appealing both to "the Christ spirit" and to the alleged fact that workmen "who had no sport on Sunday do their best day's work Monday." During the

Depression, on December 10, 1933, a *New York Times* editorial praised the economist Doctor Sprague for saying penitently of the bull-market days, "We were all miserable sinners," and Alfred E. Smith for stating that the causes of the stock-market crash were "as old as original sin." Thanks to the old Puritan heritage of American business, it sometimes shows a strange groping after the concepts of that faith.

In the making of American legends, therefore, the Puritan Fathers are often praised for contributions not very well deserved—such as religious liberalism and democracy in government—but slighted as pioneers both in State control of business and in the quite different cult of idealizing the merchant prince . . . . On the whole, the more personal qualities of the Puritan, like courage, stubborn will, and keen appreciation of the intellectual and spiritual life, have a place in legend better merited than that given to their group traits. The Puritan, in fact, seems to have been more attractive as an individual than *en masse*.

How then did the Puritan myth, somewhat at odds with the facts, arise? It was built by two forces working in contrary directions. One was the impulse of later times to exalt the first settlers as belonging to "the good old days." The other was an urge to read into Puritan life those qualities which moderns prize more than did worthies of the seventeenth century. The first was prone to measure the modern man by the Puritan yardstick; the second to give the Puritan credit for all the progressivism of a latter day. Both impulses ran to hero-worship.

Those early settlers themselves had had few individual heroes. They did not bow down before any man, choosing even in portraiture to show "the warts on Cromwell's face." Group egotism—of feeling themselves the anointed of God—they did have, but of persons they were fiercely critical. Miles Standish, nicknamed "the Hero of New England" on account of his valor against the Indians, might have stood forth as a great man in a society where the soldier was king. But in a Puritan theocracy that looked first of all to its clergymen, Standish's fame, like his physique, never reached great height. To this day New England remembers him as a doughty little man, "Captaine Shrimpe," as he was called by the irrepressible Morton of Merrymount. He owes most of his present fame to Longfellow's poem, telling of his tongue-tied courtship of Priscilla—a story for which there is no basis in fact. (To take off the dour edge of Puritan memory, the Massachusetts Development and Industrial Commission often proclaims the Old Bay State "the land of America's greatest lovers! Priscilla! John Alden! America's greatest love-match!") And there was John Winthrop, practically governor *in perpetuo* of Massachusetts, the most admired layman of his time. In funeral sermons and elegies—the Puritan equivalent of fan mail, offered when the admirer was no longer suspected of bootlicking, or the recipient of vanity—he was recalled as "the chiefest of our Peers," "New Englands Pelican," and "The Loadstone of America." Richard Greenough made a marble statue of him, Bible in hand, for the National Capitol in 1876, and another for Scollay Square in Boston, but to most Americans today he is neither an important symbol nor legend. There were eloquent divines, and the heroes of Indian captivity, and the Regicide Judges who took refuge from England in Connecticut and on account of their hiding inspired much popular folklore—but in general, colonial New England is pretty bare of individual idols.

The spirit of romance, therefore, has turned to a composite ideal called the Pilgrim Fathers or the Puritans. As early as 1676 a Boston schoolmaster named Benjamin Tompson—who seems to have been the first native-born American poet—dreamed about the first settlers and their "golden times, too fortunate to hold," when there was more praying for one's neighbors than gossiping about them, and when redskins were handled sternly—

> No sooner pagan malice peepèd forth
> But valor snubbed it. Then were men of worth,
> Who by their prayers slew thousands; angel-like,
> Their weapons are unseen, with which they strike.

As Puritanism grew still colder, early in the next century, the great preachers like the Mathers and Stoddards from their pulpits loved to praise the good old times, in summoning their flock back to the strenuous temper. They extolled the Fathers, "who for an undefiled conscience and the love of a pure Christianity, first left their native and pleasant land, and encountered all the toils and hazards of the tumultuous ocean"—but were now prone to apologize (the difference is significant) for the brusque treatment these men had meted out to the Indians. But this homage to the past had not yet grown sentimental: the first centenary of Plymouth, in 1720, for example, seems to have passed quite unnoticed.

The symbol of the Pilgrim Fathers did not become important, for the country at large, until storm clouds of the American Revolution began to gather. Then the flight of the Pilgrims, from English tyranny to the New World, was seen to have patriotic meaning. In 1768 a Marylander, John Dickinson, stirred by the recent events in Boston, wrote the most popular poem of that day, "The Liberty Song":

> *Our worthy Forefathers—let's give them a cheer—*
> *To Climates unknown did courageously steer;*
> *Thro' Oceans to Desarts for Freedom they came,*
> *And dying bequeath'd us their Freedom and Fame.*

"The Massachusetts Liberty Song" in the same year bade Americans take heart from the courage of their ancestors, who won "through deaths and through dangers," and a little later Peter St. John in his "Taxation of America" called on his countrymen to be worthy of their sires who for ideals had defied the British Crown. In January, 1769, twelve young men of Plymouth started a club to commemorate the traditions of their town; on the next December 22 they held the first dinner honoring the landing at Plymouth Rock. This spirit ran through the Revolution. The Pilgrims had now begun to be national heroes.

In Boston a scheme for annual celebration of the Pilgrims was first proposed in 1774, but was not adopted until December, 1798, when the "Sons of the Pilgrims" kept their first feast. Thereafter December 21 or 22 was observed widely in Massachusetts. The term "Pilgrim Fathers," fixed in the popular mind by this observance, soon became the usual designation for them throughout the nation. Forefathers' Day grew into a great New England tradition, with the eating of turkey and pumpkin pie and the placing of five kernels beside each plate, in memory of the daily ration said to have been allotted during the "starving time" of April, 1622. In 1820, the Bicentenary of the landing, Forefathers' Day at Plymouth reached a new high. Daniel Webster spoke one of his greatest orations, and the banquet was eaten from huge blue dinner-plates specially made by Enoch Wood & Sons of Staffordshire—showing a boatload of Pilgrims landing before the eyes of the Indians, who were standing on the Rock itself, already carved with the names of Miles Standish, William Bradford, and others. Linking this historic event with the cause of Independence were scrolls at the top and bottom of this design, reading "America Independent, July 4, 1776" and "Washington, born 1732, died 1799."

Apart from Forefathers' Day but fostering the same cult was Thanksgiving, looking back to Governor Bradford's celebrated proclamation in 1621. It was a Puritan substitute for the "Popish" or High

Church revels of Christmas—a holiday still frowned upon in Plymouth as late as 1840, when even the placing of wreaths in windows was regarded as a " 'piscopal" custom. Thanksgiving, in colonial times, was unknown outside New England. But in the tense days of the Revolution both thanksgivings and fasts were decreed by Congress, and came to be linked with the patriotic cause. In 1817 the Puritan harvest-home jumped its local borders when New York State adopted an annual Thanksgiving Day. Other states in the North followed suit, and the great tides of migration from New England to the West carried the sentiment of Thanksgiving with them—although the South looked upon the custom with suspicion, fearful lest a grain of Yankee propaganda be wrapped in the sheaves of patriotism. Not until the dark days of the Civil War—when all the states remaining in the Union were more or less friendly to New England traditions—did Thanksgiving become a national holiday, on the last Thursday of November, 1863. Lincoln's proclamation first bowed all loyal heads over the festal board, and since his time every President has set aside the feast of the Pilgrims. But . . . President Franklin D. Roosevelt's departure from the customary date in 1939 and 1940 was disapproved, in conservative New England circles, as tampering with a hallowed rule "for a purely mercenary reason," as a Republican editorial sadly remarked.

Into the West, at an early date, Pilgrim and Puritan were carried as household gods—honored not only by feasts, but also by religious and ethical homage. They had become in fact the keepers of the Protestant conscience. When Benedict Arnold had joined the British and issued a handbill urging his fellow citizens to follow, he had the effrontery to appeal to the Pilgrim Fathers:

> *What security remains for you even for the enjoyment of the consolations of that religion for which your fathers braved the ocean, the heathen, and the wilderness? Do you know that the eye which guides this pen, lately saw your mean and profligate Congress at Mass for the soul of a Roman Catholic in purgatory, and participating in the rites of a church, against whose anti-christian corruptions your pious ancestors would have witnessed with their blood?*

Arnold's handbill had little effect; many no doubt concluded that the devil could quote Calvinist scripture. But the call to prejudice is significant. With the southwest expansion that followed the Louisiana Purchase, Down East traders came into collision with an alien culture

—that part Catholic, part radical naïveté of the frontier which tended to identify sin with sharp trading and the Yankee flair for commerce. On the other hand, the Puritan Northeast began to fear lest developments in the West—Romanism, freethinking, rampant democracy and lawlessness, the saloon, the gambling table—should strangle "true Americanism." The gaiety of New Orleans and St. Louis did not seem to those sharp blue eyes the American way. Nor were the Sunday games and folk dances of Continental immigrants, nor the passion of German peasants along the Wabash for music and flowers ("a strong symptom of simplicity and ignorance," as Hulme remarked on his travels). Hence, mingled as ever with economic considerations, sprang a certain missionary impulse to claim this new Canaan for the mores of Calvin and John Cotton. The unassimilated spirit of French and Irish Catholics, brought into the Union by immigration and annexation, clashed with the Puritan heritage—and the latter took political shape in the Know Nothing party. The sons of New England were aggressive and, in this generation at any rate, polyprogenitive. The tensions of this rivalry grew taut.

Meanwhile the American schoolhouse, under the growing secularization of life, took the old place held by the church as the builder of group attitudes. Whatever his parents' church, every Protestant child attended the village school, learning his ideas of history and social consciousness from it. New England had long bred schoolmasters for America at large: even in late colonial times the Virginia aristocrat, in search of a tutor for his children, went naturally to Harvard College and Princeton. The reasons were logical enough: New England had better libraries and academies, with its stern intellectual traditions and its passion for self-improvement (even its theology, as Perry Miller has lately remarked, being based upon Ramus's theory that truth needs only to be known in order to prevail). These schoolmasters carried with them a deep respect for the New England fathers and their ways, and a creed in which Puritanism stood for the true American faith. They taught textbooks written by Noah Webster, Jedidiah Morse, William H. McGuffey—who re-enforced the young idea with the whalebone of Puritan ethics. Most of the historians and literary men in this generation sprang from New England, or were tinged by its thought. They nourished the attitude, later powerfully fostered in the North by the Civil War, that Puritan ways were synonymous with patriotism, simplicity of life, sterling worth, democracy, and all other desires of the young Republic. "For the progress and enjoyment of

civil and religious liberty in modern times," wrote Noah Webster in his
History of the United States, in 1832, "the world is more indebted to
the Puritans in Great Britain and America, than to any other body of
men, or to any other cause."

At length, therefore, the ark of the covenant brought overseas by
the *Mayflower* was speeded on its way by the Conestoga wagon—to
be set up in the little red schoolhouse of the prairies, and displayed on
the platforms of political oratory. The center of Puritanism followed
the center of population deeper and deeper into the interior, unaware
that the old homestead was mellowing in the pale sunshine of Chan-
ning and Emerson and Frothingham, or feeding the vine of Latin art
and liberalism whose shoots Yankees had lately brought home from
France, Italy, and Spain. The Puritan had become an all-American
hero. His mores filtered through to other regions. The Southerner who
assailed John Quincy Adams for setting up a billiard table in the
White House—hardly conscious of the past, when Increase Mather
had first taught that games of chance are direct appeals to God, and
hence "may not be used in trivial matters"—passed on the faith to
Adin Ballou, from Roger Williams's Rhode Island, who in the 1850's
crusaded against alcohol and tobacco, and a generation later to Carrie
Nation of Kansas, editor of *The Smasher's Mail* and *The Hatchet* who
asserted that McKinley should have recovered from the bullet "but his
blood was bad from nicotine," and grieved over the poor Yale student
who reported he had "brandy so strong on the food it made his head
dizzy." The old New England point of view set the didactic tone of
American life—decreeing that the best-loved books of the century,
supplanting Fox and Bunyan, should be *Ten Nights in a Barroom,
Uncle Tom's Cabin,* and *In His Steps.* This heritage, scattered abroad,
came to supply the pruderies and reticences of America, its absurdities
as well as its brave idealisms. Only among the gentle and wise was its
spirit of meddling sublimated into the humanitarian urge.

Not until the 1920's under the effete morality of Prohibition—age
of the bootlegger, the night club, jazz, nudism, companionate marriage, and *The American Mercury*—did "Puritanical" become an epi-
thet worse than swearing. Henry L. Mencken and Stuart P. Sherman
fought over whether the Puritans had themselves been Puritanical.
New debunking biographies of the Mathers and Jonathan Edwards
appeared. Boston, with its Watch and Ward Society, was—along with
the mores of Iowa—good for a laugh at any cocktail party. Hitting

below the Bible Belt became the chief pastime of metropolitan wit. William Jennings Bryan was widely mocked as the last Puritan. It seemed possible to blame all modern vices upon the old steeple-hatted Puritan—either as the result of, or the reaction from, his code—leaving us his grandchildren plainly helpless, in the grip of a more genial predestination to sin.

Yet even in this decade the hero-worship of the Puritan was not dead. Less sophisticated citizens, a sprinkling of fundamentalists and Klansmen, some New England brahmins of business, and the more excitable foes of Romanism still loved him, even in modern caricature. The high priest of his cult was probably that President of the United States whom William Allen White has described as "a Puritan in Babylon." In 1930 at Watertown, Massachusetts, Mr. Coolidge paid tribute to the Puritans in general: "They were a very wonderful people. . . . If they were narrow, it was not a blighting and destructive narrowness, but a vital and productive narrowness. The narrowness was like that of a mighty torrent which makes a smooth path, that after it the stream may flow on smoothly to its destination." At the decade's beginning, Mr. Coolidge had been Governor of Massachusetts, and had assisted at the Tercentenary of the *Mayflower*. This episode, reflecting the rather confused hero-worship of that day, merits description.

In spite of the proverbial punctuality of New England, preparations were not ready in time for a real jubilee on December 21, 1920; nor, fittingly to grace the occasion, had a Republican President-elect succeeded to office. Hence a kind of rehearsal, which seems to have been informal enough, was held on the actual date. Governor Coolidge was met at the Plymouth railway station by a welcoming committee. But he did not give himself into their hands, as the official Tercentenary booklet sets forth: "Gov. [*sic*] Coolidge boarded a one-man trolley car and rode away, up in front, and some of the others took the trolley cars, but the majority walked, in no special order, along Court and Main Streets to the Old Colony theatre." There Mr. Coolidge briefly praised the Pilgrims who "sailed up out of the infinite . . . sailed hither seeking only for an avenue for the immortal soul." After Mrs. Hemans's poem had been sung by a male chorus, Senator Henry Cabot Lodge spoke the oration of the day. The Senator quoted Daniel Webster's anticipation back in 1820 of this Tercentenary, when, he prophesied, "the voice of acclamation and gratitude, commencing on the Rock of Plymouth, shall be transmitted through millions of the sons of the Pilgrims; till it lose itself in the murmurs of the Pacific seas." At this juncture, we are told,

> *a telephone bell on the stage tinkled and the speaker paused. Willard Parsons, local manager of the telephone company, advanced from the wings, picked up the transmitter of the desk set and queried "Is this the Governor of California? Just a moment. I introduce to you Governor Coolidge of Massachusetts." The instrument was passed to His Excellency, and the latter took up the conversation which was fulfilling the prophetic utterances of Webster a century previous, saying, "Governor Stephens, Yes. This is Governor Coolidge of Massachusetts. Yes, I am seated in the chair of Gov. Bradford at Plymouth. I wish to say that Massachusetts and Plymouth Rock greet California and the Golden Gate, and send the voice which is to be lost in the waves and roar of the Pacific. I'll do so. Goodbye."*
>
> *As Senator Lodge resumed his discourse, he remarked: "It was the merest accident that I read that sentence." The incident had been planned as a surprise. . . . As a matter of fact, Gov. Stephens was away on a hunting trip and the conversation was with his official secretary, but the Webster prophecy had been fulfilled, nevertheless.*

In 1921 the real celebration took place, with a pageant for a cast of 1300 written by Professor George Pierce Baker of Harvard. Called "The Pilgrim Spirit," it began with the Voice of the Rock—

> *Of me, the rock in the ooze, they have made a cornerstone of the Republic.*

William Bradford is the chief actor; he reviews the noble temper of the Pilgrims. Gazing into the future of America he discovers its two greatest leaders, Washington and Lincoln, standing in a recess behind the Rock. At length a martial flourish of French and British flags that "wave and beckon," is answered by a bugle call from the *Mayflower;* the Spirit of the Rock summons America to join the Allies. Through deepening shadows the Rock speaks its benediction: "With malice toward none and charity for all. . . ."

The gala performance of the pageant was given on "Plymouth Day," when President and Mrs. Harding and some 100,000 visitors thronged the town. In his Address—delivered, to be sure, before he had seen Professor Baker's pageant—President Harding expressed America's "penitent realization" of "the wastes and the sorrows and the utter disarrangements of a cataclysmal war." Normalcy, rather than heroism, was on the march. The pageant that night, accompanied by a searchlight drill of warships in the bay, drew a mammoth crowd. In fact, because of the out-of-town invasion, the booklet recalls, there was such a run on tickets that "parties who were within reach of later productions disposed of their tickets at considerable advances." Perhaps the Fathers themselves would have understood, and forgiven.

The Rock itself, carved with the numerals "1620," remains an American shrine. Although historians long ago attacked the tradition attached to this particular boulder—pointing also to the fact that most of the Pilgrims stayed aboard ship for about a month after the *Mayflower* anchored—the Rock serves a human need for the tangible symbol. Now housed in a Greek temple of granite, it has weathered the passing of time though not without casualties. A crack "which has existed in it from Revolutionary times and probably before that," caused the Rock to split on December 20, 1920, when it was being moved to accommodate its new setting, but the fissure has been mended several times with cement. One night a few years later Plymouth Rock was painted red by stealth; alarmed citizens first reported that Communists had done this outrage, but later it was discovered to be the work of Harvard jokesters.

In truth, as the dramatist said, Plymouth Rock has become a cornerstone of American patriot lore. Today, long after the Jazz Age and Repeal, unfair blame and equally partisan praise of the Puritans have both grown fainter. Now that the vortex of national discussion has shifted from private morals to economic and international issues, the Puritan has ceased to be the object of fierce debate that he was twenty years ago. Still a somewhat blurred symbol of religious freedom and of moral intolerance, to the popular eye, he wins more respect than affection. Today it is possible more calmly to weigh his defects against his virtues. With his narrow life, his lack of beauty and poetry, his pride and bigotry, he ran counter to some of the best impulses in the modern world. But as a hero he had stern self-discipline, courage physical and moral, a sense of reality that foreswore easy optimisms, and an acceptance of the need for sacrifice—a need that the Republic, in its less complacent moods, always discovers anew for itself. By reason of these traits, and because the men who had them stand at the door of American history, Pilgrim and Puritan will not soon be forgotten in our national legendary.

29

The Puritan Legacy
KENNETH B. MURDOCK

For at least a century after the landing at Plymouth the intellectual life of the New England colonies was dominated by Puritan thought. Churches and schools followed the old patterns, and the leaders in all walks of life were at least professedly loyal to the teachings of the founding fathers. It is reasonable to suppose, therefore, that the prejudices and mental habits of the colonists must have affected somehow the behavior and attitudes of later New Englanders, and more than one critic has detected in present-day New England signs of its Puritan inheritance. The matter is of more than local interest, since men from Massachusetts and Connecticut and Rhode Island followed the advancing frontier. Some of their ideas and standards took root and flourished far west of the Hudson, and it is pretty generally admitted that somewhere in America's total cultural heritage and the complex of qualities which make up the "American character" there are traces of Puritanism.

It is very difficult, however, to be sure just what these traces are, partly because the continuing influence in intellectual history of any past "state of mind" is always hard to assess, and partly because the special "state of mind" of the New England colonists has been often misunderstood or falsely defined. The very words "Puritan" and "Puritanism" have been given so many different interpretations that they have almost lost meaning. Some critics have operated on the simple principle of calling Puritan any idea or mode of behavior of which they disapprove; others, just as emotional and no less mistaken, have been run away with by enthusiasm for the colonists' virtues and have ascribed most of the good in contemporary American civilization to the beneficent influence of the first settlers of Massachusetts Bay. The religious fundamentalist and the reactionary are still dubbed Puritans,

Reprinted by permission of the publishers from Kenneth B. Murdock, *Literature and Theology in Colonial New England* (Cambridge, Mass.: Harvard University Press, 1949). Copyright, 1949, by the President and Fellows of Harvard College.

but so, now and then, are liberals. Prohibition was glibly called a product of Puritanism, though the Puritans themselves never dreamed of a world without spirits, ale, and wine. Book censorship is decried as a survival of Puritanism by those who forget that the Puritans allowed the importation and circulation of books which in recent years have been banned here or there in this country or forbidden to enter it. Emerson and Hawthorne have been called Puritans, but so have men who disagreed with them at almost every point. Joseph Lee, in a letter to the *Boston Herald,* once summed up the confusion by writing:

> *The case against the Puritans is conclusive. We of the present genera- tion have two kinds of faults; puritanical and otherwise—especially otherwise. The former are clearly a direct inheritance from the Puritans, the latter a reaction against them. Both kinds are thus the faults of the Puritans and of no one else. We ourselves, accordingly, have no faults. This is what we have always felt, but it has never been so clearly proved before.*

Part of the confusion comes from the fact that colonial Puritanism was not static, but changed its character radically in the space of relatively few years. The earlier chapters of this book have dealt principally with what might be called its "original" or "pioneer" phase as a radical reform movement conducted by a group of devout Protestants who dissented from the practices of the English church and became leaders of a crusade for a new state and a new church which should put into effect the will of God as revealed in Holy Writ. But in New England the "movement of dissent" changed to "an institution with authority." The essentials of the formal theology and the polity persisted and hardened into a system. From the second stage of Puritanism—crystallized in a conservative and dominant church, the more rigid in its tenets the more it was threatened by new doctrines—stem most of the stiff intolerance of mind, the sterile reverence for rule as rule, the moral oppressiveness, the deference to a tradition become lifeless and bleak, which hostile critics confidently point out as marks of the Puritan heritage.

The later Puritans in New England were essentially conformists, the earlier were thorough-going nonconformists. The distinction is of great importance. It has been said that all men in all times can be divided into conformists and nonconformists, into those who reverence tradition, submerge the individual in the organization, and set form in religion above life, and those for whom man's own relation to God is the center, and individual inquiry and conviction, not corporate dogma, is the key to truth. According to this hypothesis the "original" Puritans represent the second class. It is their bequest to the future which principally concerns the intellectual historian who seeks in colonial New England for the source of a fruitful tradition.

In considering the ways in which the ideals and methods of the Puritan literary artist—or would-be artist—affected later writing and later criticism, it is important to differentiate between the pioneers of colonial New England and their more complacently orthodox successors. Such men as Shepard, Wigglesworth, Norton, Roger Williams, or the testy Nathaniel Ward, the "simple cobbler" of Ipswich, wrote with a saltiness, a homely directness, and a realism grounded in their intense conviction that anything from a mouse nibbling a book to a disastrous fire or an eclipse symbolized the relentless but ultimately benevolent reign of God. They wrote of sin, of death, of divine love, and of the miraculous stirrings of grace in the hearts of the regenerate, not as a literary exercise or a polite gesture of empty conformity but with the full fervor of passionate faith in a theology and in the grandeur and beauty of the God which it exalted. But many of their sons and grandsons lost the authentic accent because they had lost the authentic faith and had substituted for the excitements of a perilous personal quest for salvation the tamer satisfactions of a decorous acceptance of a creed and polity sanctioned rather by convention than conviction.

Others, of course, were as earnestly devout as their forefathers and wrote with something of the old stylistic energy, but even in their pages the "plain style" tends to become both plainer and more dull. They wrote for men who could no longer respond as directly as the first settlers to the presentation of simple objects of daily life as symbols of the divine and whose tastes in literature turned more and more to the placid urbanities of the sermons and essays of Queen Anne's London. "The man of Locke," Emerson said, "is virtuous without enthusiasm, and intelligent without poetry," and so were many—perhaps most—New Englanders in the early eighteenth century. They could not catch the full flavor of earlier Puritan prose, and inevitably those who preached and wrote for them had to shift their stylistic ground. For Emerson, Franklin was the type of the American become "frugal, inoffensive," and "thrifty," with "nothing heroic" in him. Certainly, many of Franklin's compatriots were no longer stirred by the old heroic conception of the Christian pilgrimage or by vision of this world as real only in its immediate relation to Heaven and Hell, Satan and God. . . .

Fortunately, in the sermon as well as in other types of writing more than mere "plainness" has survived as a stylistic legacy from the Puritans. Franklin's talent for vivid phrasing and his taste for earthy images certainly came in part from the New England of his youth. Jonathan Edwards' success in expounding his impressive and complex philosophy was made possible because he had learned to write with transparent clarity and to enlist simple phrasing and restrained diction in the service of beauty. Ralph Waldo Emerson was a master of the homely image and reverted to a familiar figure when he said of Carlyle's rhetoric, which he disliked, "The merit of glass is not to be seen, but to be seen through, but every crystal and lamina of the Carlyle glass shows." James Russell Lowell did not much like Henry Thoreau, but he thought his metaphors and images were good because they were "always fresh from the soil." Thoreau himself delighted in the "strong, coarse, homely speech" of "some of the early writers of New England" because it "brings you very near the thing itself described. The strong new soil speaks through them . . . . That generation stood nearer to nature, nearer to the facts, than this, and hence their books have more life in them."

It was the strength, the homeliness, the "life" of early colonial Puritan writing which did most for a few later literary artists in this country, not its mere simplicity and logical clarity which, however influential in their effect on the course of English style, often lent themselves after 1700 to prose both flat and dull. The strength, the homeliness, and the "life" came from the organic relation of Puritan style to Puritan concepts in the days when to be a Puritan was to be a pilgrim, a warrior, or even a tragic hero in a universal drama. The point is not that the later American artist has consciously chosen the New England colonists as literary masters, but that at times certain of their stylistic habits fixed in New England books and speech have served him well when moral or religious issues have stirred him to an ardor comparable to theirs.

A similar line of influence may be traced from the Puritan's interest in biography written with an emphasis on the portrayal of character rather than on mere events. They accented the "inner life" and in so doing helped to develop and popularize new techniques for analyzing and depicting character. It is reasonable to suppose that

American biography since colonial days has matured more rapidly than it could have if the Puritan colonists and their sympathizers abroad had not written lives with zeal and skill. Certainly in another kind of "personal literature" New Englanders have followed in the footsteps of the founding fathers. The habit of writing diaries and autobiographies persisted for generations in New England, and no doubt still persists. What is *The Education of Henry Adams* essentially but a somewhat more sophisticated and somewhat less frank variant of the analysis which the Puritan practiced in his diary or autobiography? Any reader who turns from Puritan "personal literature" to it or to the journals of Emerson or Thoreau or Hawthorne recognizes that there is a link between nineteenth-century New England and the New England of the Puritans.

As for history, the case is plainer still. Cotton Mather's *Magnalia* was followed in 1736 by Thomas Prince's incomplete history of New England, which for all its faults had some major historical virtues. Prince declared: "I cite my *Vouchers* to every Passage: And I have done my utmost first to find out the *Truth,* and then to relate it in the clearest Order." A recent historian, John Spencer Bassett, comments: "Posterity is willing to grant that he achieved his object, and it gives him a place among the most worthy of our historical scholars." The relation between the early Puritan's respect for accurate recording and Prince's insistence on "finding out the truth" is plain. So is the relation between Puritan historical standards and those of Thomas Hutchinson, "probably the best historian who wrote in the colonial period," whose history of Massachusetts began publication in 1764. Mr. Bassett says that Hutchinson's work "is broad and well balanced, details are subordinated to larger movements," and in it Hutchinson's task of creating, "as a liberal and able man of culture . . . a picture of the colony's progress," is "performed . . . in the manner of a master."

The tradition of historical writing in, and about, New England is a long and distinguished one. English critics in the days when they were just becoming conscious of the United States as a nation must have been startled to discover that however barbarous they might wish to consider this land to be, some of its historians showed maturity and skill worthy of the Old World. Wherever history is studied today the names of Motley, Prescott, and Parkman are remembered; Jeremy Belknap, Jared Sparks, George Bancroft, and a dozen other New Englanders are not so often recalled to mind nowadays, but they all partook of New England's enthusiasm for history and each of them contributed to its historical productivity and to its progress in the effective use of the best historical techniques.

The Puritans do not deserve all the credit and other districts than New England produced good histories. In quantity and quality, however, the successors of the Puritans achieved more than any other American group, and although they learned from German scholars or from other critics of, and practitioners in, historiography, it is hard to resist the conclusion that one reason for their achievement was that the local tradition gave importance to history and supported a high standard for it.

It is true that later historians abandoned one of the essential elements in the Puritan's historical attitude. He interpreted history as the revelation of God's providence, but late seventeenth- and eighteenth-century thinkers pushed God off into the position of a mere first cause. As science increasingly asserted its own ability to account for all phenomena, the role of the Almighty in history became less and less important. The historian rowed with the intellectual current and relaxed the Puritan's concentration on the providential interpretation.

Yet it is possible to trace the spirit of the Puritan's reading of history, although not its letter, among his descendants in days when his theology no longer prevailed. Is not the New England historian's liking for the history which sharply contrasts right and wrong, heroic and base, and looks on a specific series of happenings as part of a larger heroic progress, a liking which is closely akin to the Puritan's attitude? Bancroft, writing a history of this country, was "impressed . . . with . . . the grandeur and vastness of the subject." It had grandeur because "the United States constitute an essential portion of a great political system, embracing all the civilized nations of the earth. At a period when the force of moral opinion is rapidly increasing they have the precedence in the practice and defence of the equal rights of man." This confidence that the United States "were far ahead of all the other nations of the world" is very close to the Puritan's firm belief that he belonged to a people especially chosen by God. Motley's "honest love for all which is good and admirable in human character wherever he finds it, while he unaffectedly hates oppression, and . . . selfishness" smacks of the Puritan's desire to demonstrate through history the superiority of the godly and to prove that the story of mankind was one of continuous warfare between good and evil.

Motley "hated the absolute government of the Spanish monarchy, he disliked the dogmas of the Roman church, and he could not abide the repressive spirit of the Roman hierarchy." "His histories were Protestant," certainly, in their anti-Catholicism; they were Protestant, too, and Puritan, in their insistence on a moral interpretation of character and event. Parkman, the greatest of all New England historians and the one who in his personal character seems most like what we imagine the conventionally austere Puritan to have been, is a historian perhaps least like the Puritan in that he wrote with much less emphasis on religious issues. But he did share the Puritan's faith in the importance of history and a determination to pursue accuracy and truth at all costs. Moreover, the heroes Parkman most admired and painted most movingly were, although not Puritans in the theological sense, men with some traits which would have appealed to the Puritans almost as much as they did to Parkman. They faced and conquered odds by their indomitable devotion to a great cause. Religious or not, they were heroes because they had and used the qualities of character by which the Puritan himself won his successes in the wilderness.

The influence of Puritan literary theories and habits on the development of prose style and on later history and biography was in part at least beneficent, but most critics agree that with poetry the case is different. Some of the Anglican religious poets of seventeenth-century England won literary immortality; few of their Puritan contemporaries, at home or in the colonies, did. The inheritors of the American Puritan tradition, whatever their merits, have rarely pleased the critics and readers who delight in the lyrics of Donne, Herbert, and Vaughan. They were handicapped by the "Puritan distrust of plastic richness as a snare for the eye," by the Puritan's attitude toward the senses and the use of sensuous material in religious art. The situation was not improved when pioneer Puritanism hardened down into an organized and intolerant ecclesiastical and creedal system. Verse became cooler and cooler and farther from poetry. There were still versified expositions of pious precepts, rhymed paraphrases from the Bible, verse narratives of God's providential acts, and competent occasional stanzas on this or that New England worthy or event, but there was little which could not have been as well said in prose. The waning of the original rebellious spirit of Puritanism weakened the distrust of Anglican and Catholic forms of writing, and New Englanders neatly, and often ingeniously, aped the stylistic methods of the great English

religious poetry of the early seventeenth century, but they still ex-
cluded much sensuous poetic material and their verses were usually
only pale exercises in superficial imitation.

There is a kinship between the cool correctness of such poets as
Bryant—Lowell spoke of his "ice-olation"—and the tradition of Puritanism turned conventional. Longfellow too, for all his expert craftsmanship, rarely lifts his poetic moralizing above the level of calm
homage to a stereotyped formula. He was the heir not of pioneer but
of later Puritanism, which relied too much on a formal code rather
than on a deeply and personally realized belief. Emerson's occasional
inability to fuse form and content in poetry, the curious flatness of
much later New England verse, the dryness sometimes obvious in the
work of Edwin Arlington Robinson, are all examples of the weaknesses of the Puritan poetic tradition. Now and then, notably in Emily
Dickinson, something of the intensity of the pioneers flares up again,
but in other poets the fruit of the tradition is too often correctness not
vigor. Too often the flavor is bland and thin, and the effect is one of
discipline carried to the point of emotional starvation.

When James Russell Lowell said that he was

> *striving Parnassus to climb*
> *With a whole bale of isms tied together with rhyme,*

he was making fun of his New England habit of using verse to prove a
point or support a cause. That was the Puritan way, but the earliest
colonists at their best wrote with an emotional force and conviction
which, in spite of their "isms" and the handicaps of their theory, gave
off poetic sparks. Lowell's New England was painfully inclined toward the prosaic attitudes of the later diluted Puritanism, which
discouraged robustness of heart and mind.

The tangible data of literary history cast some light on the relation of Puritan writing to later American literature, but such data
never tell the whole story. The real forces in the growth of any
literature can never be measured completely by changes in conventions of style or theme or by the formal development of literary genres.
The fertilizing tradition is a matter of spirit and idea; the fruitful
heritage of the past comes from ways of thought and feeling, fundamental intellectual and emotional points of view, which have the
power to stimulate new attempts to map the changing current of life.
Such things are hard to categorize; their nature defies precise defini-

tion. Their influence comes in large part from the fact that they are living organisms, not static entities which can be exactly measured and weighed.

It is particularly difficult to be confident as to the elements in Puritanism which did most to influence, in the fundamental sense of that word, American literature and American religious thought since the seventeenth century, because Puritanism was itself a complex of many elements, and because the main stream divided into several channels as it pursued its course in America. There have been many attempts to chart those channels, and the relation of Puritanism not only to later literature and religious thought but also to the broadest aspects of social and economic life has been much discussed. The evidence is rarely conclusive enough to support dogmatic assertions, but there are bases for reasonable conjectures. Even guesses have value, since they bear upon a strain in American intellectual history the existence of which few historians would doubt even though its exact nature may be impossible to define.

Shrewd critics of Puritanism have never been at a loss to find in it qualities unfortunately suggestive of the least Christian aspects of the America which the New England colonists helped to found. Just as its literary influence, in poetry at least, may be held to have been bad, it is possible to maintain that its influence on other concerns of life has been as bad or worse. Has not the colonists' confidence in the rightness of their theology and in their position as champions of God against error fostered bitter intolerance? Has not the Puritan's emphasis on sin bred in some of his descendants, deprived of the more constructive elements of his faith, a crippling sense of guilt? Has not his intense concentration on the individual spiritual life, revealed in his diaries or autobiographies, led now and then to pathological morbidness or, more serious, to an individualism which amounts to selfishness and social irresponsibility? Cannot the misuse of such phrases as "free enterprise" to mask socially destructive greed be easily explained as the product of Puritan individualism? Cannot contemporary emphasis on material values be explained by an inherited taint of Puritanism which exalts thrift and worldly success as marks of godliness? Answer these questions in the affirmative and you have a ready-made indictment of the Puritan tradition—an indictment which American critics during the 1920's repeatedly pressed.

Except for such overenthusiastic critics, a bare affirmative answer will not do. That the colonists were intolerant, no one can question;

that their magnification of peccadilloes into major sins was, by contemporary standards, absurd, no one will challenge. The Puritan's distrust of the senses seems today like a partial denial of life; the dangers of his introspectiveness and his individualism, unless controlled by some positive principle, are painfully plain. But original Puritanism did have a positive principle. Michael Wigglesworth was tormented by his sense of his own iniquity, but he made for himself a successful and useful career as a minister, teacher, and citizen. However unhealthy his soul-searchings may seem, he never relapsed into idle neuroticism, but worked steadfastly to prove himself worthy of God's love. John Bunyan said: "No sin against God can be little, because it is against the great God of heaven and earth; but if the sinner can find out a little God, it may be easy to find out little sins." Wigglesworth and other Puritans would have agreed. Their God was a great God; the labors required of his servants were onerous. Any lapse from his laws, however trivial, could not seem trivial to men who passionately loved and feared him. The magnitude of their conception of God and of their role as his servants eclipsed everything else, and both their love and their fear were compelling motives for a constant and exciting struggle to do his will. They were individualists, but as long as they genuinely centered their lives on a "great God" and thought of New England as the country of his chosen people, they avoided the worst selfishness and the most dangerously anti-social qualities of individualism unrestrained. They were not saints, and some of them were hypocrites, but many had faith and courage enough to come nearer than most of their descendants to a truly Christian life. The harshness, bleakness, and sterility which are commonly thought of as Puritan, conquered only when the pristine ardor waned, the "great God" dwindled, and obedience to his law was no longer dictated by a deeply felt inner need.

In literature also, what is best in the tradition of Puritanism comes from its original spirit, not from the hollow conformity into which it declined. The Puritans' real gifts to later writers were not the specific contributions to the development of techniques and types of writing which have already been commented upon, but a few general religious and moral attitudes which have had significant implications for the artists. In the genuine Puritan tradition, character and morality are seen as permanent values achievable only by personal spiritual conquest, life is constantly spiritualized, and the humblest events and acts are related to a divine context. A writer who accepts such views is sure to reflect them not only in the content of his work but in his theory of style.

Samuel Sewall went to a picnic in 1697 and ate a great deal—among other things, "very good Rost Lamb, Turkey, Fowls, Aplepy." After the meal, the company sang Psalm 121, and then, he writes, "A Glass of spirits my Wife sent stood upon a Joint-Stool which, Simon W. jogging, it fell down and broke all to shivers: I said 'twas a lively Emblem of our Fragility and Mortality." In Sewall's mind there was no incongruity in following a hearty picnic by a psalm, or in reflecting piously on spilled liquor as a symbol of moral truth. Many New Englanders and many other Americans since 1697 have tried to see idealistic values in good business, have tried to link life, even in its commonplace aspects, with religion. Others have been leaders in reform and pioneers for new causes because their spiritual impulses seemed to them normally to coincide with concrete accomplishment in this world. In literature this has led to a constant emphasizing of moral values by the writers most susceptible to Puritan ways of thought. The result has been sometimes clumsy didacticism, but some major American artists have found rich suggestions for method and theme in the Puritan linking of the ideal with the concretely actual.

In Puritan theology Hawthorne found a set of concepts indispensable as the framework for his allegorical or symbolic presentations of moral drama. That he accepted neither the creed of the Puritans nor their polity mattered not at all. Their emphasis on sin, their consciousness of the adventurous struggle involved in spiritual development, and their taste for expressing the ideal in images and symbols of earth gave him not only his most characteristic themes but suggestions as to the best means of expressing concern with the inner life. Melville thought that Hawthorne's "great power of blackness" derived "its force from its appeals to that Calvinistic sense of Innate Depravity and Original Sin, from whose visitations, in some shape or other, no deeply thinking mind is always and wholly free." The last clause shows that Melville himself had felt the "force" of one basic element in Puritan thinking. Both Hawthorne and Melville "saw the empirical truth behind the Calvinist symbols" and "recovered what Puritans professed but seldom practiced—the spirit of piety, humility and tragedy in face of the inscrutable ways of God." Apart from the moot question of the extent to which the Puritans' professions were carried out in practice, it is plain that Melville in all his best work from *Mardi* to *Billy Budd* drew something from their thought. Both he and Hawthorne were influenced also by the "tendency of American idealism to see a spiritual significance in every natural fact," a tendency "far more broadly diffused than transcendentalism." Of it F. O. Matthiessen says, "Loosely Platonic, it came specifically from the common background that lay behind Emerson and Hawthorne, from the Christian habit of mind that saw the hand of God in all manifestations of life, and which, in the intensity of the New England seventeenth century, had gone to the extreme." The relation between this background and Melville's and Hawthorne's use of concrete symbols to express ideal reality is obvious.

Puritan individualism has also left an indelible mark. One of our "grand national types of personality" has been "the adventurous colonist; the Protestant sectarian, determined to worship his own God even in the wilderness." In him, as in other American types, there were good elements and bad, but his ideas have stimulated artists working in a world unlike his and in times when his theology was forgotten. His concentration on the life of the spirit as the core of character and his exaltation of the morally enlightened individual above all restraints certainly gave clues to Hawthorne and Melville, as well as to Thoreau and Emerson. All four echoed something closely akin to the Puritan's personal belief that the foundation of holiness was the personal search for truth, even when a royal government, a powerful established church, and the terrors of the wilderness seemed to bar the way.

Another aspect of Puritan individualism is reflected in the work of later writers. It is an easy step from the colonists' anxious self-analysis to Hawthorne's care "for the deeper psychology," which both Henry James and T. S. Eliot recognized. James felt a charm "even in Hawthorne's slightest allegories . . . which redeemed their stiffness for him," because they gave "glimpses of a great field, of the whole deep mystery of man's soul and conscience. They are moral, and their interest is moral; they deal with something more than the mere accidents and conventionalities, the surface occurrences of life." The Puritan had his allegories too, and their charm for him was the same as Hawthorne's for James—which suggests that one thread of influence from Puritanism stretches well beyond Hawthorne and Emerson and Melville to James and perhaps even to Eliot.

Part of the continuing power of the Puritan's ideas comes from the fact that he was not only an idealist but a nonconformist. So, in essential parts of their thought, have been most of the best New

England writers since their time. They, like him, have asserted as both a right and duty man's obligation to think and live by his moral convictions, even when they ran counter to accepted beliefs. There is much in them of the devout early colonist who was a rebel, but neither in love with rebellion for its own sake or reckless in iconoclasm. He believed that his theology and his whole intellectual scheme were soundly based on the best authority of the past, and he believed that he attacked or destroyed only things which stood in the way of what could rationally and logically be proved good. He was, he believed, not the creature of passion, but the servant of reason.

Nonconformity of this sort, coupled with Puritan idealism, accounts for some of the noblest aspects of later American thought and writing. Emerson was by no means a whole-hearted admirer of the Puritans and recognized that before his time they had "declined into ritualists," but he believed their virtues were still needed. For him the pioneer New Englanders were "great, grim, earnest men," who had "solemnized the heyday of their strength by the planting and liberating of America." "This town of Boston has a history," he said.

> *It is not an accident, not a windmill, or a railroad station, or crossroads tavern, or an army-barracks grown up by time and luck to a place of wealth; but a seat of humanity, of men of principle, obeying a sentiment and marching loyally whither that should lead them. . . . I do not speak with any fondness, but the language of coldest history, when I say that Boston commands attention as the town which was appointed in the destiny of nations to lead the civilization of North America.*

Emerson is thinking of the moral tradition of Boston, as the Puritans did, and his very imagery suggests theirs. Just as they loved to symbolize themselves as an army of righteousness, so he pictures his men of principle as "marching loyally." And just as the Puritans reverenced history and believed that the success of their colonial venture was proof that they were carrying out God's will, so Emerson is sure that Boston was by destiny appointed to lead civilization on this continent. The terms are shifted from the theological, but the spirit remains the same.

Emerson also touches specifically on the Puritan tradition of idealism and of nonconformity. "These Englishmen," he says of the pioneer settlers, "with the Middle Ages still obscuring their reason, were filled with Christian thought. They had a culture of their own

. . . . They were precisely the idealists of England; the most religious
in a religious era." He drives his point home with an image of just the
sort which the Puritans themselves delighted in. He writes: "An old
lady who remembered these pious people said of them that 'they had
to hold on hard to the huckleberry bushes to hinder themselves from
being translated.' " "As an antidote to the spirit of commerce and of
economy," Emerson goes on, "the religious spirit—always enlarging,
firing man, prompting the pursuit of the vast, the beautiful, the unat-
tainable—was especially necessary to the culture of New England." As
for nonconformity,

> *Boston never wanted a good principle of rebellion in it, from the plant-
> ing until now; there is always a minority unconvinced . . . some pro-
> tester against the cruelty of the magistrates to the Quakers . . . some
> defender of the slave against the politician and the merchant; some
> champion of first principles of humanity against the rich and luxurious
> . . . some pleader for peace; some noble protestant, who will not stoop
> to infamy when all are gone mad, but will stand for liberty and justice,
> if alone, until all come back to him.*

Of course, Emerson admits that New England's history contains many
dark chapters of cruelty and injustice, but he insists that it should be
judged by its best, which, as he defines it, bears the unmistakable
marks of its Puritan heritage. Boston "is very willing to be outnum-
bered and outgrown" by other cities, "full of its blood and name and
traditions," if those cities will "carry forward its life of civil and
religious freedom, of education, of social order, and of loyalty to law
. . . . It owes its existence and its power to principles not of yesterday,
and the deeper principle will always prevail."

Today the Puritans' dream of what the New England colonies
might become is unrealized, and the Boston which Emerson praised
has ceased to be—if, indeed, it ever existed. The United States bears
little resemblance to anything that the colonists or Emerson thought a
great nation should be. Much good Puritan seed fell on ground so
barren that the fruit was dwarfed and sour. Too often only the
narrowness and intolerance of Puritanism survived; too often its more
generous spirit was lost. In practice, when it commanded the hearts
and minds of the colonists, it "was the most strenuous of creeds" and
"the greatest of the Puritans, far from yielding fatalistically to some
superior will, asserted their own wills at every turn with the resolute-

ness and vehemence of men for whom freedom is an unchallenged reality." Today little of their moral robustness persists, and it is hard to find any faith, or even any intellectual system, which is as stimulating and as productive of useful action as was the faith and system of the Puritans when they laid the foundations of their Bible commonwealth. . . .

Recommended Reading

I. The Puritan Vision

BARITZ, LOREN, *City on a Hill* (New York: John Wiley and Sons, Inc., 1964), Ch. 1

BATTIS, EMERY, *Saints and Sectaries: Anne Hutchinson and the Antinomian Controversy in the Massachusetts Bay Colony* (Chapel Hill: Univ. of North Carolina Press, 1962)

EMERSON, EVERETT H., *John Cotton* (New York: Twayne, 1965; New Haven: College and Univ. Press, 1965)

HASKINS, GEORGE LEE, *Law and Authority in Early Massachusetts* (New York: Macmillan, 1960)

MACLEAR, JAMES F., " 'The Heart of New England Rent': The Mystical Element in Early Puritan History," *Mississippi Valley Historical Review*, XLII (March, 1956), 621–52

MILLER, PERRY, *The New England Mind: The Seventeenth Century* (New York: Macmillan, 1939)

——, *Orthodoxy in Massachusetts* (Cambridge: Harvard Univ. Press, 1933)

MORGAN, EDMUND S., *The Puritan Dilemma: The Story of John Winthrop* (Boston: Little, Brown and Co., 1958)

——, *The Puritan Family* (new ed., rev. and enl.: New York, Harper and Row, 1966)

——, ed., *Puritan Political Ideas, 1558–1794* (Indianapolis: Bobbs-Merrill, 1965)

——, *Roger Williams: The Church and the State* (New York: Harcourt, Brace and World, Inc., 1967)

——, *Visible Saints: The History of a Puritan Idea* (New York: New York Univ. Press, 1963)

MORISON, SAMUEL ELIOT, *Builders of the Bay Colony* (Boston and New York: Houghton Mifflin Co., 1930)

NIEBUHR, H. RICHARD, *The Kingdom of God in America* (New York: Harper and Bros., 1957)

PETTIT, NORMAN, *The Heart Prepared: Grace and Conversion in Puritan Spiritual Life* (New Haven and London: Yale Univ. Press, 1966)

SEIDMAN, AARON B., "Church and State in the Early Years of the Massachusetts Bay Colony," *New England Quarterly*, XVIII (June, 1945), 211–33

SIMPSON, ALAN, *Puritanism in Old and New England* (Chicago: Univ. of Chicago Press, 1955)

WALZER, MICHAEL, *The Revolution of the Saints* (Cambridge: Harvard Univ. Press, 1965)

ZIFF, LARZER, *The Career of John Cotton: Puritanism and the American Experience* (Princeton: Princeton Univ. Press, 1962)

————, "The Social Bond of the Church Covenant," *American Quarterly*, X (Winter, 1958), 454–62

Numerous scholars are engaged in rewriting the local and institutional history of seventeenth-century New England. Their findings are presented in the following books and articles:

BROWN, B. KATHERINE, "Freemanship in Puritan Massachusetts," *American Historical Review*, LIX (July, 1954), 865–83

————, "A Note on the Puritan Concept of Aristocracy," *Mississippi Valley Historical Review*, XLI (June, 1954), 105–12

————, "Puritan Democracy: A Case Study," *ibid.*, L (Dec., 1963), 377–96

————, "Puritan Democracy in Dedham, Massachusetts: Another Case Study," *William and Mary Quarterly*, 3rd ser., XXIV (July, 1967), 378–96

DEMOS, JOHN, "Families in Colonial Bristol, Rhode Island: An Exercise in Historical Demography," *ibid.*, XXV (Jan., 1968), 40–57

————, "Notes on Life in Plymouth Colony," *ibid.*, XXII (1965), 264–86

FOSTER, STEPHEN, "The Massachusetts Franchise in the 17th Century," *ibid.*, XXIV (1967), 613–623

GREVEN, PHILIP J., JR., "Family Structure in Seventeenth-Century Andover, Massachusetts," *ibid.*, XXIII (1966), 234–256

————, "Historical Demography and Colonial America," *ibid.*, XXIV (1967), 438–54

————, "Old Patterns in the New World: The Distribution of Land in 17th Century Andover," *Essex Institute Historical Collections*, CI (April, 1965), 133–48

LANGDON, GEORGE D., JR., *Pilgrim Colony: A History of New Plymouth, 1620–1691* (New Haven and London: Yale Univ. Press, 1966)

LOCKRIDGE, KENNETH A., "The History of a Puritan Church: 1637–1736," *New England Quarterly*, XL (1967), 399–424

———, "Land, Population and the Evolution of New England Society, 1630–1790, " *Past and Present,* No. 39 (April, 1968), 62–80

———, "The Population of Dedham, Massachusetts, 1636–1736," *Economic History Review,* 2nd ser., XIX (August, 1966), 318–344

———, and ALAN KREIDER, "The Evolution of Massachusetts Town Government, 1640 to 1740," *William and Mary Quarterly,* 3rd ser., XXIII (1966), 549–74

MORGAN, EDMUND S., "New England Puritanism: Another Approach," *ibid.,* XVIII (April, 1961), 236–242

OBERHOLZER, EMIL, JR., "The Church in New England Society," in James M. Smith, ed., *Seventeenth-Century America: Essays in Colonial History* (Chapel Hill. Univ. of North Carolina Press, 1959), 143–165

POWELL, SUMNER CHILTON, *Puritan Village: The Formation of a New England Town* (Middletown, Conn.: Wesleyan Univ. Press, 1963)

RUTMAN, DARRETT B., *Husbandmen of Plymouth: Farms and Villages in the Old Colony, 1620–1692* (Boston: Beacon Press, 1967)

———, *Winthrop's Boston* (Chapel Hill: Univ. of North Carolina Press, 1965)

SIMMONS, RICHARD C., "Freemanship in Early Massachusetts: Some Suggestions and a Case Study," *William and Mary Quarterly,* 3rd ser., XIX (1962), 422–28

WALL, ROBERT E., JR., "A New Look at Cambridge," *Journal of American History,* LII (December, 1965), 599–605

WINSLOW, OLA ELIZABETH, *Meetinghouse Hill, 1630–1783* (New York: Macmillan, 1952)

IIA. The Vision Refracted

ADAMS, JAMES TRUSLOW, *The Founding of New England* (Boston: Atlantic Monthly Press, 1921)

BUSHMAN, RICHARD L., *From Puritan to Yankee: Character and the Social Order in Connecticut, 1690–1765* (Cambridge: Harvard Univ. Press, 1967)

DUNN, RICHARD S., *Puritans and Yankees: The Winthrop Dynasty of New England, 1630–1717* (Princeton: Princeton Univ. Press, 1962)

ERIKSON, KAI T., *Wayward Puritans: A Study in the Sociology of Deviance* (New York: John Wiley and Sons, Inc., 1966)

GAY, PETER, *A Loss of Mastery: Puritan Historians in Colonial America* (Berkeley & Los Angeles: Univ. of California Press, 1966)

HAROUTUNIAN, JOSEPH, *Piety Versus Moralism: The Passing of the New England Theology* (New York: Henry Holt and Co., 1932)

MILLER, PERRY, "Declension in a Bible Commonwealth," in *Nature's Nation* (Cambridge: The Belknap Press of Harvard Univ. Press, 1967), pp. 14–49

_____, The New England Mind: From Colony to Province (Cambridge: Harvard Univ. Press, 1953)

SHIPTON, CLIFFORD K., New England Life in the 18th Century (Cambridge: The Belknap Press of Harvard Univ. Press, 1963)

WERTENBAKER, T. J., The Puritan Oligarchy (New York: Charles Scribner's Sons, 1947)

IIB. God Profit

BAILYN, BERNARD, The New England Merchants in the Seventeenth Century (Cambridge: Harvard Univ. Press, 1955)

FULLERTON, KEMPER, "Calvinism and Capitalism," Harvard Theological Review, XXI (1928), 163–95

GREEN, ROBERT W., ed., Protestantism and Capitalism: The Weber Thesis and Its Critics (Boston: D. C. Heath and Co., 1959)

GRISWOLD, A. WHITNEY, "Three Puritans on Prosperity," New England Quarterly, VII (1934), 475–93

HUDSON, WINTHROP S., "The Weber Thesis Reexamined," Church History, XXX (March, 1961), 88–99

MICHAELSEN, ROBERT S., "Changes in the Puritan Concept of Calling or Vocation," New England Quarterly, XXVI (Sept., 1953), 315–36

PERRY, RALPH BARTON, Puritanism and Democracy (New York: The Vanguard Press, 1944), Ch. 12

TAWNEY, R. H., Religion and the Rise of Capitalism (New York: Harcourt, Brace and Co., 1926)

WEBER, MAX, The Protestant Ethic and the Spirit of Capitalism (London: George Allen and Unwin Ltd., 1930)

IIC. God Land

EAST, ROBERT A., "Puritanism and New Settlement," New England Quarterly, XVII (1944), 255–64

HALLER, WILLIAM, The Puritan Frontier (New York: Columbia Univ. Press, 1951)

NASH, RODERICK, Wilderness and the American Mind (New Haven & London: Yale Univ. Press, 1967), Ch. 2

SHIPTON, CLIFFORD K., "The New England Frontier," New England Quarterly, X (1937), 25–36

WILLIAMS, GEORGE, Wilderness and Paradise in Christian Thought (New York: Harper Co., 1961)

III. The Puritan Legacy

AHLSTROM, SYDNEY E., "The Puritan Ethic and the Spirit of American Democracy," in George L. Hunt, ed., Calvinism and the Political Order (Philadelphia: The Westminster Press, 1965), Ch. 5

BALDWIN, ALICE M., *The New England Clergy and the American Revolution* (Durham, N. C.: Duke Univ. Press, 1928)

DEGLER, CARL N., *Out of Our Past* (New York: Harper and Bros., 1959), Ch. 1

GABRIEL, RALPH H., *The Course of American Democratic Thought* (New York: The Ronald Press Co., 1940)

HALLER, WILLIAM, "The Puritan Background of the First Amendment," in Conyers Read, ed., *The Constitution Reconsidered* (New York: Columbia Univ. Press, 1938), 131–41

HEIMERT, ALAN, *Religion and the American Mind: From the Great Awakening to the Revolution* (Cambridge: Harvard Univ. Press, 1966)

HOFFMAN, FREDERICK J., "Philistine and Puritan in the 1920s," *American Quarterly*, I (Fall, 1949), 247–63

MCLOUGHLIN, WILLIAM G., "Piety and the American Character," *American Quarterly*, XVII (Summer, 1965), pp. 163–86. Reprinted in Hennig Cohen, ed., *The American Experience* (Boston: Houghton Mifflin Co., 1968), pp. 39–63.

MEAD, SIDNEY E., *The Lively Experiment: The Shaping of Christianity in America* (New York: Harper and Row, 1963)

MILLER, PERRY, "From the Covenant to the Revival," in *Nature's Nation* (Cambridge: The Belknap Press of Harvard Univ. Press, 1967), 90–120

———, "From Edwards to Emerson," in *Errand into the Wilderness* (Cambridge: The Belknap Press of Harvard Univ. Press, 1956), Ch. 8

MUZZEY, DAVID S., "The Heritage of the Puritans," in *Report* of the American Historical Association for 1920 (Washington, D. C., 1925), 237–49

NICHOLS, JAMES HASTINGS, *Democracy and the Churches* (Philadelphia: The Westminster Press, 1951)

NOBLE, DAVID W., *Historians Against History* (Minneapolis: Univ. of Minnesota Press, 1965)

PERRY, RALPH BARTON, *Puritanism and Democracy* (New York: The Vanguard Press, 1944)

ROSSITER, CLINTON, *Seedtime of the Republic* (New York: Harcourt, Brace and Co., 1953), Ch. 2

SCHNEIDER, HERBERT W., "The Puritan Tradition," in F. Ernest Johnson, ed., *Wellsprings of the American Spirit* (New York & London: Institute for Religious and Social Studies, 1948), Ch. 1

SHIPTON, CLIFFORD K., "Puritanism and Modern Democracy," *New England Historical and Genealogical Register*, CI (July, 1947), 181–98

SMITH, CHARD POWERS, *Yankees and God* (New York: Hermitage House, 1954)

STEPHENSON, G. M., *The Puritan Heritage* (New York: Macmillan, 1952)

WARREN, AUSTIN, *The New England Conscience* (Ann Arbor: Univ. of Michigan Press, 1966)

WILDER, AMOS N., "The Puritan Heritage in American Culture," *Theology Today*, V (1948), 22–33

WILLSON, LAWRENCE, "The Puritan Tradition in American Literature," *Arizona Quarterly*, XIII (1957), 33–40